Wittgenstein within the Philosophy of Religion

Wittgenstein within the Philosophy of Religion

Thomas D. Carroll
Xing Wei College, People's Republic of China

palgrave
macmillan

First published 2014 by
PALGRAVE MACMILLAN

Palgrave Macmillan in the UK is an imprint of Macmillan Publishers Limited, registered in England, company number 785998, of Houndmills, Basingstoke, Hampshire RG21 6XS.

Palgrave Macmillan in the US is a division of St Martin's Press LLC, 175 Fifth Avenue, New York, NY 10010.

Palgrave Macmillan is the global academic imprint of the above companies and has companies and representatives throughout the world.

ISBN: 978–1–137–40789–4

This book is printed on paper suitable for recycling and made from fully managed and sustained forest sources. Logging, pulping and manufacturing processes are expected to conform to the environmental regulations of the country of origin.

A catalogue record for this book is available from the British Library.

A catalog record for this book is available from the Library of Congress.

For Don and Joy

Contents

Acknowledgments

The motivation for this project began with questions I first asked as an undergraduate at Occidental College, especially concerning the relevance of philosophy to clarifying the ideals of multiculturalism in education, ethics, and politics. It was also at Occidental that I first read some of Wittgenstein's writings. I will always appreciate the faculty members of the Philosophy Department (at the time, Marcia Homiak, Hal Lauter, William Neblett, and Saul Traiger) as well as Dale Wright in Religious Studies for challenging me to express myself more clearly, to read more carefully, and to work harder than I had ever worked before. I would like to thank in particular Professor Lauter who supported my plans to pursue graduate studies in philosophy. I also appreciate the opportunities I had in the MA program at San Francisco State University to study with Donald Provence and Peter Radcliff and to speak on many occasions with fellow students David Dell'Agostino and Julian Friedland about Wittgenstein and philosophy of language. I am especially grateful to Dr. Provence for his painstaking attention to detail in supervising my thesis on theories of truth.

The ideas and arguments that grew into this book emerged during my doctoral studies at Boston University. I am indebted to Juliet Floyd, who served as my dissertation director, for facilitating my exploration of the historicity of interpretations of Wittgenstein within the philosophy of religion and her extensive comments on multiple drafts. I am deeply grateful to Alan Olson, my second reader and academic advisor, who has guided me from my first semester to graduation and beyond. I am also thankful to Diana Lobel, Allen Speight, and Robert Cohen for graciously agreeing to serve as committee members.

During the years of my doctoral study, I also worked closely with John Clayton, whose posthumous book, *Religions, Reasons and Gods* (Clayton, 2006), Anne Blackburn and I prepared for publication. Clayton's project of tracing of the context-specific ends of theistic arguments throughout history and showing their differences from other philosophical ends, continues to inspire me in considering how contextually attentive philosophy of religion may be helpful for understanding human diversities. I am appreciative of conversations during these years with Anne Blackburn as well as with fellow students Bradley Herling and Timothy

Knepper about what philosophy of religion at the boundaries of the fields of philosophy and religious studies could become.

During this time, I also presented papers relating to my project at conferences hosted by organizations such as the American Academy of Religion, the American Philosophical Association, and the European Society for Philosophy of Religion. Financial support from Boston University enabled me to attend these conferences. I would especially like to thank Hans Adriannse, Richard Amesbury, Ingolf Dalferth, Patrick Horn, John A. Knight, Andrew Rawnsley, Andy Sanders, Olli-Pekka Vainio, and Ludger Viefhues-Bailey for probing questions and good conversations. Out of these conference presentations emerged parts of various chapters as well as the article, 'The Traditions of Fideism', *Religious Studies* 44/1 (2008): 1–22 (Copyright © 2008 Cambridge University Press); I am grateful to Cambridge University Press for permission to reprint that article as Chapter 4 of this book. I also thank the Institut für die Wissenschaften vom Menschen in Vienna, Austria for a Junior Visiting Fellowship in the Spring of 2007. This fellowship enabled me to write about half of the dissertation while living a short distance from the Wittgenstein Haus.

This book has developed significantly since its first iteration as my doctoral dissertation. Over the last five years, living and teaching in Boston and Shanghai have affected the development of the book. I am grateful to my students in these two major cities for the indirect influence they have exerted on the book through the questions and philosophical problems they raised in a variety of courses. Teaching topics in ethics and philosophy of religion with an eye to multicultural and cross-cultural dynamics in academic conversation in these two contexts has illustrated to me the ongoing relevance of Wittgenstein's writings to problems arising from lack of clarity about the use of language.

Lastly, I would like to thank those closest to me who have encouraged me over the years in pursuing this project. I thank my partner Amalia Jiva for her companionship, wise counsel, and good humor. I also thank my parents, Don and Joy Carroll, to whom this book is dedicated, who did not flinch when their son told them he wanted to pursue an academic career in philosophy and religious studies, and my sister Elizabeth Carroll, who having received her PhD in Art History, still understands well how to advise her younger brother. I hope I have succeeded in writing this book with some awareness of the generosity of so many. Despite my best intentions and the efforts of many helpful interlocutors, remaining errors and infelicities in the finished book are mine.

Introduction: On Reading Wittgenstein on Religion

Wittgenstein belongs to history. He began his philosophical studies at Cambridge over one hundred years ago, published his first book (the only to be published during his lifetime) more than ninety years ago, and, following a philosophically abundant period of just over two decades, died more than sixty years ago. While there is considerable disagreement in the philosophical community over the value of Wittgenstein's philosophy, frequently he is listed as the, or among the, most important philosophers of the twentieth century. He is still widely read, if not quite as widely as during the decades of his students' lives and influence (Biletzki, 2003, p. 190). Much of twentieth century philosophy was undertaken within his wake (whether with gratitude or scorn). Wittgenstein is surely important to study as a recent historical figure, but what is his importance today? The ultimate goal of this book is to respond to this question in connection with contemporary philosophy of religion. The motivation for this study stems, in part, from the observation that religions are human phenomena of great significance to contemporary events (on local, national, and global levels) and that Wittgenstein's philosophy has much to offer in reevaluating what the philosophy of religion could be at this moment in history.

Over the course of his life, Wittgenstein wrote or dictated a large number of manuscripts and typescripts, yet as has been much discussed, these texts must be read carefully because of their unusual form and largely unpublished state. Despite the fact that Wittgenstein did not write in the essay form, readers often feel compelled to search for a main argument or to discern below the surface of his writings a philosophical theory or at least a method for doing philosophy. This way, readers can more easily determine what Wittgenstein's concrete contributions or objections would be to current issues or research programs. In so far as the mainstream of contemporary philosophy is in the business of building theories or articulating methods, it seems only reasonable that Wittgenstein, qua philosopher, would have something to contribute to mainstream philosophical projects. Yet, Wittgenstein's writings tend to call into question approaches to philosophy that seek to build theories. Even so, readers of Wittgenstein may be preoccupied with their own philosophical projects while reading his work, and thus, they may be unable to detect subtle but recurrent themes in his writing. The hermeneutical use of a phenomenological *epoché*, while clearly appropriate in studies of culturally or historically distant texts, might seem to be extravagant in interpretation of the writings of a twentieth century philosopher central to the early development of analytic philosophy. Readers who do not apply an *epoché* to Wittgenstein's texts may not see what his questions were and see how he developed those questions over his philosophical career. In the philosophy of religion, the preoccupation of readers with their own philosophical problems has been no less pronounced when reading figures from the history of philosophy (including Wittgenstein). Is his philosophy anti-metaphysical? Is Wittgenstein an anti-realist with respect to religious language? An expressivist? Is Wittgenstein a fideist? A relativist? Is his philosophy of any use to Jewish or Christian philosophers and theologians?

The approach to reading Wittgenstein on religion advanced in this book is a variation on the ethical-therapeutic interpretations developed by Stanley Cavell, James Conant, Cora Diamond and Stephen Mulhall. This reading involves three steps or, perhaps better, movements, since they do not need to proceed consecutively or in linear progression; instead, the movements are spread across the seven chapters of the book. The first movement is the thorough application of historicist *epoché*. One reason for applying an *epoché* in any study is to suspend longstanding presuppositions and questions in order to diminish their influence in reading a text. The idea here is that sometimes longstanding presuppositions and questions can get in the way of understanding the aims of a text, especially when that text is historically or culturally distant from the reader. This may be difficult to do particularly when these presuppositions or questions motivate one to approach a text in the first place; even so, if one is to understand a philosopher like Wittgenstein fairly, and if one hopes to gain insight or assistance for addressing one's philosophical problems reliably, then a careful approach to reading is needed. One area in which the present book strives to apply this *epoché* is to the history of philosophy itself, whether it be the history of analytic philosophy or of philosophy of religion, or the history of key terms, such as 'fideism' or 'religion'. The value of attending to the history of critical terms in order to discern their suitability for comparison is, I take it, a lesson one may draw from Wittgenstein's thought.

The second movement argues that Wittgenstein's corpus is directed to a particular philosophical end; that end is a searching clarity or perspicuity. His concern for clarity of expression in the *Tractatus Logico-Philosophicus* and the place of language within the flow of human social life in later sources such as *Philosophical Investigations* exemplify this pursuit of what I term his ethic of perspicuity. I contend that after studying Wittgenstein's philosophy in concert with his biography, it can readily be seen that Wittgenstein took the moral duty to uncover clarity to be of the utmost importance. Not only was this a philosophical goal, but it was also the means by which he established and maintained a sense of integrity. Wittgenstein's philosophy famously went through various phases, but what is found throughout is an overarching intellectual aspiration to achieve a transparency of meaning that relieved confusion. To formulate this ethic definitively would be to suggest that Wittgenstein's thought may be essentialized or that his thought may be summarized in virtue of the achievements of one period of his philosophical development, but when an ethic of perspicuity is turned towards the study of Wittgenstein's thought, it is evident that such essentializing typically runs counter to the duty to notice differences and development. We are left then with an interpretive circularity: the ethic, by means of which Wittgenstein's corpus is to be interpreted, cannot be easily formulated because of the diversity of his corpus, a diversity recognized frequently when one raises as a value the perspicuity pursued variously but repeatedly in Wittgenstein's writings. Instead of defining the ethic, I will refer to Wittgenstein's various instantiations of it across numerous sources.

When confronted with the goal of clarifying one's concepts, one may find that they are not as helpful for addressing one's philosophical problems as it may have appeared at first, that some modification to thought is required to address one's problems. One may even discover that one's formulation of a problem is itself senseless. The third movement stems from this insight; it is the reformulation of philosophical projects and problems through the conversation. It is in engaging Wittgenstein in conversation that his work has the most to offer contemporary philosophers of religion. In this sense, through reading his texts Wittgenstein emerges as a philosophical conversation partner, much like Plato's Socrates. *What are the problems of philosophy of religion?* The question is not to be read as 'what are the classical problems?' Instead, it is *where is there conceptual confusion regarding religions?*

The reevaluation of some of the standard questions asked about Wittgenstein and the philosophy of religion comprises the third movement of the book. I argue that this reevaluation should issue in a new course for philosophy of religion. Unlike analytic philosophy, philosophy of religion at present has cause to embrace philosophical and religious traditions around the world as being relevant to both its self-conception and its subject matter. Indeed, the heightened profile of religions in local, national, and international affairs in recent decades only increases the importance of this reconceiving of the subdiscipline.

Scholarship on the history of analytic philosophy has had to overcome the apparent ahistorical tendencies of this tradition of philosophy. Hans Sluga, in his review of Peter Hacker's *Wittgenstein's Place in Twentieth Century Analytic Philosophy* emphasizes this tension. Sluga asks lucid questions that bring to mind what a Wittgensteinian approach to the history of philosophy might look like. As Sluga notes, what the name 'analytic philosophy' refers to is itself a contested matter. More recently, Hans-Johann Glock has argued the contested concept of 'analytic philosophy' should be understood according to both historical and genetic factors as well as a family resemblance approach to understanding the methods, problems, doctrines, and styles of the philosophical tradition.[1] Which philosophers do or do not fit the classification is likewise contested. Sluga holds that these contests should themselves be part of the story that is told in histories of the movement:

> The arena of history has been widely neglected by analytic philosophers, though historical facts are in principle as worthy of philosophical attention as the facts of set theory or quantum mechanics. This lack of historical consciousness has led to curious distortions and limitations in analytic discussions of historical phenomena. Past philosophers are read as if they were writing today; ethics and politics are discussed only in terms of abstract principles, not in terms of the lives that human beings actually lead; the fact that concepts are historical structures is ignored in favor of a vague Platonism. The philosophy of science has been at the forefront of trying to break these preconceptions, but elsewhere – in the study of logic, language, mathematics, and, as just said, in ethics, politics, and even the history of philosophy – they linger on. (Sluga, 1998, p. 130)

Surely this picture of the state of philosophy has improved somewhat in the last decade and a half, but the continuing ring of truth to Sluga's criticisms indicates more work is yet to be done in drawing the attention of analytic philosophers to historical-contextual studies of philosophers or philosophical movements. Sluga not only suggests how history of philosophy might be aided by conceptual analysis but also how conceptual analysis may be aided by the history of philosophy. Indeed, extending Sluga's criticisms to philosophy of religion shows how much preconceptions about Wittgenstein or about the nature of philosophy itself 'linger on'.

Sluga suggests some avenues where conceptual analysis could effectively engage the history of philosophy. Examples of terms he identifies as being ripe for philosophical analysis are 'authors', 'philosophers', the 'development' of a philosopher, 'interpretations', 'texts', 'work' as a whole, 'schools', 'movements', and 'traditions' (Sluga, 1998, p. 104). Sluga offers some sobering remarks on the very classification of 'analytic philosophy', suggesting that 'analytic philosophy is to be characterized in terms of overlapping circles of family resemblances and causal relations of "influences" that extend in all directions and certainly far beyond the boundaries we hope to draw' (Sluga, 1998, p. 107). For Sluga, the act of drawing boundaries in the history of philosophy is itself a philosophical matter, an act that ought to be subject to critique: 'So our question should not be: what precise property do all analytic philosophers share? But: how can we draw the boundaries of analytic philosophy most naturally and most usefully and to what uses are we putting the term when we draw them in one way rather than another?' (Sluga, 1998, p. 107). The same can be asked for philosophy of religion. In contrast, we might ask, paraphrasing and adapting Sluga: how can we draw the boundaries of philosophy of religion most naturally and most usefully and to what uses are we putting the term when we draw them in one way rather than another?

A key aim of the first movement of the book is to complicate the sense of familiarity many philosophers and scholars of religions have had with respect to Wittgenstein's thought and its bearing on the philosophy of religion. Anat Biletzki writes in *(Over)Interpreting Wittgenstein* on the state of scholarship on Wittgenstein and religion: 'More commentators by far deal with religion as a language-game or as a form of life than any other interpretive gesture; and so our perusal of religion as language-game and form of life is, accordingly, densely populated by interpretive heroes' (Biletzki, 2003, p. 131). Neither Biletzki, nor recent historians of philosophy of religion Eugene Thomas Long and Charles Taliaferro, claim that interpreting religions as language-games or forms of life is the only or best way of understanding Wittgenstein's import for the philosophy of religion; however, each of them notes the dominant presence such interpretations of Wittgenstein have had in the field (Taliaferro, 2005, pp. 361–2; Long, 2003, pp. 265–6, 407–8). It is time for a reassessment of Wittgenstein and philosophy of religion.

The seven chapters of this book together present a reassessment of the reception of Wittgenstein in the philosophy of religion. Chapter 1: 'Problems of Interpretive Authority in Wittgenstein's Corpus' identifies a variety of problems involved in developing a principled reading of Wittgenstein. In setting the stage for the book, this chapter explores hermeneutical problems of reading Wittgenstein's works with an eye to their relevance to philosophy of religion. Because many of the sources now available to scholars were not prepared to Wittgenstein's satisfaction for publication, or indeed, were ever meant for it, study of these works – and his thought on religion contained within – should be guided by an appreciation for the conditions of the writing of the sources consulted.

Next, I explore the merits of some interpretive schemes readers have used in approaching Wittgenstein's body of work, locating my hermeneutic with respect to other approaches. While some of the sources that concern religions include private diaries and correspondences never intended for publication, these important but problematic texts merit close attention. I argue that these sources should be read against the central themes and arguments of the texts Wittgenstein did prepare for publication. One such central theme, the ethic of perspicuity, coordinates my readings of his corpus.

Chapter 2: 'Wittgenstein, Biography, and Religious Identity' addresses a number of philosophical problems that arise from taking Wittgenstein's extended corpus and biography seriously. An intriguing feature of Wittgenstein's corpus is that while his more prepared philosophical works rarely mention religious phenomena, less prepared and private sources reveal a longstanding interest in a wide variety of religious phenomena. Furthermore, Wittgenstein's own religious identity appears to have been complicated and even vexed by his Jewish and Catholic religious inheritances all amidst a life spanning decades scarred by rising anti-Semitism.

For many philosophers and on many topics, knowing their biographical details or historical context is strictly speaking irrelevant to understanding their philosophical achievements or shortcomings, but for Wittgenstein and the topics of religion and the nature of philosophy, this is not so. The reasons why are because: (a) for Wittgenstein, philosophy was a personal practice as much as an academic discipline and one can see this practice in action in his life, and (b) the fragmentary and enigmatic remarks on religion can be better appreciated against the background of Wittgenstein's life. The purpose of this chapter is to better appreciate the sources of discontinuity between Wittgenstein, who appears to have been alienated and possibly self-loathing, and his philosophy, which contains powerful resources for dismantling the very forces that bewitched him. Understanding this tension will prove helpful for later chapters that contemplate what challenges the ethic of perspicuity reading of Wittgenstein's philosophy may bring to contemporary philosophy of religion and to learning to live well amidst myriad human differences.

Chapter 3: 'A History of Wittgenstein and the Philosophy of Religion' traces the reception of Wittgenstein in the philosophy of religion in order to show how prevailing philosophical problems can affect the interpretation of philosophers and to assess the obstacles to advancing Wittgensteinian philosophy of religion today. It is now commonplace to find characterizations of fideism that identify Wittgensteinian philosophy of religion as exemplifying the category, just as it is common to see characterizations of Wittgensteinian philosophy of religion that invoke the category of fideism. In 1967, when Kai Nielsen first categorized Wittgensteinian philosophy of religion as fideistic, philosophy of religion influenced by Wittgenstein had been emerging in published and unpublished form for nearly a decade. By the time Nielsen used the term 'fideism' to classify what he saw as a movement, it seemed to many readers to name a real phenomenon in middle to late twentieth-century analytic philosophy of religion; thus the name 'Wittgensteinian fideism' remains with us to the present day.

In this chapter, I show how the ideas Nielsen associated with Wittgensteinian fideism are just one possible avenue in the development of a philosophy of religion after Wittgenstein. The ideas in Wittgenstein's philosophy that have been most influential in twentieth century philosophy of religion are clearly those associated with 'meaning as use', 'language-games', and 'forms of life'. These ideas were of interest to philosophers of religion in the middle to late twentieth century because of the influence of verificationist tendencies in theories of meaning and austere naturalistic metaphysics. Many critics have detected an intellectually evasive or protective trend in Wittgensteinian philosophy of religion, and interpretations of Wittgenstein that suggest or propose a strong identification of language-games with religions clearly ought to be left behind. Insight into the development of the 'fideist' reading of Wittgenstein on religion may be helpful also in overcoming the sense of interpretive inevitability accompanying the long-standing received interpretations of other philosophers.

Chapter 4: 'The Traditions of Fideism' presents a perspicuous approach to the histories of philosophy and theology through tracing the genealogies of the critical term 'fideism' used in philosophical and theological classification and appraisal. Contemporary philosophers and theologians acknowledge that 'fideism' is difficult to define but rarely agree on what the best characterization of the term is. The diverse and sometimes conflicting individual definitions of fideism call out for some philosophical housekeeping if the term is to be useful academically. This preliminary investigation into the genealogy of fideism shows that the meaning of the term is not at all clear in either philosophical or theological discourse. Because of this confusion, academic investigations into the fideism of, for example, Wittgenstein, Kierkegaard, or philosophers influenced by them are often disconnected from the historical origins of the term. The goal of this chapter is to suggest some ways towards clearing up this confusion and identifying the uses of the term that are fruitful in academic discourse. Taking a cue from Wittgenstein, I propose that it is best to see how the term was actually used in its original context and to construct extensions of the term carefully from this original use. I investigate the history of use of the word among philosophers and theologians to explore why its meaning has been so contested and thus why it has not always been helpful as a term of classification. I trace the use of 'fideism' from its origins in French Protestant and Catholic theological discourses to its current uses in philosophy, concluding that the term is helpful in interpretations only when philosophers scrupulously acknowledge the tradition of use that informs their understanding of the word.

Chapter 5: 'On "Fideism" as an Interpretive Category' considers the adequacy of 'fideism' for approaching Wittgenstein through comparisons with analyses of James and Kierkegaard. Building on the work of Chapters 3 and 4, in this chapter I investigate the use of the term for the interpretation of philosophers. In particular, I compare the case of Wittgenstein with the cases of William James and Søren Kierkegaard with respect to using 'fideism' as an interpretive term. What emerges from this historical study of reception and interpretation is that the meaning of this critical term has continued to shift through twentieth century philosophical scholarship, and thus the question of whether or not any particular philosopher is a fideist is not straightforward. By neglecting the history of use of the term, critics of particular philosophers and theologians have unwittingly introduced confusion into their interpretations; this helps explain the unwillingness of those thus criticized to accept the 'charges'. While a narrative may be traced showing threads of late nineteenth century French Protestant fideism in James's writings, connections with Kierkegaard and various traditions of fideism remain speculative and liable to introduce more misunderstanding than clarity. Unless narrowly circumscribed, use of the term 'fideism' in interpreting Wittgenstein is likely to introduce more confusion than insight.

Even if 'fideism' is not helpful, the problem remains over whether Wittgenstein's philosophy provides resources that may be used to epistemically isolate and protect religious beliefs and practices from public criticism; this is the topic of Chapter 6: 'Religions, Epistemic Isolation, and Social Trust'. Critics of some Wittgensteinian philosophers of religion are right to warn against the temptation to isolate religious discourses from outside critique out of the otherwise laudable goal of doing justice to the particularity of those religious discourses. Against the view held by Kai Nielsen and others that Wittgensteinian philosophy of religion characterizes religious belief and language as being intellectually isolated from outside rational criticism, I argue that a central theme in Wittgenstein's philosophy – the social nature of linguistic meaning – is incompatible with the idea that religious discourses are conceptually cut off from other discourses. The first part of the chapter explores the remarks on pain and the idea of a private language in *Philosophical Investigations* in order to show how the isolationist reading of Wittgenstein on religion does not fit well with central features of his developed philosophy. Drawing on the work of Stanley Cavell on social attunement and Annette Baier on the ethics of trust, I argue that trust is a requirement for establishing and maintaining the cooperative venture of language; moreover, trust plays a critical role in the process of interpretation. An appreciation for the fragility of trust goes some ways towards dispelling the apparent relativism some have thought implicit in Wittgenstein's treatment of meaning as use. Boundaries of language-games are not barriers preventing outsiders from understanding; rather, the boundaries between instances of language are practical. Without such trust, barriers to communication become, practically speaking, too great to cross, and lack of trust characterizes misunderstandings across cultural and religious divides. While uses of language associated with religions may not be immediately transparent to those seeking to interpret them, the possibility always remains that interpretive ventures will succeed.

Chapter 7: 'Wittgenstein's Ethic of Perspicuity and the Philosophy of Religion' considers the prospects of the perspicuity reading of Wittgenstein for contemporary philosophy of religion. A number of interpreters of Wittgenstein and philosophers of religion influenced by Wittgenstein have articulated philosophical goals inspired by Wittgenstein's quest for perspicuity. In this chapter, I will survey some of these approaches, including Stephen Mulhall's therapeutic reading of Wittgenstein, D. Z. Phillips' conception of contemplative philosophy, and John Clayton's ideal of clarification of defensible differences. Then, I locate my understanding of Wittgenstein's ethic of perspicuity with respect to these philosophical ends. I also explore H. H. Price's early criticisms of analytic philosophy as expressed in his 1945 lecture 'Clarity is Not Enough'. Price argues that philosophers have duties to their students and to the public that go beyond the mere analysis of concepts. Bringing together Price and Wittgenstein, I contemplate the role perspicuous philosophy of religion could play at a time in global history characterized by unprecedented contact across cultures and between peoples and in which traditionalist religious movements appear to be on the rise. In short, I argue that the philosophical work of an exile (to borrow from James Klagge's recent study of Wittgenstein's life and philosophy) may prove helpful in approaching cross-cultural conversations in philosophy that seek to recognize human diversities, such as those involving the place of religions in people's lives.

Reconsidering philosophy of religion in light of his ethic of perspicuity will open up new possibilities for what the subdiscipline might be. Much recent work in analytic philosophy of religion concerns the evidential support for a/theism and the logical status of divine attributes. But there are other questions scholars might ask at the intersection of philosophy and religions. The ethic of perspicuity reading downplays the relevance of the various uses of 'fideism' for understanding Wittgenstein's thought on religion and the bearing of his philosophy on philosophy of religion. Reconsidering what philosophical reflection on religions ought to involve is a matter of current urgency. As Kwame Anthony Appiah has written, 'The world is getting more crowded: in the next half a century the population of our once foraging species will approach nine billion. Depending on the circumstances, conversations across boundaries can be delightful, or just vexing: what they mainly are, though, is inevitable' (Appiah, 2006, p. xxi). It is in light of observations of the importance of conversations across boundaries that I take it Wittgenstein's philosophy has a great deal to teach us today. As much as Wittgenstein's ethic is concerned with achieving transparency of meaning, it also involves a questioning of one's own aims and motives as a philosopher. To some, it has seemed that Wittgenstein's philosophy aims at frustrating cross-cultural conversation, but that is not the reading pursued in this book. Instead, I concur with Appiah that

> The problem of cross-cultural communication can seem immensely difficult in theory, when we are trying to imagine making sense of

> a stranger in the abstract. But the great lesson of anthropology is that when the stranger is no longer imaginary, but real and present, sharing a human social life, you may like or dislike him, you may agree or disagree; but, if it is what you both want, you can make sense of each other in the end. (Appiah, 2006, pp. 88–9)

A topic that should receive renewed attention following on the perspicuity reading of Wittgenstein on religion is the developing of an ethic for living well in culturally and religiously pluralistic contexts. Wittgenstein's ethic of perspicuity draws the reader's attention to the pluralism of our social contexts and can aid efforts to delineate points of difference or similarity between beliefs, values, and social practices. Furthermore, the pursuit of clear thinking is itself necessary to discover and overcome one's own prejudices; and discoveries of this sort can be aided by the critical stances taken by reliable interlocutors. Wittgenstein's ethic of perspicuity may inspire those who also value clarity to pursue a searching knowledge of cultural variance and thus contribute to contemplation of what it means to live well amidst cultural diversity.

Despite the potential in Wittgenstein's philosophy for navigating communities with cultural and religious diversities, there is obvious distance between Wittgenstein's historical moment and ours. Wittgenstein followed a convention that most others also have used in the philosophy of religion up until the present day: referring to the philosopher's object of study as 'religion' (that is, in the singular). The term 'religion' has shown itself notoriously difficult to define comprehensively; Jonathan Z. Smith and Talal Asad contend it is a relatively modern and distinctly Western construction.[2] These studies of the category of 'religion' are not of great concern for the study of Wittgenstein as such, insofar as he is a relatively modern and distinctly western philosopher, and he did not aspire to develop a theoretical approach to the study of religions. However, some of Wittgenstein's readers have sought out just what Wittgenstein might have to contribute to methodology debates in religious studies. 'Could "religion" be a family-resemblance term?' 'In what ways are religions like games?' While I do not read Wittgenstein as offering a robust view of 'religion' or 'religious', I observe that a key feature of Wittgenstein's mature philosophy is an emphasis on the diversity and distinctiveness of instances of language use. Wittgenstein's philosophy would seem to be naturally aligned with approaches such as these in religious studies that take into consideration the social and historical context of words, and thus a word such as 'religion'.[3] While Wittgenstein might be read to recapitulate pre-critical use of the term 'religion', I read his philosophy as spurring readers to challenge easy classifications that blur otherwise salient distinctions. Wittgenstein's ethic of perspicuity should tame the instinct to reach instinctively for generality. Hermeneutical study of contexts of ascriptions of the term 'religion' and philosophical investigation of problems and puzzles arising from these contexts of ascription would be an appropriate way to conduct inquiries in the philosophy of religion.

Contrary to those who would hold that Wittgensteinian philosophy ought only to be descriptive, I hold that it does not renounce normative endeavors. After all, the pursuit of perspicuity *is* a normative endeavor. Wittgenstein was deeply concerned that some of his contemporaries did not practice philosophy with the seriousness and sincerity he understood himself to bring to the topic. Philosophy drawing on themes explored in Wittgenstein's writings can help contribute to the building of an ethical discourse that consists in identifying and describing nuances among superficially similar instances of language use. I do not read Wittgenstein as precluding the identification of similarities across instances of language use or social practice, but he tends to be a pessimist about the viability of such identifications (Klagge, 2011, pp. 75–6). Wittgenstein spent a great deal of time in his writings contemplating the value in searching for differences; similarities we are already tempted to see.

1
Problems of Interpretive Authority in Wittgenstein's Corpus

The present study of Wittgenstein begins with texts. Wittgenstein's first wave of influence in philosophical circles was through his *Tractatus Logico-Philosophicus*, but during his philosophical career from 1929 to his death in 1951, a second wave of influence came through his teaching, conversation, and charismatic philosophical persona. During this time he scrupulously composed and revised numerous manuscripts, typescripts, and diaries; none of these texts ultimately achieved sufficient clarity to satisfy Wittgenstein's powerful self-criticism. Yet after his death, these texts have slowly been prepared for publication and have been issued to a larger reading philosophical public, thus instigating a third wave of influence (Kenny, 2006, pp. 382–96). Effects from these three waves continued to affect philosophers through the middle decades of the twentieth century; yet, as the first two waves have receded into history, the third wave (increasing progressively in its volume as further texts from Wittgenstein's corpus have become more widely available and easier to access) defines the presence of Wittgenstein in philosophy today, supplemented by biographical and historical scholarship on the development and interpretation of Wittgenstein's corpus. Secondary research on how to read Wittgenstein continues to be a vibrant area of philosophical work relating to Wittgenstein; hermeneutical work is enriching much of philosophy beyond the writings of Wittgenstein and is aiding analytic philosophers in approaching difficult and problematic texts as well as historical texts and issues. The present book is situated within this body of hermeneutical work.

Developing a principled approach to Wittgenstein's corpus is no simple task, for while he wrote extensively on philosophical topics,

Wittgenstein did not publish very much of his writings during his lifetime. The body of work scholars have been left with is made up of different genres and executed with varying levels of preparation and editing. Most of what Wittgenstein wrote does not overtly concern religious phenomena, but what does concern religion has inspired much scholarly reflection.[1] Yet how should Wittgenstein's thought on religion affect one's reading of the more straightforwardly philosophical material, if at all, and vice versa?

Many of the sources now available to scholars were not prepared to Wittgenstein's satisfaction for publication, or indeed, were not ever meant for it. The need for contextual work is made apparent by the fact that generally, early interpreters of Wittgenstein in philosophy of religion were not seeking to place his remarks on religion within the context of his wider philosophical interests; far from it, the earliest group of interpreters of Wittgenstein on religion, spread across the second and third waves as we will see in Chapter 3, did not have access to some of the main sources for Wittgenstein's remarks on religion – 'Remarks on Frazer's *Golden Bough*', 'The Lectures on Religious Belief', *Culture and Value*, and 'Movements of Thought: Diaries 1930–1932, 1936–1937' and thus formed their interpretations based on works like the *Tractatus*, the *Blue and Brown Books*, and *Philosophical Investigations*. Philosophers of religion of earlier decades interpreted Wittgenstein in light of the dominant philosophical questions of their time. Now that the philosophical controversies of those days have passed to some degree, it is possible to investigate Wittgenstein's thought on religion without being swept up into those controversies.

1.1 Sources for Wittgenstein and philosophy of religion

Despite the fact that books and articles have been written with variations on the title, it is debatable to what extent it makes sense to speak of Wittgenstein's philosophy of religion. Since the 'phenomena' of religion were not obviously major topics in his philosophical output, it is better to speak of his having thoughts about religion and occasionally about topics in the area of philosophy now named as philosophy of religion.[2] By 'phenomena of religions', I have in mind not Husserlian phenomenology but the meaning the term has in the phenomenology of religions. Ninian Smart writes of phenomenology of religions as delineating 'the various manifestations of religions in complex ways. It discusses a number of themes – about myths, doctrines, art, rituals, experiences, organizations, ethics, law – and a certain amount of religion, politics and economics.' (Smart, 1999, p. 2) A Wittgensteinian philosophy of religion is the kind of thing that later scholars have constructed from the available source texts.

The principal sources for Wittgenstein's thought on religion may be divided into two groups, those that deal explicitly with phenomena of religions and those that have only an implicit bearing on philosophy of religion. The first group itself also may be divided into two again; there are those sources that deal primarily with the topic of religion and those that contain occasional remarks or asides dealing with religion. In what follows, I will outline the manner in which I approach these three kinds of sources for philosophy of religion in Wittgenstein's corpus.

1.1.1 Sources primarily concerned with phenomena of religions

The texts concerned explicitly with religions include the 'Remarks on Frazer's *Golden Bough*' (Wittgenstein, 1993) and 'The Lectures on Religious Belief' (Wittgenstein, 1967a). These two texts provide the lengthiest treatments of phenomena of religion in Wittgenstein's corpus and, among sources dealing explicitly with religion, have received much attention in secondary literature. However, one must be careful in studying these texts as Wittgenstein did not seek to publish the 'Remarks on Frazer' and the notes on the 'Lectures on Religious Belief' were published long after Wittgenstein's death.

Begun in 1931 with additions in 'not earlier than 1936 and probably after 1948' (Rhees, 1984, p. 119), the 'Remarks on Frazer's *Golden Bough*' contain numerous short critical reflections on James G. Frazer's classic text in anthropology. A recurring theme in Wittgenstein's criticism of Frazer is the latter's interpretive idea that religious beliefs are proto-scientific in nature; that is, in Wittgenstein's reading, Frazer believes that expressions of religious belief are inchoate attempts at descriptions of the forces that operate in the world. One might call magical and religious beliefs, as Frazer conceives them, folk science. Frazer understands the conceptual connection of spirits or souls with powerful forces in the world to be the beginning of science. Likewise, Frazer understands modern observers to know better and not make such elementary mistakes and simultaneously thinks it is only natural that more 'primitive' cultures should make blunders in their initial epistemological forays.

Frazer first published his book *The Golden Bough* (2 volumes) in 1890. Subsequent editions and expansions were published in 1900 (3 volumes), 1906–15 (12 volumes), and 1922 (abridged edition). The various editions of the book had a wide impact and readership. Wittgenstein would have been most likely familiar with the 1922 abridged edition, although he had some familiarity with the 1915 edition. (Wittgenstein, 1993, p. 115) In the seminal book, Frazer sought to articulate the motivation lying behind the varying manifestations of religion and guiding the evolution of this human cultural phenomenon. In the preface to the 1922 edition, Frazer identifies fear of the human dead as the primary factor driving the evolution of religion in what anthropologists then termed 'primitive' cultures. The idea that religions and cultures evolved from a primal state to their contemporary forms was a commonly held thesis among European and American anthropologists, historians, and philosophers of religion during the late nineteenth and early twentieth century, although the nature of this development was contested among the different theories offered. Oswald Spengler, a thinker who influenced Wittgenstein's view of the history of cultures, espoused something of an evolutionary view of the history of cultures, and such a view was defended by thinkers now recognized as among the most influential theorists in the development of the academic study of religions (for example, Herbert Spencer, and E. B. Tylor).

In holding Frazer up to criticism, is Wittgenstein rejecting whole-cloth the idea of evolution of culture or religion? Given his appreciation for Spengler, I think it unlikely. Not that evolution would insure greater sophistication or value (say, as teleological versions of the evolution of culture and religion would have it). It seems likely that the evolutionary hypothesis would be misleading by Wittgenstein's lights insofar as the hypothesis might tempt those using it to perceive similarities where scrupulous investigation would show divergences. Also potentially problematic for Wittgenstein would be Frazer's use of the expression 'primitive culture'. It is not so much the descriptive use of the expression, which was quite common as an anthropological category at the time of Frazer's writing, which would have bothered Wittgenstein as the use of it specifically to indicate the intellectual distance between primitive peoples and modern observers. As much as Wittgenstein was keen to point out differences, he was also concerned to rebuff arrogant pronouncements that a nationality, race, or epoch might immunize its people from error, stupidity, or moral failure.[3] In any case, Wittgenstein's pessimism about the modern era may have made such a comparison dubious (Klagge, 2011, pp. 70–1). Such delusions about 'modern' sophistication make the possibility of moral and intellectual failure all the more likely (but as discussed in Chapter 2, Wittgenstein was not free of these tendencies in his own thinking for much of his life).

In the Remarks, Wittgenstein pays particular attention to the nature of explanation. Frazer's method comes off as roughly empirical. Frazer hopes to identify a general theory of religious development based upon study of particular cases. This will enable him to form a theory of the essence of religion as well as to trace the history of the evolution of religions than can subsequently be applied to novel cases. Nevertheless, Frazer seems to welcome the possibility of revision of hypotheses if new countervailing evidence arises.

However, Wittgenstein takes issue with what he takes to be Frazer's myopia regarding the pervasiveness of ritual in 'modern' life. Wittgenstein might well have enjoyed Frazer's attention to the details of cultural practices. Monk notes that Wittgenstein turned to reading Frazer's *Golden Bough* because of Wittgenstein's long-standing interest in magic as a primitive expression of religious feeling (Monk, 1990, p. 310). According to Monk, Wittgenstein's interests in religion and magic can be thought of as analogous to his fascination with 'the desire to run up against the limits of our language,' that is, the same desire that gives rise to metaphysics (Monk, ibid.). Monk does not read Wittgenstein's use of the term 'primitive' as bringing along pejorative connotations that are sometimes associated with the term or entailing an attitude of cultural superiority. Indeed, one overarching theme of Wittgenstein's 'Remarks on Frazer's *Golden Bough'* is that a strict distinction between the 'modern' and 'primitive' in human culture is not tenable. Rituals and magical thinking pervade much ordinary human experience as Wittgenstein frequently remarks.

In the Remarks, Wittgenstein repeatedly explores the nature of explanation. Frazer's approach to the study of religions is preoccupied with explanation. Wittgenstein writes:

> The very idea of wanting to explain a practice – for example, the killing of the priest-king – seems wrong to me. All that Frazer does is to make them plausible to people who think as he does. It is very remarkable that in the final analysis all these practices are presented as, so to speak, pieces of stupidity. (Wittgenstein, 1993, p. 119)

Wittgenstein observes something contemptible in Frazer's analysis. Frazer's explanatory project treats magic and religion as proto-scientific cultural artifacts. According to Wittgenstein, in doing so Frazer depicts practitioners of magic and of religion as unintelligent (that is, because they do not have our common-sense naturalist worldview), while Wittgenstein detects something deep in religious and magical practices.

The 'Remarks on Frazer's *Golden Bough*' provides some *prima facie* support for the view that religious practices (and thus the beliefs they presuppose) do not need justification. Just before the passage quoted above, Wittgenstein remarks on what he takes to be a concept of error in Frazer's interpretive epistemology:

> Frazer's account of the magical and religious views of mankind is unsatisfactory: it makes these views look like *errors*.
>
> Was Augustine in error, then, when he called upon God on every page of the *Confessions*?
>
> But – one might say – if he was not in error, surely the Buddhist holy man was – or anyone else – whose religion gives expression to completely different views. But *none* of them was in error, except when he set forth a theory. (Wittgenstein, 1993, p. 119)

Consider the final sentence of the quotation above. The sentence conveys a conception of the nature of error: theories are among the kinds of things by means of which one may be in error. Of course, one may be in error about the facts too, but the point is that truth and falsity are properties of certain sorts of expressions or thoughts. The view Wittgenstein seems to be putting forward is that religious practices are not the kinds of things one can be in error about, except when those practices do follow on an erroneous belief or theory, or unless or until one tries explicitly to form an interpretation about values or beliefs presupposed in the practices. We can get a sense as to how this criticism might go by seeing what Wittgenstein has to say further about the nature of explanation: 'I believe that the attempt to explain is already therefore wrong, because one must only correctly piece together what one knows, without adding anything, and the satisfaction being sought through the explanation follows of itself' (Wittgenstein, 1993, p. 121). Several remarks later, Wittgenstein adds: 'Nothing is so difficult as doing justice to the facts.' This seems to suggest a two-tiered assessment of Frazer's efforts. No doubt, Wittgenstein was interested in what Frazer had to offer regarding observations of the practices of various tribes and civilizations; however, it is to the theoretical organization of those facts that Wittgenstein directs his attention primarily.

Many of Wittgenstein's ideas recur in multiple sources, and the 'Remarks on Frazer's *Golden Bough*' are not unique in this respect. While discussions of explanation and error reappear in sources such as *Philosophical Investigations* and *On Certainty*, the theme of the tenacity of religious belief is also addressed in passages from *Culture and Value* and implied in the 'Lectures on Religious Belief'. While these multiple sources can and should be read in concert with one another, we should not assume that these different texts will always converge on these topics in the same way or that they present a completely synoptic view of Wittgenstein's philosophy of religion.

That said, a common theme that emerges in these three sources is that religious belief is of a different kind than the ordinary mental states conventionally called beliefs. Wittgenstein is inspired in part by the thought of Kierkegaard, Tolstoy and others, including Lessing. The difference between beliefs that may be thought of as 'religious' and those that are 'ordinary' is developed more fully in 'The Lectures on Religious Belief' than in other sources, although this theme may be found in 'Movements of Thought: Diaries 1930–1932'(Wittgenstein, 2003b) and *Culture and Value*. Wittgenstein suggests that religious faith is not the same type of subjective state as is historical belief. A belief about a state of affairs in history may be judged true or false depending on the evidence. Apportioning one's credence to propositions as they tend to be supported by the evidence is the epistemic principle of evidentialism. However, evidentialism suggests that degree of belief should be proportioned to the evidence in favor of the belief. Beliefs that are merely probably true are not the right state of mind upon which a life may be built or changed. Instead, Wittgenstein argues that religious faith needs an entirely different kind of ground; here he is in agreement with Kierkegaard and Lessing.

'The Lectures on Religious Belief', constitute the second lengthy key source for Wittgenstein's ideas on religion. The text itself, published in 1966, contains not Wittgenstein's notes for the 1938 lectures but instead a compilation from the notes of several students.[4] As one might expect from notes, the text of the lectures is really a loose collection of instances where Wittgenstein turned his gaze on some of the peculiarities of religious belief and its linguistic expression. In this way, the notes show a familiar manner of leading discussions for Wittgenstein. The following remark, opening the notes to the first lecture, shows this approach: 'An Austrian general said to someone: "I shall think of you after my death, if that should be possible." We can imagine one group who would find this ludicrous, another who wouldn't.' (Wittgenstein, 1967a, p. 53) One theme of the lectures is the difference between those who hear an expression with religious content and share its frame of reference and those who do not. Wittgenstein seems especially interested in the distance that lies between the standpoints of different hearers of expressions.

Another theme in the lectures seems to be a lack of sympathy for philosophers – or sophisticated religious thinkers themselves – who are tempted to offer rational criticisms of foundations for religious beliefs. Both critics and apologists are apparently missing something important about the meaningfulness of religious utterances. In connection with thoughts such as these, Wittgenstein is sometimes interpreted as being fideistic in his apparent advocacy for the rational autonomy of religious beliefs (McGovern and Szabados, 2002; Richter, 2004). Yet, one might wonder whether Wittgenstein intended to defend the thesis that religious beliefs are rationally autonomous. He is very critical of a certain Father O'Hara who had recently given an apologetic lecture at Cambridge earlier in the 1930s:

> It has been said that Christianity rests on an historical basis.
>
> It has been said a thousand times by intelligent people that indubitability is not enough in this case. Even if there is as much evidence as for Napoleon. Because the indubitability wouldn't be enough to make me change my whole life.
>
> It doesn't rest on an historic basis in the sense that the ordinary belief in historic facts could serve as a foundation.
>
> Father O'Hara is one of those people who make it a question of science.
>
> Here we have people who treat this evidence in a different way. They base things on evidence which taken in one way would seem exceedingly flimsy. They base enormous things on this evidence. Am I to say they are unreasonable? I wouldn't call them unreasonable.
>
> I would say, they are certainly not reasonable, that's obvious.
> 'Unreasonable' implies, with everyone, rebuke.
> I want to say: they don't treat this as a matter of reasonability.
>
> Anyone who reads the Epistles will find it said: not only that it is not reasonable, but that it is folly.
>
> Not only is it not reasonable, but it doesn't pretend to be.
>
> What seems to me ludicrous about O'Hara is his making it appear to be reasonable. (Wittgenstein, 1967a, p. 57–8)

Setting aside for now the question of the fairness of Wittgenstein's interpretation of Father O'Hara (Davies, 1982; Diamond, 2005), Wittgenstein is here drawing a distinction between beliefs for which it is acceptable to give reasons and beliefs for which the giving of reasons undermines the character of the belief. What is Wittgenstein getting at – if not a recapitulation of the old opposition between rational philosophy and irrational faith?

As with many of Wittgenstein's writings, the lectures offer largely critical remarks on some of the prevalent ways in which the topic in question has been dealt with in philosophical or academic discourses. Wittgenstein is not presenting a theory of religious belief or an argument for a particular conclusion. O'Hara's style of apologetic remains fairly common in contemporary philosophy of religion and interdisciplinary discourse between theology and science. In the lectures, Wittgenstein seeks to address some of the differences he detects between ordinary perceptual and religious beliefs in order to portray some of the conceptual confusion surrounding how people talk about religion. Wittgenstein criticizes religious apologists who seek to defend the evidential support for religious beliefs, for ignoring salient features of religious beliefs, and for treating them as if they were ordinary beliefs about the existence or nature of things in the world. In offering these criticisms, Wittgenstein suggests that beliefs of a religious sort tend to function differently in people's belief systems than do beliefs concerning mundane matters.

Generally, Wittgenstein does not defend theses regarding religion, or the philosophy of religion, so much as he seeks clarity regarding some of the ways people use language in the context of religious phenomena. This concern shows something about what Wittgenstein's understands philosophy to be. For him, philosophy is a discipline that responds to a lack of clarity; it is *occasional*. Wittgenstein seems to have been provoked by something he heard or read in Frazer and O'Hara. It is important to observe that Wittgenstein never really seems to diverge from this overarching conception of philosophy as the seeking of clarity about the workings of language in his writings, conversations, or lectures, no matter how formal or informal. Wittgenstein is critical of religious believers' use of reason when it strives for an appearance of reasonableness. He seems to find those efforts insincere. For Wittgenstein, a religious thinker like O'Hara is going beyond what a religious discourse ought to be. To use a concept like religion is to presuppose a particular understanding of what the meaning of that term is, an extension that one takes one's conversation partners to more or less share.

As for what sort of positive message scholars or philosophers of religion should take from Wittgenstein's lectures, a word of caution that is repeated throughout concerns how easy it is to let one's desires, as philosopher or scholar, lead one past salient differences towards a misleading sense of univocity between instances of language use or social practice.

In this sense, the principal lesson of the Lectures is similar to that of the 'Remarks on Frazer's *Golden Bough*' and many other texts Wittgenstein wrote. Wittgenstein counsels restraint when it comes to theorizing about religious phenomena (whether as scholars or as practitioners). We, as scholars, are often intellectually or socially quite distant from those who participate in religious ways of life, and it is all too easy for our own prejudices and desires for intellectual unity to lead us astray; yet practitioners may be tempted to draw on the reputation of rigor in science to theorize about their faith, but this move all too easily becomes a form of alienation. According to Wittgenstein, attention to particulars and vigorously seeking after clarity are marks of the responsible philosopher and sincere practitioner of a religion.

1.1.2 Private sources of remarks on religions

Occasional remarks on religious phenomena can be found in sources throughout Wittgenstein's corpus, but some of Wittgenstein's most provocative remarks on religion are found in his private diaries and notes taken on conversations by friends and colleagues. During World War I, Wittgenstein kept a series of notebooks in which he wrote both personal and philosophical material. The philosophical material, published under the title: *Notebooks: 1914–16,* is better known than the personal, published as *Geheime Tagebücher: 1914–16*. Throughout Wittgenstein's *Nachlass* are other coded remarks, some of which have been published as *Culture and Value*. While that collection does contain a remark from the war diaries, the content of *Culture and Value* is almost entirely written after 1929.

The diaries provide a window into Wittgenstein's private thoughts during a deeply personally shaking – and philosophically productive – period during his life. In these diaries, readers can see the seriousness and earnestness with which Wittgenstein addressed God during his prayers:

> [7.4.16] Torture, from which I am only temporarily released, in order to remain sensitive to further torments. A range of terrible torments. An exhaustive march, a night of ceaseless coughing, a company of drunks, a company of common and stupid people. Do good deeds and rejoice about your virtue. Am ill and have a bad/poor life. God help me. I am a poor unfortunate man. God hear me and give me peace. Amen.[5]

What is seen here is not the God beyond the limits of the sayable that one might anticipate from Wittgenstein's official philosophical writings stemming from the time but instead a God that Wittgenstein addresses directly in prayer. And indeed, the last lines are reminiscent of the traditional Jesus Prayer: 'Lord Jesus Christ, Son of God, have mercy on me, a sinner.' It is difficult to know what to make of Wittgenstein's own apparent wartime religiosity or his attachment to Tolstoy's rendering of the Gospels. Was his prayer produced by the daily anxieties and dreadful experiences of life at war? Does Wittgenstein's occasional religiosity have any bearing on his philosophical work at the time?

It may well be that Wittgenstein's occasional religiosity did not move beyond Monk's appraisal: 'In William James's terms, the question is whether it helps to heal the "sick soul". And the "it" here is not a belief but a practice, a way of living' (Monk, 1990, p. 121). Monk continues on the next page:

> The idea that the essence of religion lay in feelings (or as Nietzsche would have it, instincts) and practices rather than in beliefs remained a constant theme in Wittgenstein's thought on the subject for the rest of his life. Christianity was for him (at the time) 'the only sure way to happiness' – not because it promised an after-life, but because, in the words and the figure of Christ, it provided an example, an attitude, to follow, that made suffering bearable. (Monk, 1990, p. 122)

While I would avoid talk of 'essences' when discussing Wittgenstein's philosophical views on just about any topic, the force of this remark by Monk seems right to me. The faith shown in the diaries from the war is earnest. Wittgenstein wrote of Christianity here because he found it helpful in dealing with both the suffering he had known before the war and the extreme stress experienced at the front.

During the 1930s, Wittgenstein kept diaries that his sister gave to Rudolf Koder upon Wittgenstein's death (Wittgenstein, 2003b, p. 3); subsequently, they have come to be known as the Koder Diaries. These diaries became generally available in German in 1997 and in English in 2003b under the title 'Movements of Thought: Diaries 1930–1932, 1936–1937' in James Klagge and Alfred Nordmann's *Wittgenstein: Public and Private Occasions*. Klagge and Nordmann take pains to note that unlike the diaries from World War I, there is no clear point of demarcation between public and private voices with respect to these diaries. These diary entries are another window into the mind of Wittgenstein during a time of dramatic transition in his philosophy. To what extent do the remarks here shed new light on Wittgenstein's thought? Upon reading the diaries, several features present themselves.

During the time in which the first entries of the Koder diaries were written (1930–32), Wittgenstein was considering writing an autobiography

(Wittgenstein, 2003b, pp. 4–5). Editors Klagge and Nordmann compare these early reflections to Augustine's *Confessions*. (Wittgenstein, 2003b, p. 5) Klagge and Nordmann observe that Wittgenstein sought to arrive at 'clarity and truth' regarding his life:

> The remarks of manuscript 183 [the MS for the diaries] constitute a spiritual act, but one that cannot be divorced from Wittgenstein's philosophical practice, his rejection of all things impure and superstitious in the serious and rigorous quest for clarity and truth. In this regard, Wittgenstein's Confessions are indeed akin to those of Augustine or Rousseau. Instead of writing a 'secret' diary, Wittgenstein subjects apparently personal concerns to the same scrutiny, the same movements of thought, the same standards of written expressions as he does more overtly philosophical matters. (Wittgenstein, 2003b, p. 4)

Klagge and Nordmann suggest that the diaries are an early attempt at autobiographical writing. This makes them an important resource for further reflection on Wittgenstein's philosophical method and for how he thought about his own religious dispositions. Klagge and Nordmann observe in their introduction that '[a]s opposed to his other notebooks and the so-called secret diaries of 1914–16, the Koder diaries are unique precisely in that they do not set off the private from the public at all' (Wittgenstein, 2003b, p. 3).

This blending of the personal and philosophical is reflected in the very first sentence of the diaries: 'Without a little courage one can't even write a sensible remark about oneself' (Wittgenstein, 2003b, p. 9). Why does it take courage? Perhaps it is because we are so often not transparent to ourselves. We may wish to be other than we are. It takes work to consider critically the images we construct of ourselves. The courage to find the right words does not come easily:

> Often I feel that there is something in me like a lump which, were it to melt, would let me cry or I would then find the right words (or perhaps even a melody). But this something (is it the heart?) in my case feels like leather & cannot melt. Or is it only that I am too much a coward to let the temperature rise sufficiently? (Wittgenstein, 2003b, p. 11)

Note the interplay between courage and cowardice with respect to clarity. Clarity requires courage. Lack of clarity may be due to bad luck or a bad day; it might be a sign of moral vice. Here we see an emphasis on epistemic virtue that is not distant from moral virtue. Wittgenstein himself seems not to be clear on whether the source of unclarity is sin (variously conceived) or something more mundane and ordinary. Consider the following:

> The only thing that at some point might break in me & I am sometimes afraid of that, is my intellect.
>
> Sometimes I think that at some point my brain won't take the strain on it & will give out. And given what its strength is, it is frightfully strained – at least that's how it often seems to me. (Wittgenstein, 2003b, p. 13)

In the passage, the source of confusion is a mind that is heavily taxed. However, the previous passage seems to link a lack of clarity with a lack of virtue. In these passages, not all unclarity is moral failing, but to the extent that the intellect obeys the will, one might infer from the above that Wittgenstein thinks here that human beings are responsible for the clarity they pursue or the unclarity they tolerate.

While I do not think Wittgenstein's writings should be read *strictly* synoptically, themes and modes of expression recur across Wittgenstein's corpus. Sincerity appears again as a religious virtue as Wittgenstein contemplates being an 'apostle'. Repeatedly, Wittgenstein seeks to emphasize the thoroughness of religious commitment:

> To be an apostle is a life. In part it surely expresses itself in what he says, but not in that it is true but in that he says it. Suffering for the idea defines him but here, too, it holds that the meaning of the sentence 'this one is an apostle' lies in the mode of its verification. To describe an apostle is to describe a life. What impression this description makes on others must be left to them. Believing in an apostle means to relate toward him in such & such a way – relate actively. (Wittgenstein, 2003b, p. 81–2)

Again, Wittgenstein wishes to emphasize the practical consequences of, rather than the intellectual elaborations on, religious commitments. Wittgenstein also includes some candid remarks on his own relationship to religion, his awareness of his peculiarity in this regard:

> I am doing right when I proceed to a more spiritual plane on which I can be a human being – while others can be human also on a less spiritual one.

> I just don't have the right to live on that floor as they do & on their plane feel my inferiority rightfully. (Wittgenstein, 2003b, p. 95)

Wittgenstein seems to sense in himself a disposition towards spiritual cultivation. Yet, he recognizes that this stems from his aspiration to be a flourishing human being. Wittgenstein seems to evince a humanism as the ethic he strives for, and in order to reach this goal, he judges that pursuing 'a more spiritual plane' is the means by which he can achieve it. Others might not need this help; however, Wittgenstein recognizes that he cannot keep in mind his own failings – something he takes to be a condition of his own moral flourishing – without the 'spiritual plane'.

In addition to these private sources for Wittgenstein's views on religion, there are texts that do not come directly from Wittgenstein; these include the memoirs and correspondence with students, colleagues, and friends. Friends such as Maurice O'Conner Drury, Norman Malcolm, Rush Rhees, and O. K. Bouwsma took notes following conversations with Wittgenstein, and some of these conversations were concerned with the topics of religion, ethics, and the relationship between the two. For example, Bouwsma took extensive notes on conversations he had with Wittgenstein during the last two years of Wittgenstein's life (Bouwsma, 1986). These conversations show a preoccupation with the nature of genuinely virtuous living, be it religious or otherwise. Topics under consideration drifted from abstract virtues, moral theories, to the possibility of religious practice and belief. Bouwsma includes not just Wittgenstein's remarks but also his own responses, questions, and after-the-fact critical reflections. Among other things, what these conversation notes reveal is that Wittgenstein did not think of religion being any one thing; instead, he understands religions to be like languages: they show a remarkable diversity. The conversations also show the normative standpoints that are present in Wittgenstein's private remarks on religion. Wittgenstein evidently thought that religiosity based on (cognitive) belief was of less value than religion based on (passionate) practice.

From these recollections of others, we may be reminded of the fact that Wittgenstein was at times very ambivalent about religion. Recall the remark of Wittgenstein's Drury reports: 'I am not a religious man, but I cannot help seeing every problem from a religious point of view' (Rhees, 1984, p. 94). Malcolm held this to be 'analogous to a religious point of view' (1993, p. 1); the analogy lies in the paralleling of grounding belief in God to the grounding of meaning in grammar. Neither for

Wittgenstein stands in need of justification or explanation. Malcolm writes:

> When Wittgenstein said that all he wanted was that his philosophical work 'should be God's will', he would certainly have considered any question as to why it should be God's will as nonsensical.
>
> The analogy to philosophy is that reasons, justifications, explanations, reach a terminus in the language-games and their internally related forms of human life. The assumption that everything can be explained filled Wittgenstein with a kind of fury. (Malcolm, 1993, pp. 84–5)

Also analogous to a religious point of view is the tendency to feel a sense of wonder at the very existence of the world; this, Malcolm contends, runs parallel to Wittgenstein's wonder at the existence of particular language-games. Malcolm notes a parallel between the idea that certain religious emotions point to something fundamentally wrong with human beings and Wittgenstein's tendency to use metaphors of illness or disease in making sense of philosophical confusion. According to Malcolm, Wittgenstein attaches no value to the traditional theistic proofs. Analogous to these would be arguments directed to the skeptic purporting to prove the existence of other minds or of the external world. One should not put too much stock into these early reminiscences of Wittgenstein, but neither should they be ignored. These early reflections on Wittgenstein provided the initial evaluation of Wittgenstein's life before full-length biographies were available.

1.1.3 Sources that are otherwise relevant to philosophy of religion

Most texts in Wittgenstein's philosophical corpus treat topics that are related, at most, indirectly to issues in the philosophy of religion. These sources include some of Wittgenstein's most polished and widely read writings: the *Tractatus*, *Philosophical Investigations*, and *On Certainty*. While some of these texts include occasional remarks having to do with religion (such as the reference to 'praying' among the 'multiplicity of language-games' and the 'Theology as grammar' aside in *Philosophical Investigations*[6]), these texts are of importance for philosophers of religion because of their bearing on problems common to many areas of twentieth century philosophy. Other texts included in this category may be less well polished by Wittgenstein but may have significant consequences for philosophy of religion.

In the *Tractatus*, Wittgenstein famously relegates ethics, aesthetics, and talk of God to the sphere of what cannot be said. The irony of the *Tractatus* is that Wittgenstein holds these topics to be of great importance; nevertheless, he held that language involving these ideas runs up against the limits of what is sayable. The *Tractatus* might not seem to be a fruitful text for philosophy of religion, except insofar as it seems to make the *philosophy* of religion an impossible exercise (save for keeping silent, a feature of the text that has generated interest among philosophers of mysticism).

The reading of the *Tractatus* as showing but not saying that which is inexpressible is strengthened by Wittgenstein's correspondence with Paul Engelmann. In one well-known segment of their correspondence during World War I, Engelmann sent Wittgenstein a poem by Ludwig Uhland, 'Count Eberhard's Hawthorn', which Wittgenstein read with much delight; he felt the poem was able to express a life without straying into metaphysical explanation.[7] For him, the poem illustrated precisely the decorum with which one should speak of the world and show what is of value.

A text that is sometimes used to shed light on both the *Tractatus* and Wittgenstein's views on ethics and the limits of expressibility is the 'Lecture on Ethics'. Wittgenstein's lecture was given before The Heretics group at Cambridge in either 1929 or 1930 but not published until 1965. This lecture provides some insight into the ideas of Wittgenstein during a period of creativity and change in his thought. In the lecture, Wittgenstein provides some conceptual clarifications on the use of value-laden language, how some uses of words like 'good' and 'right' are ethical and others are merely utilitarian. Wittgenstein distinguishes between statements of relative value and statements of absolute value. Statements of relative value (for example, 'This is a good chair.') are essentially statements of fact; whereas statements of absolute value (for example, 'You should have behaved better.') are not.

Wittgenstein also discusses what would have to be the case in order for people to sensibly use expressions such as 'the absolute good'. For example, Wittgenstein writes: 'No state of affairs has, in itself, what I would like to call the coercive power of an absolute judge. Then what have all of us who, like myself, are still tempted to use such expressions as "absolute good," "absolute value," etc., what have we in mind and what do we try to express?' (Wittgenstein, 1965, pp. 7–8). In response to his own question, Wittgenstein replies:

> I will describe this experience in order, if possible, to make you recall the same or similar experiences, so that we may have a common ground for our investigation. I believe the best way of describing it is to say that

> when I have it I wonder at the existence of the world. And I am then inclined to use such phrases as 'how extraordinary that anything should exist' or 'how extraordinary that the world should exist.' I will mention another experience straight away which I also know and which others of you might be acquainted with: it is, what one might call, the experience of feeling absolutely safe. I mean the state of mind in which one is inclined to say 'I am safe, nothing can injure me whatever happens.' Now let me consider these experiences, for, I believe, they exhibit the very characteristics we try to get clear about. And there the first thing I have to say is, that the verbal expression which we give to these experiences is nonsense! (Wittgenstein, 1965, p. 8)

These remarks seem to resonate with Wittgenstein's statements on the inexpressible in the *Tractatus*. Indeed, the lecture seems to say more explicitly what lay implicit in his early work about the limits of language. One might see in the lecture some evidence for readings of Wittgenstein that stress the idea of ineffability in semantics.

His final remarks in the lecture on ethics and religion on the one hand and the sciences on the other clearly display Wittgenstein's appreciation of the limits of language, but also of reason:

> I see now that these nonsensical expressions were not nonsensical because I had not yet found the correct expressions, but that their nonsensicality was their very essence. For all I wanted to do with them was just to go beyond the world and that is to say beyond significant language. My whole tendency and I believe the tendency of all men who ever tried to write or talk Ethics or Religion was to run against the boundaries of language. This running against the walls of our cage is perfectly, absolutely hopeless. Ethics so far as it springs from the desire to say something about the ultimate meaning of life, the absolute good, the absolute valuable, can be no science. What it says does not add to our knowledge in any sense. But it is a document of a tendency in the human mind which I personally cannot help respecting deeply and I would not for my life ridicule it. (Wittgenstein, 1972, pp. 11–12)

Wittgenstein does not here expand on why he holds this respect for ethics and religion, but these closing remarks of the lecture are coherent with Wittgenstein's early thought that what is of value lies outside the propositions of natural science, that is, outside of what can be said. Perspicuity here is the recognition of nonsense as nonsense. Yet ethical attitudes ought to be respected and even revered.

Another source providing some insight into Wittgenstein's thought on religion, as well as the development of his philosophy over time, is the collection published in English as *Culture and Value*. The text contains miscellaneous remarks Wittgenstein made across his corpus concerning topics not generally considered to be philosophical in nature. How this editorial decision was made reflects a positive view of the nature of philosophy that Wittgenstein might or might not have shared. The book must be read with great care as some of the original sources are private journals and others manuscripts Wittgenstein had been working on. The fact that these remarks are published together can give the impression of a unified work (despite the prefatory comments to the contrary by the editors).

With one exception from 1914, *Culture and Value* covers writings from the period following Wittgenstein's return to philosophy in 1929 until his death in 1951. In this collection, one sees Wittgenstein work with ideas regarding the nature of truth and meaning, the development of the idea that meaning correlates with use, and various remarks on the place of clarity in philosophy. Because of the temporal scope of the book, one can glean from it a sense of Wittgenstein's development. Sometimes, one sees him playing with an idea that might be further developed in the *Philosophical Investigations* or in *On Certainty* or in other private sources. One theme that presents itself almost immediately is the central importance Wittgenstein places on clarity for its own sake. Clarity was not just the means of doing philosophy for Wittgenstein; it was the end as well (one end instead of others). Consider the following remark from 1930:

> Our civilization is characterized by the word progress ... Typically it constructs. Its activity is to construct a more and more complicated structure. And even clarity is only a means to this end & not an end in itself.
>
> For me on the contrary clarity, transparency, is an end in itself
>
> I am not interested in erecting a building but in having the foundations of possible buildings transparently before me.
>
> So I am aiming at something different than are the scientists & my thoughts move differently than do theirs. (Wittgenstein, 1998, p. 9)

Wittgenstein took himself to be after a sort of philosophical insight that ran counter to the propensity towards progress and construction in Western civilization. Wittgenstein is critical of the ends of philosophy 'typical' of our era.

As can be seen from *Culture and Value*, various sources in Wittgenstein's *Nachlass* are of interest, as they show the development of Wittgenstein's views on the methods of philosophy and on the relationship between language and world. These sources shed light upon the gradual development of Wittgenstein's methods and views. They may help us construct a picture of the career of Wittgenstein the philosopher, and this would be of help in coming to understand the place of remarks on religion in his body of work.

For example, TS 213, the so-called 'Big Typescript' shows Wittgenstein's mind at work as he returned to themes familiar from the *Tractatus* after his return to Cambridge in 1929. While the typescript never quite found completion as a book or essay ready to be published, it does show hints of where this thought would go. Wittgenstein's care in seeking proper turns of phrase and order of the remarks likewise shows his preoccupation with achieving clarity and resolution of philosophical confusion (Kenny, 1976). The attitudes towards language and philosophy are familiar to readers of Wittgenstein's later works, such as *Philosophical Investigations* and *On Certainty*, However, this work contains connections between themes about the nature of philosophy, the nature of meaning, understanding, and explanation, as well as the nature of mathematics and logic. The typescript contains early reflection on familiar notions such as language-games, rule following, the privacy of experience and the public nature of language.

Philosophical Investigations is a text widely understood to be the most polished of the writings from Wittgenstein's later career. It is difficult to overstate the influence of this book on how Wittgenstein is read on religion, and indeed because this text can rightly be read as a culmination of Wittgenstein's philosophical activity in the last two decades of his life, it makes sense that the text would loom large in philosophy of religion self-consciously following Wittgenstein's lead. The book focuses upon many of the same general topics as the *Tractatus* – the relationship between language and the world, the nature of logic, the nature of philosophy – but this time there is more explicit focus on the particularities of language use and the plurality of ways in which philosophy may work to clarify confusion. Scholars of philosophy of religion, theology, and religious studies have paid much attention in the secondary literature to the ideas of 'grammar', 'meaning is use', 'language-games' and 'forms-of-life'.[8]

Early characterizations of Wittgenstein on religion treated religions as language-games – on occasion, philosophers would refer to 'the religious language-game' – and thus utterances asserted within 'religious language-games' were held to be meaningful insofar as they had a use. While this view staved off verificationist criticism of religious language, it also came to be seen as being too similar to fideism, anti-realism, and relativism. Yet, a central theme of *Philosophical Investigations* is the idea that language is a social practice, where meaning is found publicly; configurations of religious language as being rationally cut off from other areas of human life seems to miss a key feature of Wittgenstein's thought.

The book *On Certainty* was written between 1949 and Wittgenstein's death in 1951, partly in response to G. E. Moore's 'Proof of an External World'. The text is concerned largely with questions regarding belief and doubt. The relevance of the text for the philosophy of religion seems to be indirect; however, given the importance of belief and doubt for some religions, the ideas in *On Certainty* are quite provocative when explored in connection with topics in philosophy of religion. Consider the following remarks:

> 115. If you tried to doubt everything you would not get as far as doubting anything. The game of doubting itself presupposes certainty. (Wittgenstein, 1972, p. 18e)
>
> 142. It is not single axioms that strike me as obvious, it is a system in which consequences and premises give one another mutual support. (Wittgenstein, 1972, p. 21e)
>
> 160. The child learns by believing the adult. Doubt comes after belief.
>
> 161. I learned an enormous amount and accepted it on human authority, and then I found some things confirmed or disconfirmed by my own experience. (Wittgenstein, 1972, p. 23e)

These remarks, as others in *On Certainty*, deflate the idea that one may be capable of the radical doubting of a global skeptic. Instead, doubting takes place against a background of accepted beliefs. These ideas clearly have consequences for epistemology, in general, and epistemology of religion, in particular.

What might the picturing of belief in *On Certainty* teach us about the conditions of religious belief or religious doubt? Furthermore, rather than being in a position to consider the justification of each of the many beliefs we may hold at any given time, Wittgenstein reminds the reader that much of what a person may believe is accepted on trust. Among other things, Wittgenstein depicts persons as living in epistemic communities; relationships of trust and authority are relevant to understanding how beliefs are acquired, revised or rejected. We rely on other people all the time in our forming of beliefs. Indeed, this is part of what it means to be a social being. The way in which the passages quoted above emphasize the place of language within social practices – and the primacy of trust to doubt – have been very influential and will deeply inform arguments to come in later chapters.

1.2 Interpretive schemes and Wittgenstein's corpus

Given the wide variety and nature of the Wittgenstein texts now available to scholars, determining which sources should be authoritative or corrective when there are differences between the treatments of various topics is a challenge. While Wittgenstein's approach to philosophy may have changed over the years, his philosophical goals remain the same. Time and again, he is concerned above all to seek out clarity about the workings of language because of its tendency to induce philosophical confusion.

Klagge argues that Wittgenstein should be read as an exile, as someone who has no home. In this vein, Wittgenstein's writing has no general audience. Klagge argues that Wittgenstein was profoundly aware of the lack of a suitable audience and he could not write, save in a handful of texts, to a general audience. If Wittgenstein was in this way self-critical, then it is important to understand his concern over the adequacy of his own texts. What he was trying to say did not immediately present itself to him, a fact I take it is shown both in his lecturing, conversational, and writing styles. Nevertheless, with occasional identification of connections between Wittgenstein's biography and his philosophy, I believe the various sources in Wittgenstein's corpus can be placed into a fruitful conversation with one another. What must be guarded against however is the desire to find a prooftext for a particular interpretive thesis. Instead, heeding Wittgenstein's words in a separate context: 'Don't think but look!'(Wittgenstein, 2001, §66), it may be that the various types of sources (private and public) can give readers a better sense of the interplay and methods used by this philosopher to seek clarity both in his larger philosophy as well as in his person.

Anat Biletzki's *(Over)Interpreting Wittgenstein* (2003) offers an overview of the many ways Wittgenstein has been interpreted across the last century. Her book is a valuable corrective against the ambitions of scholars who might seek to definitively interpret Wittgenstein. When considering how best to approach Wittgenstein's corpus, one is immediately confronted with the considerable volume of interpretations of

Wittgenstein that have developed since the initial publication of the *Tractatus*. Biletzki depicts five successive 'stations' of Wittgenstein interpretation through the history of analytic philosophy and also surveys the topics that dominate discussion of Wittgenstein within various subdisciplines (such as logic, ethics, or religion).

Biletzki begins the book with a study of the main approaches philosophers have taken in the study of Wittgenstein in the then eight decades following the publication of the *Tractatus*. The first station identifies what had been a highly influential interpretation of Wittgenstein in the early decades of analytic philosophy: the logico-linguistic. Biletzki understands this station to include Wittgenstein's very first interpreters, including Bertrand Russell, Frank Ramsey, and the members of the Vienna Circle. While Russell and Ramsey emphasized the centrality of the discussion of the compositionality of propositions, the so-called 'Picture Theory' of meaning, and the anti-metaphysical tendencies of the work, they downplayed the importance of what they took to be the mysterious propositions at the end of the book:

> 6.44 It is not *how* things are in the world that is mystical, but *that* it exists.
>
> 6.45 To view the world sub specie aeterni is to view it as a whole – a limited whole.
>
> Feeling the world as a limited whole – it is this that is mystical.
>
> 6.54 My propositions serve as elucidations in the following way: anyone who understands me eventually recognizes them as nonsensical, when he has used them – as steps – to climb up beyond them. (He must, so to speak, throw away the ladder after he has climbed up it.)
>
> He must transcend these propositions, and then he will see the world aright.
>
> 7 What we cannot speak about we must pass over in silence. (Wittgenstein, 2001, pp. 88–9)

Members of the Vienna circle such as Rudolf Carnap and Moritz Schlick took inspiration from Wittgenstein's demarcation of physicalist language from evaluative language and his discussion of logic (especially tautologies). Biletzki writes:

> Where Russell or Ramsey focused on the logico-linguistic center of the *Tractatus* and gingerly addressed its meta-philosophical implications,

> making scant note of its 'extraneous' themes (bundled under 'the mystical'), the Vienna Circle did more than focus – they excluded from their interpretation anything not having to do with the positivistic framework ordered by their focus. (Biletzki, 2003, p. 46)

Biletzki notes that while these first station readings were influential throughout what would eventually become known as analytic philosophy, these interpretations can prevail only when readers reject the importance of both the framing remarks in Wittgenstein's preface to the book and the remarks on the mystical and the limits of language in the 6's and in proposition 7.

Biletzki understands the second station of interpretations to develop a more sophisticated version of metaphysics in light of the critical stance the *Tractatus* and *Philosophical Investigations* each take towards metaphysics. Interpreters of the second station include philosophers such as G.E.M. Anscombe or Max Black who sought to identify just what Wittgenstein understood by the word 'object' in the *Tractatus*. The problem arises from Wittgenstein's compositional account of meaning.[9] According to the *Tractatus*, facts are the basic constituents of the world and are that to which true propositions correspond. Interpreters of the second station wonder if facts are composed of objects and relations among those objects and in what sense those objects are understood to exist. Does the existence of objects depend on their being embedded within facts, or is their existence independent of their contributing to the constitution of facts?

Biletzki thinks of the second station of Wittgenstein interpretation as including both the sophisticated metaphysical interpretations of the *Tractatus* as well as the early reception of Wittgenstein's 'later' philosophy. This initial reflection on the notions of 'private language', 'language-games', 'family resemblances', and 'meaning-as-use' emphasizes the replacement of one metaphysical attitude (exemplified in the early Wittgenstein) with a more sophisticated variant (drawn from the later). Second station interpreters take license from Wittgenstein himself: Wittgenstein presents the *Philosophical Investigations* as a criticism of what he understood to be mistakes in his earlier views. Biletzki writes:

> These mistakes include the representational character of language vis-à-vis the world, the logically one-dimensional character of any language, the workings of ostensive definition, the Augustinian picture of meaning, and many others – petty or, more to the point, principled. Their rejection seems to lead, naturally, to the new positions

> espoused in the *Philosophical Investigations*: language as made up of language-games (rather than pictures of the world) and meaning as use (rather than as reference). (Biletzki, 2003, p. 55)

Contending with the discontinuity in Wittgenstein's appraisal of his own philosophical development has been one of the central tasks of all Wittgenstein interpreters after the first station.

Biletzki's third station, 'Reasonable Meta-Readings' rises above the early, more conventional readings of Wittgenstein, and comes to identify themes that run through both his 'early' and 'later' periods. According to Biletzki, interpreters of the third station include some of the most distinguished Wittgenstein interpreters, including P.M.S. Hacker and Jaakko Hintikka. Those at the third station bring to light the very remarks in the 6's and 7 of the Tractatus that philosophers of the first two stations downplayed or ignored. But what follows from taking seriously Wittgenstein's remarks on silence, nonsense, and the limits of language? In order to formulate an answer, philosophers of the third station lean on what is known as the show/say distinction (Biletzki, 2003, p. 62). Consider for example these remarks from the *Tractatus*:

> 4.121 Propositions cannot represent logical form: it is mirrored in them.
>
> What finds its reflection in language, language cannot represent.
>
> What expresses *itself* in language, *we* cannot express by means of language.
>
> Propositions *show* the logical form of reality.
>
> They display it.
>
> 4.1212 What *can* be shown, *cannot* be said. (Wittgenstein, 2001, p. 31)

The apparent anti-metaphysical themes of the *Tractatus* are understood as counseling silence regarding truths that can be shown but not said. Interpreters of the third station emphasize a metaphysics of ineffability in Wittgenstein, whether it be in terms of the truths of logic (as in the *Tractatus*) or in terms of the nature of grammar (as in the *Philosophical Investigations*). Biletzki also notes that readers of this station, along with the second, emphasize overarching interpretive positions, that is, the idea that Wittgenstein is a realist (or an anti-realist) as well as the greater interpretive importance of the *Philosophical Investigations* for reading Wittgenstein.

Biletzki's fourth and fifth stations 'Taking Nonsense Seriously' and 'Over the Deep End, Or the Ethical Reading', respectively, are closely related, and I will explore them jointly. The fourth station moves beyond the early/late Wittgenstein (or anti-metaphysical/metaphysical) distinction common to the first three and reads the framing remarks of the *Tractatus* as being of the utmost importance for discerning the meaning of the content of the book. Biletzki understands the fifth station to extend beyond the fourth to consider what the philosophical point may be of taking nonsense seriously. Biletzki writes, 'the sharp division between the two Wittgensteins, or even the duller developmental distinction between the two connected by the middle, now gives way to a strongly unified Wittgenstein wherein one can ascertain necessary forerunners of the second within the very differently interpreted first' (Biletzki, 2003, p. 83). Biletzki observes that the roots of the fifth station can be found in the early writings of Stanley Cavell among others. In his work from the 1960s, Cavell emphasizes the therapeutic dimensions of the *Philosophical Investigations*.[10] Biletzki writes of the significance of Cavell's interpretation:

> Though other, earlier (in stations, not in dates) interpreters, recognize the primacy of language-games (vs. the picture theory), of forms of life (vs. a metaphysics), of the particular (vs. the general), of description (vs. theory), it was Cavell's readings that presented a vigorously dissimilar Wittgenstein whose idea of therapy involves not only giving up our earlier pictures, but also realizing our 'being in the grip' of such pictures. (Biletzki, 2003, 89–90)

Taking nonsense seriously in the *Tractatus* can have a therapeutic effect, one that is similar to the effect one finds in the *Investigations*, that of leading the mind away from chronically problematic patterns of thinking. Cavell's therapeutic reading could also be at home in the fifth station. Biletzki presents these five stations of Wittgenstein interpretation as a way to organize the disparate threads of research on Wittgenstein's philosophy over the last century. This does not mean that all Wittgenstein scholarship neatly fits into these stations; nevertheless, Biletzki provides a useful overview of the immense body of secondary scholarship.

In what follows, the reading of Wittgenstein I offer is closest to the fourth and fifth stations (that is, the ethical-therapeutic readings). This approach presents itself from studies of Wittgenstein's texts in concert with study of his biography. Wittgenstein seeks to steer himself, his readers, conversation partners, and students away from some of the pitfalls of confused philosophical thinking. This approach to the practice of philosophy I term Wittgenstein's *ethic of perspicuity*. Perspicuity is more than clarity; it is a searching clarity or a clarity that is achieved by working away at problematic assumptions embedded in ordinary habits of thought or action. Sometimes the terms *Durchsichtigkeit* and *Übersichlichkeit* are translated as 'clarity', 'transparency', 'perspicuity', 'surveyability', and 'synoptic view'.[11] I prefer to use the words 'perspicuity' and 'transparency', because they render the idea that ordinary ways of using language may be unclear, clarity is thus something that must be worked for and achieved.

Looking at the Wittgensteinian corpus, one may judge some texts to be of greater authority than others. The more authoritative texts I understand to have been those that Wittgenstein prepared for publication (primarily, the *Tractatus Logico-Philosophicus, The Big Typescript, Philosophical Investigations* and *On Certainty*); the less authoritative sources include those Wittgenstein did not develop for publication, those he abandoned, and lecture notes and personal diaries. I will follow the hermeneutical principle that the less authoritative texts ought to be read in concert with the more, the rationale being that the latter survived Wittgenstein's stringent criticism more or less to his satisfaction. If a conflict arises within Wittgenstein's corpus, that fact – if it is a fact – ought to be recognized; ultimately, the more authoritative texts may trump the less authoritative, but the less authoritative may venture approaches to topics not broached in the more authoritative sources. This is one reason why less authoritative sources may be of interest to philosophers.

Wittgenstein's ethic of perspicuity emerges from many places across his corpus, and I will use it to guide my reading both of these sources as well as less authoritative sources. The singular term 'ethic' is not ideal as it may imply a strict unity across Wittgenstein's corpus. That would be misleading. It is not that Wittgenstein has a particular ethical standpoint concerning philosophy that is reiterated in various texts throughout his philosophical career; however, the texts across Wittgenstein's corpus each pursue the goal of clarity as an end in itself.

As Biletzki's recounting of Wittgenstein interpretations shows, the early interpretive scheme of the first and second stations, of the 'early' and 'later' Wittgensteins – characterized by the authoritative texts *Tractatus* and *Philosophical Investigations* – has been modified or revised to such an extent that some contemporary scholarship on Wittgenstein tends to downplay perceived differences between the earlier and later periods in his corpus. The stark contrast between early and later Wittgensteins has been leavened by the gradual public appearance of additional sources from Wittgenstein's corpus in the decades following his death and more recently the 1997 and 2000 publications of Wittgenstein's *Wiener Ausgabe* and *Nachlass*, previously available only in the Wittgenstein archives. Earlier posthumous publications, such as the *Blue and Brown Books, On Certainty, Remarks on the Foundations of Mathematics, Last Writings on the Philosophy of Psychology*, and so on, have been profitably used to gain further insight into the evolution of Wittgenstein's thought as well as the relevance of Wittgenstein's ideas for various areas of philosophy beyond the study of language and logic.

Perhaps the tendency to divide among different Wittgensteins has been significantly undermined by the publication of McGuinness's and Monk's biographies, along with subsequent biographical essays. After all, conceiving of texts as the product of a life which has its own narrative will naturally encourage a reading of those texts that searches for continuity. This is not to say that one should approach the life of another as a coherent narrative. The question of the utility of biography for philosophical study comes down to whether biographical, or for that matter historical-critical, study will help interpreters avoid misinterpretations of otherwise distant or obscure work. Because so much of what Wittgenstein wrote was not prepared for publication by him, and this is especially true of the works that contain references to religious phenomena, biographies may be relevant to these texts' interpretation.

One can rarely appeal to independent philosophical criteria in establishing a philosophical method. Instead, methods are judged according to their fruits. An interpretation may be judged as reasonable given its expressive power. As with other readers of Wittgenstein, I argue that an interpretation of Wittgenstein ought to take seriously the situations in which the texts interpreted were written. This contextualism, which is inspired in part by Wittgenstein's own attention to context in understanding the workings of language, will suggest recurrent themes throughout Wittgenstein's career and trace how those themes are articulated in the various sources under investigation. Some of these themes are philosophical temptation and therapy, examination of the meaning of words as a source for resolving philosophical problems, and the relationship between language and thinking. I understand these themes to all meet in Wittgenstein's ethic of perspicuity, his unrelenting sense of there being a moral and intellectual duty to strive for clarity, honesty, and integrity. When turning one's attention to the phenomena of religions, this will emphasize a search for clarity about descriptions of practices, rituals, beliefs, doctrines, ethical commitments, institutions, myths, and so on, but it will also focus one's attention on one's own will, on the vicissitudes of one's own commitments to clarity, honesty, and integrity. Sometimes descriptions of our social worlds may give rise to confusion and it is especially then when Wittgenstein's philosophy has the most to offer philosophy of religion.

2
Wittgenstein, Biography, and Religious Identity

2.1 The uses of biography in philosophical study

It might seem obvious that the philosopher, while perhaps intrigued by details of biography or history, need not consult these disciplines when *doing philosophy*. After all, the validity of an argument is not affected by who asserted it and what he or she was really like as a person. To suggest otherwise invites concern that an interpreter may be committing an *ad hominem* fallacy or may be otherwise losing track of the important things – claims and reasons. The view just described is common sense, but like all sensible principles, it admits of exceptions, or so I argue. For many philosophers and on many topics, knowing their biographical details or historical context is strictly speaking irrelevant to understanding their philosophical achievements, but for Wittgenstein and the topics of religion and the nature of philosophy, this is not so. The reasons why are because for Wittgenstein, philosophy was a personal practice as much as an academic discipline, something that can be readily seen in biographies; and because the fragmentary and enigmatic remarks on religion, typically coming from sources that were not prepared for publication, can be better appreciated against the background of Wittgenstein's life. This chapter argues for a pair of claims regarding the use of biography and historical-contextual study for interpreting Wittgenstein's philosophy. The first, modest claim is that context may help scholars avoid misinterpretations of Wittgenstein's philosophical texts; this strategic use of historical-contextual study is common in the history of philosophy. The second, perhaps more controversial claim is that context can aid in interpreting claims that have philosophical import that come from fragmentary sources, such as Wittgenstein's remarks on Judaism and Christianity.

Biographer Ray Monk, too, was drawn to link the person and the philosopher, having the sense that the latter would be better understood through knowledge of the former. As Monk writes in his Introduction to *Ludwig Wittgenstein: The Duty of Genius*, 'I hope to make it clear how this work came from this man, to show – what many who read Wittgenstein's work instinctively feel – the unity of his philosophical concerns with his emotional and spiritual life' (Monk, 1990, p. xviii). Commenting on Monk's biography, James Conant observes, 'Wittgenstein neither wanted to, nor thought he could, separate the task of becoming the sort of human being he wanted to be from the task of becoming the sort of philosopher he wanted to be' (Conant, 2001, p. 29). Wittgenstein's philosophical work was bound up with a life of intellectual and moral striving, and one can see this striving both in works prepared for publication as well as in private sources, such as diaries, correspondence, and memories of conversations.

The claim that study of Wittgenstein's life is relevant to understanding his philosophy is hardly new, but the present chapter undertakes to consider the consequences of this claim for approaching Wittgensteinian philosophy of religion. Brian McGuinness' study on the first half of Wittgenstein's life, *Wittgenstein A Life: Young Ludwig 1889–1921*, and Monk's biography have displayed the effectiveness of studying Wittgenstein's life for understanding his philosophy. McGuinness begins the preface to his book connecting his scholarly interest in the *Tractatus* with a need to know more about the philosopher beyond his published words. McGuinness writes:

> I do not here pretend to publish a reference book containing all that is known (and nothing but what *is* known) of Wittgenstein. Rather I attempt to present his life (part of it, at first) as an intelligible whole, as something capable of being seen as a unity, as the development of just such a *Daimon* as Goethe describes in a favourite poem of Wittgenstein's ... I believe that Wittgenstein wanted to see his own life in such a way: what I have to describe is as much the character he tried to create as the character he was (if the two are really distinct). (McGuinness, 1988, p. xi)

In seeking to portray 'an intelligible whole' to Wittgenstein's life and philosophy, note here that McGuinness observes two characters of Wittgenstein: first, 'the character he tried to create', and second, 'the character he was'. I claim that we should think of the first as being fashioned by the ethic of perspicuity running through Wittgenstein's developed philosophy and the second as the character of Wittgenstein the man, who holds views that are scrutinized and may be superseded by the first. This dichotomy is useful for considering the overall aspirational or dialectical character of philosophy for Wittgenstein. Philosophy was something that Wittgenstein applied to himself and his own tendencies of thought. He observed this distance between his own inclination of thought and where philosophy ought to take him. Stanley Cavell famously detects the styles of confession and dialogue in *Philosophical Investigations*, but this dynamic can be found throughout his entire corpus (Cavell, 1966, pp. 183–4).

2.2 Wittgenstein and religiosity

Wittgenstein's most widely read texts make almost no mention of religious phenomena. In these texts, like the others, only a few scattered remarks have anything overt to do with phenomena of religions. It might seem to some then that the best option for the philosopher of religion in determining Wittgenstein's import for the subfield is to examine Wittgenstein's philosophy in general as expressed and developed in these well-prepared sources and then to apply it to the particular case of philosophy of religion (much like one might do with philosophy of mind or epistemology). What becomes of the meaning of language involving gods, souls, and the like given a picture theory of meaning or an understanding of language games? A major strand of development in Wittgensteinian philosophy of religion (and especially early Wittgensteinian philosophy of religion) has followed precisely this approach. Of course, this approach to Wittgensteinian philosophy of religion was also the only practical alternative for those philosophers in the 1950s and early 60s who did not know Wittgenstein personally.

During this time, only a small subset of the works now widely published were readily available to scholars. Wittgenstein's philosophy was to be found in a handful of texts that gradually found publication. It should not be surprising that Wittgensteinian philosophy of religion was largely devoted to explicating the pictures of language developed in the *Tractatus* and *Philosophical Investigations* and applying these explications to the cases of religious language. As numerous additional sources, including Wittgenstein's *Nachlass*, correspondence, and diaries, have shown, religion was a topic with which he was deeply concerned. Brian McGuinness's and Ray Monk's biographies and Norman Malcolm's memoirs portray Wittgenstein's life as being periodically deeply and personally concerned with religion.[1] While one could overinterpret this observation, the fact that Wittgenstein wrote about religious topics should be taken into consideration by both philosophers of religion interested in Wittgenstein's relevance to the subfield and interpreters of Wittgenstein generally.

If biographical materials are relevant to studies of Wittgenstein's philosophical practice, the question immediately arises how connected Wittgenstein's life and philosophy really are. New interpretive problems arise when philosophers consider texts outside the prepared, primary texts of Wittgenstein's corpus. When one considers sources that were not intended for publication such as *Geheime Tagebücher, Culture and Value* and 'Movements of Thought', further questions arise rather dramatically concerning Wittgenstein's conflicted relationship to his Jewish heritage and ambivalence about Christianity.

Sources that contain remarks about religious phenomena such as the 'Remarks on Frazer's *Golden Bough*', the 'Lectures on Religious Belief', or the 'Lecture on Ethics' were unpublished during Wittgenstein's lifetime. Because he did not prepare them for publication, the extent of their authority in his corpus is problematic. Reading these sources in connection with biographical material on Wittgenstein may help situate them within Wittgenstein's life and among other sources in Wittgenstein's corpus. For occasional, unsystematic remarks spread through the (mostly unpublished) corpus of a philosopher (like Wittgenstein) whose thought was in motion, recourse to biography may be helpful in deterring some misreadings and suggesting points of connection with non-philosophical figures who may have influenced the philosopher in question.

As discussed in Chapter 1, a text that has become very important to philosophers of religion interested in Wittgenstein is *Culture and Value* (first published in 1978/80 and published in a revised edition in 1994/98). Along with reflection on topics such as music and religion, in *Culture and Value* one sees Wittgenstein work with ideas regarding the nature of truth and meaning, the development of the idea that meaning may be connected with use, and the place of clarity in philosophy. Where one finds recurrence of ideas, it suggests a long term interest in those ideas or conceptions of philosophical activity.

Wittgenstein's stances towards various aspects of religiosity were complicated and changed over time. It is not easy to answer a seemingly straightforward question such as 'Was Wittgenstein religious?' It is best to pause and consider what definition of religion is relevant here. Furthermore, it is not clear how to measure religiosity (as if one measure would fit all religions). Wittgenstein's passion for honesty when it comes to religious beliefs and practices shows a level of commitment to the perceived integrity of religious traditions that neither all critics, nor all practitioners would share. One might then ask a more narrow question, 'Was Wittgenstein a Jew?' or 'Was he a Christian?' Any discussion of Wittgenstein's relationship to Christianity or Judaism runs the risk of essentializing just what it is to be a Christian or a Jew. Yet, I would not want to suggest there are no limits to these categories, only that limits are drawn in particular places and times and for particular purposes. In his more philosophical than personal writings, Wittgenstein located religiosity not merely or even primarily in the espousing of a belief but also in the social practices prescribed by the religion and in the seeing of one's life in a way changed by religious ideas, practices, and experiences.

In recent decades, increased attention has been placed on Wittgenstein's social context in early twentieth-century Vienna, his intellectual influences, and his experiences during World War I.[2] Furthermore, correspondence from the period (for example, with Paul Engelmann) and Wittgenstein's personal writings (for example, *Notebooks*, *Geheime Tagebucher*) show many of the topics – philosophical, religious, literary – with which Wittgenstein was preoccupied while he wrote the *Tractatus*. In *Wittgenstein's Vienna* (1973), Allen Janik and Stephen Toulmin opened new avenues for interpreting Wittgenstein through their reading of the *Tractatus* against the background of the high culture of fin-de-siècle Vienna. After providing a rich description of some of the artistic, political, literary, and musical movements of Vienna of the time, Janik and Toulmin argue that the unsayable in the *Tractatus* in fact engages the values and concerns of avant-garde Viennese culture. Consider for example the following passage:

> In order to have had the same thoughts as the author of the *Tractatus Logico-Philosophicus*, one would have to have lived in the milieu of fin-de-siècle Vienna; but, more than that, one would have to have undergone the experiences that Ludwig Wittgenstein himself had undergone during the First World War. For it was during that war that these thoughts – drawn from Kraus and Loos, Hertz and Frege, Schopenhauer, Kierkegaard and Tolstoy – coalesced into the unity which was the man Ludwig Wittgenstein. (Janik and Toulmin, 1973, p. 200)

The provision of historical and social context of Vienna of the 1900s is of great value, and their work has inspired later biographical and historical-contextual study in approaching Wittgenstein. Yet, as an early reviewer notes, Wittgenstein made extensive reference to Russell and Frege in the *Tractatus*; downplaying their influence on the *Tractatus* while highlighting the signal importance of fin-de-siècle Viennese culture would seem to be an overcorrection (Linsky, 1975). What this episode suggests to me is that philosophers should not appeal to historical and biographical material to fill-in content (for example, that which is unsaid) perceived to be missing from a work, but these contextual studies may contribute to the plausibility of one interpretation over another.

Studying the writings of those who influenced Wittgenstein may help philosophers appreciate the forms of religious thought Wittgenstein found plausible and inspiring. An example of just such an influence is Tolstoy's *Gospel in Brief*, which Wittgenstein discovered in a bookshop in Tarnow, very soon after World War I had begun. As Monk and McGuinness describe in their respective biographies, this discovery was highly significant for the young Wittgenstein's views on religion. McGuinness writes:

> At the time he was a byword among the soldiers for carrying it – 'the one with the Gospels' he would be called. The Christianity that he found in Tolstoy seemed to him the only sure way to happiness, but it was not an easy way. Man must renounce the flesh, the gratification of his own will, must make himself independent of outward circumstances, in order to serve the spirit which is in himself and in all men. This spirit makes all men the sons of God and the only true life for a man is communion with that spirit, without any concern for his own wishes or for the past or future: the only true life is life in the present. For a man living not the personal but the common life of the spirit, there is no death. (McGuinness, 1988, pp. 220–1)

Tolstoy's *Gospel* is written as a single narration divided into twelve chapters corresponding to segments from the Lord's Prayer. In Tolstoy's *Gospel*, Jesus is presented as a teacher and moral exemplar and God is the source of a meaningful, ordered life. This variation on Christianity is meant to satisfy the existential longings of an unsentimental soul for whom ideas like miracles and divine providence distract from the 'essential' message of the possibility of personal moral perfectibility. The transformation of Tolstoyan Christianity is a this-worldly, moral transformation, not the sanctification of traditional Catholicism or salvation by faith of Protestant Christianity. Tolstoy writes in his introduction to the text:

> I sought a solution to the problem of life, and not of a theological or historical question; and that is why I was indifferent to know

> whether Jesus Christ is or is not God, and from whom proceeds the Holy Spirit. And it is just as unimportant and unnecessary to know when and by whom such and such a Gospel was written, and whether such and such a parable came from Jesus Himself or not. For me, the only important concern was this light, which, for eighteen hundred years, has shone upon mankind; which has shone upon me likewise, and which shines upon me still. (Tolstoy, 1997, p. 24)

For Tolstoy, the Biblical Gospels are neither 'sacred books emanating from the Holy Spirit,' nor 'mere historical monuments of religious literature' (Tolstoy, 1997, p. 22). It is better to say that Tolstoy considers the Gospels to provide a resource for living in a meaningful way. Tolstoy takes himself to have offered a revision of the Biblical Gospels, a revision that removes the traces of 'Hebraism' that form part of the social and religious milieu of the Gospel writers as well as the traces of the influence of the early Church (Tolstoy, 1997, p. 23). Tolstoy sought to remove above all else elements in the Gospels that struck him as superstitious (Tolstoy, 1997, p. 32).

The Christ that Tolstoy depicts in his *Gospel* saves by practicing a piously moral life of love and self-sacrifice and then teaching it; in these teachings and practical examples are the resources for salvation. Through rigorous effort, one may achieve similar moral perfection. Here, there are no illusions of miraculous salvation – illusions which, one wonders, might impede the full development of one's moral character – just one's self and one's own actions. Consider the following passage:

> And Jesus called the people to him, and said: 'Hearken all, and understand: There is nothing in the world that, entering a man, could defile him; but that which goes forth from him, this defiles a man. Let love and mercy be in your soul, then all will be clean. Try to understand this.'
>
> And when he returned home his pupils asked him: 'What do these words mean?' And he said: 'Do you also not understand this? Do you not understand that everything external, that which is of the flesh, cannot defile a man? The reason is, it enters not his soul, but his body. It enters the body, and afterward goes out from it. Only that can defile a man which goes out from the man himself, from his soul. Because from the soul of man proceed evil, fornication, impurity, murder, theft, covetousness, wrath, deceit, insolence, envy, calumny, pride, and every kind of folly. All this evil is out of the soul of man and it alone can defile a man.' (Tolstoy, 1997, p. 49–50)

For Tolstoy, sin (that which defiles) comes from action. One stands in need of salvation because of one's own lack of discipline in the will. The personal discipline of love and mercy is what brings salvation[3], through deterring the actions that would defile. This discipline of love finds its completion in the raising of the temple: 'The living temple is the whole world of men when they love each other' (Tolstoy, 1997, p. 51).

Wittgenstein's attraction to Tolstoy shows contemporary scholars a sort of religiosity that Wittgenstein found plausible and inspiring during the war years. This may well be of some help in better understanding the import for ethics and religion Wittgenstein's writings from the period have. That said, since the *Tractatus* is in many ways the culmination of Wittgenstein's early philosophical work, Tolstoy should not be used to fill-in information on ethics or religion that is taken to be missing from the text (for example, that about which Wittgenstein remains silent). Wittgenstein clearly did not take Tolstoy's pacifism to heart (at least, not at this time in his life), and Wittgenstein found his fellow soldiers to be contemptible. What Wittgenstein did find accessible in Tolstoyan Christianity may or may not be in fact something he ultimately transcends in climbing the philosophical ladder of the *Tractatus*.

2.3 The *Tractatus*, the mystical and Wittgenstein's ethic of perspicuity

Wittgenstein's *Tractatus* is sometimes read as contemplating what it is to think clearly about the relationship between propositions and the facts that the propositions picture. In the text, Wittgenstein relegates ethics, aesthetics, and God to that which is 'higher'. Putative propositions about what is 'higher' are nonsensical, yet this does not mean for Wittgenstein that moral, aesthetic, and religious matters are ignored or overlooked in the book. Far from it, in a widely noted letter to his publisher Ludwig von Ficker he famously describes his book as ethical (Wittgenstein, 1979). While a number of interpretations of the *Tractatus*, under the rubric of 'resolute' or 'austere' readings of nonsense, have directed their attention to the ethical aspects of the work, more attention ought to be paid to references to the 'mystical', as a putatively religious phenomenon.

What I find most tempting in reading the *Tractatus* is to regard the references to 'the mystical' in the 6.4s and 6.5s as some sort of gesture towards a deep sense of ineffability in Wittgenstein's early thought (in line with Biletzki's third station of interpretation). However, it is precisely this temptation that resolute readings of nonsense in the *Tractatus* call into question as a straightforward doctrine of the book.

Nevertheless, the references to 'the mystical' (*Mystische*) seem to offer *prima facie* textual evidence for a deep sort of nonsense or ineffability. After all, isn't ineffability closely connected with mysticism? Here we ought to be careful, for expressions involving 'the mystical' or 'mysticism' have a wide variety of connotations; it is hard to know exactly what Wittgenstein meant by the expression – he used it just three times in the *Tractatus* and once in the *Notebooks* – so great care should be observed in interpreting the *Tractatus* on this matter. What I suggest is that these references to 'the mystical' should be seen as penultimate examples of what must be climbed through in pursuing Wittgenstein's ethic of perspicuity. According to a resolute reading of the *Tractatus*, Wittgenstein is not putting forth a theory of mysticism or even preparing a place for mysticism within his philosophy; instead, he is holding the mystical up as an ultimate instance of nonsense that may grow naturally out of certain questions, puzzlements, or experiences. In the end, however, such descriptions must be given up in the pursuit of perspicuity.

Many readers have been puzzled or enticed by Wittgenstein's talk of 'the mystical' and 'the inexpressible' in this early work. Debate between 'traditional' interpreters of Wittgenstein (up to the third station in Biletzki's categories) and proponents of the 'new' Wittgenstein (including the fourth and fifth stations) centers around how to understand the nature of 'nonsense' and the 'inexpressible' in the *Tractatus*. Remarks such as the following have fueled these debates:

6.44 It is not *how* things are in the world that is mystical, but *that* it exists.

6.45 To view the world sub specie aeterni is to view it as a whole – a limited whole.
Feeling the world as a limited whole – it is this that is mystical.

6.52 We feel that even when all *possible* scientific questions have been answered, the problems of life remain completely untouched. Of course there are then no questions left, and this itself is the answer.

6.521 The solution of the problem of life is seen in the vanishing of the problem.
(Is not this the reason why those who have found after a long period of doubt that the sense of life became clear to them have then been unable to say what constituted that sense?)

> 6.522 There are, indeed, things that cannot be put into words. They *make themselves manifest*. They are what is mystical. (Wittgenstein, 2001, pp. 88–9)

Upon meeting with Wittgenstein in The Hague in 1919, Bertrand Russell wrote to Ottoline Morrell that Wittgenstein 'has penetrated deep into mystical ways of thought and feeling, but I think (though he wouldn't agree) that what he likes best in mysticism is its power to make him stop thinking' (Russell, 1999, p. 199). This quotation provides additional *prima facie* support for the idea that Wittgenstein was a mystic and sought to preserve room for mysticism (whatever that might be) in his philosophy. It might then seem that the traditional view of the *Tractatus* is well supported.

Traditional interpreters of Wittgenstein such as Hacker understand Wittgenstein to hint at deep inexpressible truths in the *Tractatus*, truths which can only be shown, not said. Examples of these deep ineffable truths are the truths of logic. While logical form is shown in language and cannot be expressed, these 'truths' yet persist; they are inexpressible but nevertheless a genuine representation of reality is had through them. The traditional reading of nonsense has its parallel in philosophy of religion with respect to 'the mystical'. Traditional readings of the *Tractatus* and mysticism retain the idea of a deep ineffability lying behind notions like 'the mystical' and 'nonsense'. 'New' Wittgensteinians such as Cora Diamond, Juliet Floyd and James Conant read remark 6.54 resolutely: 'My propositions serve as elucidations in the following way: anyone who understands me eventually recognizes them as nonsensical, when he has used them – as steps – to climb up beyond them' (Wittgenstein, 2001, p. 89). On resolute readings, emphasis is placed on the idea that what Wittgenstein said was nonsense really is nonsense. To 'chicken out' as Diamond writes in her essay 'Throwing Away the Ladder: How to Read the Tractatus' (in Diamond, 1995) is to imply that Wittgenstein did not really mean what he said in remark 6.54. Against such traditional readings, Diamond counsels resolve in treating as nonsensical what Wittgenstein implies in this remark. As Diamond concludes her essay, 'The idea of a science of logic is, on Wittgenstein's account, nothing but illusion' (Diamond, 1995, p. 201). The point, or ethic, of the *Tractatus* then involves curing readers of philosophical illusions. The very idea of a science of logic is then an illusion, for which the *Tractatus* is an intended cure. This ethic has been called 'perfectionist' by Cavell (and further elaborated on by Conant), and indeed one finds resonance here with the moral perfectionism of Tolstoy, whom Wittgenstein so admired.

But what did Wittgenstein mean by '*Mystische*' and what is its bearing on the discussion of nonsense? McGuinness wishes to deter conflation of Wittgenstein's use of the term 'mysticism' in the *Tractatus* with the uses of the term commonly found in scholarship on the history or psychology of religions, as may be found in William James's *The Varieties of Religious Experience*, for example. McGuinness also notes there is no evidence Wittgenstein read Bertrand Russell's 1914 essay 'Mysticism and Logic' before the war (McGuinness, 2002, p. 140). Nevertheless, McGuinness notes 'a considerable coincidence' between the references to 'the mystical' in the *Tractatus* and 'Mysticism and Logic'.

For the Russell of that essay, mysticism is an aspect of human experience inspiring philosophy alongside science. However, what Russell understood by 'mysticism' was a human impulse to believe in a special, direct insight into reality granting an experience that reality is one, time is unreal, and good and evil are illusory (Russell, 1917). Russell writes, 'Metaphysics, or the attempt to conceive the world as a whole by means of thought, has been developed, from the first, by the union and conflict of two very different human impulses, the one urging men towards mysticism, the other urging them towards science' (Russell, 1917, p. 1). He continues, 'Some men have achieved greatness through one of these impulses alone, others through the other alone... But the greatest men who have been philosophers have felt the need both of science and of mysticism' (Russell, 1917, p. 1). While Russell remains leery of full-blown expressions of mysticism (as a 'creed'), he maintains respect for it as 'an attitude towards life'. McGuinness finds much in Russell's analysis of mysticism to dovetail with Wittgenstein's references in the *Notebooks* and ultimately, the *Tractatus*, and McGuinness turns to the 'Lecture on Ethics' as a source to further fill in just what this mysticism might amount to and to show how Wittgenstein's mysticism resonates with Russell's description.

In the Lecture, McGuinness finds three possible experiences that could qualify as mystical experiences for Wittgenstein:

> First, is what he calls his experience par excellence in which he wonders at the existence of the world. Second is the experience of feeling absolutely safe: 'nothing can injure me whatever happens'. Third is the experience of feeling guilty, about which he says very little. (McGuinness, 2002, pp. 157–8)

McGuinness conjectures that some sort of mixture of the three is the best way of rendering what Wittgenstein meant by the term. According to McGuinness, it would seem then that the personal sense of having a meaningful life, the resolution of one's character, and wonder at the existence of the world together make up the array of experiences which Wittgenstein may have had in connection with his use of the word 'mysticism'. Wittgenstein's mysticism – a potentially misleading expression, to be sure – would be mysticism about the very idea of the world and of one's place in it. McGuinness notes that the God mentioned in the *Tractatus* and *Notebooks* is at best a pantheistic God; thus, mystical union would be also a union with the world.

The mysticism McGuinness describes has moral efficacy. Prayer or philosophical contemplation of the world as a whole might bring one's will into alignment with God's. McGuinness's treatment of 'the mystical' in Wittgenstein raises problems for resolute readings of nonsense. After all, how is it possible to speak sensibly about union with God or the world? Are these not matters concerning ineffability? McGuinness's interpretation looks to be an exemplary case of the *Tractatus* gesturing towards deep ineffable truths. What would a resolute reading of 6.54 suggest about approaching Wittgenstein's use of 'the mystical'?

Over the last two decades, disputes over the resolute reading of nonsense in the *Tractatus* have been prominently featured in Wittgenstein scholarship. While Diamond has led the charge, Conant has been a frequent partisan in favor of the reading, especially as it bears on 'the ethical' aspects of the text. In a contribution to the Phillips-edited volume, *Religion and Wittgenstein's Legacy*, titled 'What "Ethics" in the *Tractatus* is Not', Conant criticizes various interpretations of the *Tractatus* that treat its ethical 'content', rather than seeing the ethical force of the work lying in the very act of working one's way through the text.

A great obstacle to reading the book ethically seems to lie in what Conant and Floyd call 'departmentalism', an idea they borrow from Diamond. One misses significant aspects of Wittgenstein's views on, for example, the philosophy of mathematics if one looks only for passages or remarks that deal with a departmental conception of the subdiscipline. The principle could be adopted with respect to other subdisciplines in philosophy, such as ethics or the philosophy of religion.[4] Departmentalism with respect to 'the ethical' would entail a reading that looks for Wittgenstein's propositions explicitly about ethics and seeks to interpret them, either in light of themes from moral philosophy or in light of various influences we know from biographers that can fill-in what is held to be the missing or incomplete content. Conant mentions appeals to Kierkegaard, Schopenhauer, Tolstoy, and Kraus as sources for such readings. One might interject that there are legitimate insights to be gained from study of these figures for understanding Wittgenstein's literary ambitions, but the problem lies not in the insight given as in the refusal to read the *Tractatus* resolutely. Remark 6.54 casts all that has passed in the work as nonsense; yet from Wittgenstein's letter to von Ficker, we are to understand that the work has ethical force of considerable importance. Conant does not present a positive account of what the ethical is in the *Tractatus*. Indeed, not extrapolating content from the work but understanding that reading the work can have ethical value is for Conant the point in pursuing Wittgenstein's wandering path, through analyses of propositions to the final remarks explicitly mentioning the problem of life.

What I would like to suggest when approaching Wittgenstein's references to 'the mystical' in the *Tractatus* is that we approach them first as being akin to references to 'the ethical' or the 'higher'. These are preliminary expressions that, whatever their value, are cast aside as nonsense, as rungs in a ladder are stepped through and over. If there is a mysticism to be found in Wittgenstein's *Tractatus*, according to a resolute reading, this mysticism will not come from reflection alone on the three remarks that mention 'the mystical'.

However, a problem arises that prevents a straightforward parallel treatment of 'the mystical' with 'the ethical'. While Wittgenstein explicitly mentions the ethical dimensions of the work and later gives a lecture on the topic, he rarely discusses mysticism before, during, or after the writing of the *Tractatus*. Wittgenstein offers no framing remarks on the *Tractatus* that refer to mystical dimensions of the work. Following Conant and Floyd, one should beware departmental readings of mysticism; however, insofar as the *Tractatus* can have an effect on its reader, one may be struck with a feeling of insight upon reading the text, perhaps even a sense of piety at having responsibly followed through the pursuit of clarity towards its end.

Whatever 'the mystical' is, it presents itself through the practice of perspicuity (the climbing of the ladder in the *Tractatus*). Because of its variant connotations the expression 'the mystical' would seem to present more of a problem to resolute readings of the *Tractatus* than does 'the ethical'; however, as references to 'the mystical' come before remark 6.54, they too are among the propositions that must be climbed out through, on, and over.

Tractarian silence involves philosophical as much as moral, aesthetic or perhaps, in some sense, religious reverence. As Diarmuid Costello writes in '"Making Sense" of Nonsense: Conant and Diamond Read Wittgenstein's *Tractatus*',

> [T]he silence to which the book's last proposition refers is not a pregnant silence guarding an ineffable truth. It is an injunction not to speak unless one means something by one's words, not because there is anything that we are debarred in principle from meaning, but because we are frequently given to meaning nothing at all. (Costello, 2004, p. 115)

Nevertheless, deference to the world is a part of this perspicuity as well. Perspicuity in the *Tractatus* means scrupulously attending to what can be said. Perhaps this is why the book begins with the proposition, 'The world is everything that is the case' (Wittgenstein, 2001, p. 31). Throughout Wittgenstein's corpus, one sees this deference and the *Tractatus* is particularly useful in that it reminds readers of the seriousness with which Wittgenstein practiced philosophy. He persisted in this feeling of reverence, but varied in how to live with it. Wittgenstein felt the duty to pursue clarity strongly, and he was likewise offended when other philosophers did not take such seriousness as an ethic in their own work. I do not think it an exaggeration to say that, for Wittgenstein, the pursuit of clarity was a sacred duty and that achieving this philosophical goal was itself the proper response to a sense of wonder at the world.[5]

Wittgenstein retained a seriousness about the practice of philosophy throughout his life, but in the *Tractatus*, perspicuity seems to involve especially a great economy of expression. Among other things, what he is able to accomplish in his varied numbered remarks is an impressive systematization and compression of ideas. In his later writings, Wittgenstein was far more occasional in his thinking and not as obviously systematic in his thinking. Throughout his career, a sense of intellectual and moral duty permeates Wittgenstein's thought.

2.4 Perspicuity about Wittgenstein's religious identity

Wittgenstein's philosophical work is commonly divided into two periods, his early work and his later work. Yet, when one approaches his thought through the lens of the ethic of perspicuity, one sees continuity as well as development. When Wittgenstein returned to Cambridge in 1929, his return to philosophy was anchored by this ethic. In a remark dating from 1930, Wittgenstein describes the place of clarity in his philosophy:

> Our civilization is characterized by the word progress... Typically it constructs. Its activity is to construct a more and more complicated

> structure. And even clarity is only a means to this end & not an end in itself.
>
> For me on the contrary clarity, transparency, is an end in itself[.]
>
> I am not interested in erecting a building but in having the foundations of possible buildings transparently before me.
>
> So I am aiming at something different than are the scientists & my thoughts move differently than do theirs. (Wittgenstein, 1998, p. 9e)

Wittgenstein understood himself to be searching after a sort of philosophical insight that ran counter to what he took to be the propensity towards progress and construction in Western civilization. In James Klagge's analysis, this tendency marks out Wittgenstein as an exile (Klagge, 2011). Wittgenstein identifies his philosophical approach as being more in the spirit of surveying architectural plans than in construction. One can see glimpses of this view of philosophy in remarks from other moments in Wittgenstein's life:

> [1929] I myself still find my way of philosophizing new, & it keeps striking me so afresh, & that is why I have to repeat myself so often. It will have become part of the flesh & blood of a new generation & it will find the repetitions boring. For me they are necessary. – This method consists essentially in leaving the question of *truth* and asking about *sense* instead. (Wittgenstein, 1998, p. 3e)
>
> [1931] Work on philosophy – like work in architecture in many respects – is really more work on oneself. On one's own conception. On how one sees things. (And what one expects of them.) (Wittgenstein, 1998, p. 24e)
>
> [1946] Grasping the difficulty *in its depth* is what is hard. (Wittgenstein, 1998, p. 55e)
>
> For if you interpret it in a shallow way the difficulty just remains. It has to be pulled out by the root; & that means, you have to start thinking about these things in a new way. The change is as decisive e.g. as that from the alchemical to the chemical way of thinking. – The new way of thinking is what is so hard to establish.
>
> Once it is established the old problems disappear; indeed it becomes hard to recapture them. For they are embedded in the way we express ourselves; & if we clothe ourselves in a new form of expression, the old problems are discarded along with the old garment. (Wittgenstein, 1998, p. 55e)

Perspicuity does not merely show everything as it is; it frees one from ways of looking at the world that are distorted. Rather than clarity and precision being the means of philosophical inquiry; the intellectual release of freedom from convoluted or confused ways of thinking is the end.

During the 1930s, Wittgenstein kept a series of diaries which were later entrusted to his friend, Rudolf Koder. This text, edited and translated by James Klagge and Alfred Nordmann in 2003, as 'Movements of Thought: Diaries 1930–1932, 1936–1937' proves important to scholars examining Wittgenstein's views regarding religion. Yet the fact that these were diaries, raises questions immediately about their proper place within an interpretation of Wittgenstein. While Wittgenstein's wartime notebook contained private coded and public philosophical remarks on opposing pages, 'Movements of Thought' shows no such dichotomy. Klagge and Nordmann remark in their introduction:

> The remarks of manuscript 183 constitute a spiritual act, but one that cannot be divorced from Wittgenstein's philosophical practice, his rejection of all things impure and superstitious in the serious and rigorous quest for clarity and truth. In this regard, Wittgenstein's *Confessions* are indeed akin to those of Augustine or Rousseau. Instead of writing a 'secret' diary, Wittgenstein subjects apparently personal concerns to the same scrutiny, the same movements of thought, the same standards of written expression as he does more overtly philosophical matters. (Wittgenstein, 2003b, p. 5)

In these diaries, the scholar finds not just information about Wittgenstein's thought on religion or about the importance of perspicuity in philosophy, but also importantly information about the place of philosophical clarity within Wittgenstein's life.

Yet, given the remarks now available to scholars, Wittgenstein's pursuit of clarity regarding his religious and ethical life appears significantly unfinished. This philosophical incompleteness is perhaps most obviously found in a number of remarks from the 1930s in 'Movements of Thought' and in manuscripts drawn on for *Culture and Value* that generalize about 'the Jews'. Some of these remarks contain anti-Semitic tropes. These remarks divide interpreters. Some, like Bela Szabados and Ranjit Chatterjee see in them expressions of criticism of the anti-Semitism they invoke.[6] Indeed, Chatterjee and Szabados are helpful in pointing out that at least some of the remarks are performatively ambiguous. Indeed, their structure is not unlike those parts of Wittgenstein's writing found elsewhere, entertaining an idea, exploring its entailments, evaluating it, and rejecting it. Yet I am not convinced by their accounts, which together depict a life that is too neat. Others, like Ray Monk, Sander Gilman, David Edmonds and John Eidinow, and James Klagge, hold the straightforward view that these remarks show that Wittgenstein was either an anti-Semite or a self-hating Jew. While on balance, I think the self-hatred thesis has greater plausibility, I think the anti-Semitism resistance thesis helpfully reminds readers that Wittgenstein was an acute rhetorician (especially in his diaries). The diaries must be read with care as the reflective sources they inevitably are.

Wittgenstein did not achieve resolution about his relationship to Judaism despite the importance of pursuing clarity in his philosophical practice. Some readers may conclude from the presence of these remarks in Wittgenstein's corpus that he is not to be trusted on this and related ethical matters, that he had internalized anti-Semitic tropes and was callously indifferent to the increasingly dire plight of European Jews in the 1930s. That interpretation could be apt, but I suggest readers remain open to viewing these remarks as emanating from a part of the character of Wittgenstein that he would have sought to challenge philosophically, had he recognized these remarks as philosophically or morally problematic. As Chatterjee and Szabados note, the pragmatic effect of these remarks tends to be obscure; so it is not clear exactly what Wittgenstein is saying by them (especially given their incidental nature and presence in sources he did not prepare for publication). Even so, the remarks are cause for regarding Wittgenstein as a thinker whose internal dialectic on religion remained unfinished. Wittgensteinian philosophy of religion ought to work harder to be more scrupulous about the use of language than Wittgenstein himself was able to be when it came to Judaism.

The relationship between the Wittgenstein family and the religions of Germany and Austria of the nineteenth and early twentieth centuries was complicated by their assimilated status. Three of Wittgenstein's grandparents were born into Jewish families but would later come to identify with one or another form of Christianity. According to Monk, Hermann Christian Wittgenstein (1802–1878), Wittgenstein's paternal grandfather and a Christian convert, married Fanny Figdor (1814–1890), 'the daughter of an eminent Viennese Jewish family...but before their wedding in 1838 she too converted to Protestantism' (Monk, 1990, p. 5). Ludwig's maternal grandfather, Jakob Kalmus, (b. 1814) was raised Catholic despite his prominent Jewish heritage and Ludwig's grandmother Marie Stallner (b. 1825) came from an established Austrian Catholic family (Monk, 1990, p. 7). But just what was the significance of these conversions? Did the grandparents' generation understand themselves to be performing the final act of cultural assimilation as opposed to making an un-coerced choice of value, practice, or belief? If they were like their peers, then it would seem to be the former. As McGuinness writes,

> Jews of the assimilation, particularly in what became the German Empire, not only took pains to lose all traces of the old culture themselves but viewed its manifestations in others and even viewed the race itself as a sort of taint from which only good fortune and self-mastery had managed to free them, in so far as they were free. (McGuinness, 1988, p. 2)

But of course, the nations to which their generation hoped to assimilate would not accept them. Were it not for the fortune Wittgenstein's father Karl had gained in the late nineteenth century, members of the Wittgenstein family would very likely have experienced the same persecution, displacement, and destruction as the vast majority of Vienna's Jews under National Socialism.

Wittgenstein was not a religious person in a conventional sense, but for the most part neither was he irreligious. One sees the presence of particular religions emerging here and there in his life and thought. As a child, perhaps due to the pressure of social conformity and later as a young man fighting on the eastern front in World War I, Wittgenstein appears to have embraced forms of Christian piety. Especially during the war, he maintained an interest in religion that went well beyond mere intellectual curiosity. Whether it was his gratitude for how Tolstoy's *The Gospel in Brief* or James's *The Varieties of Religious Experience* helped him cope with life during the war or an appreciation for the moral edification religions make possible, or something else entirely lost to biographers, Wittgenstein retained throughout the rest of his life the respect of a sympathetic observer. Calling him an observer of religion does not mean to suggest that Wittgenstein remained on the sidelines; he was repeatedly moved by Christian philosophical, theological, and liturgical texts as well as what were then called 'primitive' religious ceremonies. It has become a commonplace to recite Drury's quote of Wittgenstein: 'I am not a religious man, but I cannot help seeing every problem from a religious point of view' (Rhees, 1984, p. 94). What could it mean to describe someone as, or as not, 'religious'? It might refer to belief, practice, tradition, ritual, marriage, citizenship, acceptance of certain narratives or social institutions as being normative. In short, it could mean so many things, if read as referring to religion *in general*, that it would be meaningless. In Drury's sense, it must mean something more specific.

While Wittgenstein's remarks on indigenous religious practices or Christian piety are characteristically hermeneutically subtle, his remarks on Judaism seem coarse by comparison. Consider for example the following statements from 1931 collected in *Culture and Value*:

> How should we feel if we had never heard of Christ?
> Should we feel left alone in the dark?
> Do we not feel like that only in the way a child doesn't when he knows there is something in the room with him? (Wittgenstein, 1998, p. 15e)

> The saint is the only Jewish 'genius'. Even the greatest Jewish thinker is no more than talented. (Myself for instance.) (Wittgenstein, 1998, p. 16e)

> It has sometimes been said that the Jews' secretive & cunning nature is a result of their long persecution. That is certainly untrue; on the other hand it is certain that, despite this persecution, they continue to exist only because they have the inclination towards this secretiveness. As we may say that such & such an animal has escaped extinction only because it has the possibility or capability of concealing itself. Of course I do not mean that one should commend this ability for such a reason, not by any means. (Wittgenstein, 1998, p. 19e)

In the first remark, Wittgenstein seems to contemplate the virtues of conversion from Judaism to Christianity, that Christ provides salvation. On a closer reading, it seems to contemplate the untapped life potential in Jews, potential that may be obscured by Christian paradigms which, of necessity, would downplay the narrative power of Judaism. A remark like this is consistent with the anti-Semitic resistance thesis. In the second remark, the implication is that Jews are not prone to genius, that genius is un-Jewish and that Jews have a merely reproductive form of intelligence (a Weiningerian theme Gilman identifies as running throughout Viennese anti-Semitism and Jewish self-hatred) with the exception of sainthood, a strangely Christian aspiration for Jewish would-be geniuses (Gilman, 1986, p. 215). The remark is also ambiguous as it posits an 'autonomous' standard for genius within Judaism. The passage itself, or part of it, is frequently cited in studies of Wittgenstein because it is here that Wittgenstein lists a number of influences. A parallel arises here that bears mentioning – between Wittgenstein as a 'reproductive' and as a clarifying thinker. If the work of clarification is occasional, then reproduction would be too. Wittgenstein's thinking about Judaism may have provided an alternative means to consider the place of clarification within philosophy. The last remark reinforces the association between secrecy, cunning, and the Jews. Wittgenstein contemplates different directions of causality and rejects the view that secrecy or cunning could be virtues (even if they have survival value).

In my estimation, none of this textual evidence supports a definitive conclusion that Wittgenstein was anti-Semitic or self-hating, but it links Wittgenstein's thought with tropes that arose in the anti-Semitic culture of Vienna. It is possible he was engaging these tropes critically, as Chatterjee and Szabados have it, but nevertheless, the lacunae in Wittgenstein's writings about the plight of the Jews in Europe suggests another view.

As with Judaism, Wittgenstein had a complicated relationship to Christianity; however, while his relationship to Judaism was complicated by the rampant anti-Semitism of Austrian society and the assimilated status of his family, his relationship to Christianity was complicated by his Protestant and Catholic religious inheritance, his sympathy for certain elements of the religion (for example, the self-sacrifice of the Christ he read about in Tolstoy's Gospel) and his conviction that one be unsentimental in one's beliefs (again, a theme developed by Tolstoy). Clearly, Wittgenstein found much in terms of inspiration in the Christian gospels; yet, while Wittgenstein was baptized as a Catholic, he does not seem to have embraced Catholic piety and practice.[7] Perhaps in the first quotation he is writing generally of the experience of awareness of both the need for and the means of salvation and resolution.

It is remarkable that later on the same page is a passage that seems to reverse the association:

> I look at the photographs of Corsican brigands and reflect: these faces are too hard & mine too soft for Christianity to be able to write on them. The faces of the brigands are terrible to behold & yet they are certainly no more distant from a good life & are simply situated on a different side of it than am I. (Wittgenstein, 1998, p. 16e)

What is particularly notable is that this passage comes from the same manuscript as the previously quoted remark from *Culture and Value*. Here Wittgenstein seems to recognize the distance between his identity and anything that Christianity might be able to transform. Taken with the previous remark, Wittgenstein's thoughts seem to point to a person who is musing over a religion, wondering to what extent it has something to say to him. But above such existential concerns, we see Wittgenstein writing of Christianity as not being able to affect certain sorts of persons: those too soft or too hard. The emphasis here is on the practical benefit of a particular religion for morally edifying a person. For Tolstoy, the point of Christianity is to save the soul, but for unsentimental souls, stories of miracles will not do. The idea seems to be that for some people, their identities are so formed that one religion has nothing to say to them while another may speak profoundly. Christianity seemed to lure him and to provide for him something towards which it was beneficial for him to strive. Wittgenstein understood himself to be too soft to accept a conventional form of Christianity, and Judaism was never really a live option for him given his family history, assimilated status, disconnect from modern forms of Judaism (Bouwsma, 1986, p. 33), and possible internalization of Gentile suspicion of Jews. Judaism was both inseparable from his identity and irretrievable. According to Gilman, this is the double bind of the *Mischling* (Gilman, 1986).

At one point, it was thought that all evidence of Wittgenstein's stereotyping of Jewish people ended in 1931 (Monk, 1990, p. 316); yet consider the following remark from 1937, collected in 'Movements of Thought':

> Jews! for the longest time you haven't given the world anything for which it is grateful to you. And that, not because it is ungrateful. Since one doesn't feel gratitude for every contribution just because it is useful to us.
>
> So give it something again for which you deserve not cold recognition but warm gratitude.
>
> But the only thing it needs from you is your submission to fate.
>
> You might give it roses that will blossom, never wilt. (Wittgenstein, 2003b, p. 215)

Wittgenstein seems to acknowledge the persecution and destruction of German Jews already under way, but he seems to shift the moral responsibility to the Jews for not producing 'roses that will never wilt', which I interpret to be things of clearly evident value to society. He almost seems to chide Jews for not being sufficiently assimilated. It is possible that Wittgenstein writes here in a tone of rueing the inevitable disaster, as if something so simple as a gift would reverse the social forces marshaling.

In these passages, Wittgenstein employs the trope of Jews as a cancerous growth on the body politic[8] and stereotypes of Jewish character and intellectual capacity as well as the notion of a minority as being responsible for its hated status. The remarks are all the more surprising given Wittgenstein's chiding of Norman Malcolm when at the beginning of World War II Malcolm spoke informally in defense of the British 'national character'.[9] Were Wittgenstein so sensitive *generally* to the perils of stereotyping peoples, one would think he would have scrupulously avoided the use of such stereotypes altogether, that his philosophy would have sought to mitigate tendencies to think in unreflective, clichéd and potentially dehumanizing ways. These remarks on 'the Jews' conflict with the overarching tendencies of Wittgenstein's philosophy to move away from essentializing and towards acknowledging differences. Szabados sees this as a dawning discovery of Wittgenstein's; it could be that Szabados is right, but the absence of sympathetic or hermeneutically generous remarks on Judaism or Jews is notable.

The remarks on Judaism, appearing as they do in unpublished and personal sources, would be largely unintelligible without some understanding of Wittgenstein's biography. Contemporary critics have assessed Wittgenstein's troubled relationship to his Jewish heritage. Some have claimed that Wittgenstein was a self-hating Jew or a Jewish anti-Semite (Stern, 2001, p. 238). Even with study of Wittgenstein's life, the remarks remain difficult, but it may be helpful to compare Wittgenstein's stereotyping of Jews with Gilman's analysis of the 'Jewish Self-Hatred' of Karl Kraus and Otto Weininger, two Viennese writers who influenced the young Wittgenstein.

As is well known, Kraus was a literary figure who influenced Wittgenstein and whom Wittgenstein admired. Like Wittgenstein, Kraus had a Jewish heritage yet was linked to Catholicism (in Kraus' case through his own conversion). In his writings for his periodical *Die Fackel*, Kraus used anti-Semitic tropes to criticize (fellow) Jewish journalists. The targets of his criticism were Jewish journalists he took to exemplify the Jewish identity he wished to distinguish himself from. Gilman writes: Kraus 'is one of the most complex examples of the creation of the Jewish Other as a substitute for the hatred of the self. For Kraus's self-selected enemies were Jews, and they represented the essence of the Jewish language' (Gilman, 1986, p. 233). Kraus' criticism of Viennese Jewish identity focused on the use of language by Jews. The trope Kraus appeals to is the idea that the language of the Jews is a corruption. Gilman writes, 'Kraus attempts to distance his rhetoric from that of the Jewish, liberal journalist, whom he views as part of a conspiracy to alienate European Jews from their Western culture' (Gilman, 1986, p. 233). Kraus is indeed a complex case. He holds onto what is obviously now a delusion about the security of the circumstances fin-de-siecle Jews faced in Austria and elsewhere in Europe. Kraus seeks to distinguish himself from other Jewish writers through his command of the German language, as if aesthetic and rhetorical demonstration would be sufficient to silence the anti-Semites. Yet at times, Kraus displays a spirit of resistance in his publishing anti-Semitic criticisms of his own writing in *Die Fackel* (Gilman, 1986, p. 235). The 'double bind' of self-hating Jews stemmed from their 'accepting the linguistic standards of German or Austrian society concerning minority or liminal languages' (Gilman, 1986, p. 242). Writers like Kraus 'created a situation in which they were writing in a "borrowed" tongue, since these racist views of language denied such groups the true ability to alter their modes of expression'. Gilman continues: 'The double bind that resulted forced such Jews to undertake the role of language critics for all of society and provided them with the hidden motivation to prove their ability to transcend that which was perceived as unalterable, their language' (Gilman, 1986, p. 242–3). Kraus's famous economy of language in his aphorisms thus appears to have been, at least in part, a result of his Jewish self-hatred.

Weininger seems a less complicated case of self-hatred. His 1903 book, *Sex and Character* influenced Wittgenstein. In that book, Weininger espouses numerous views of the essence of 'Man' and 'Woman' as well as 'Aryan' and 'Jew'. Weininger writes:

> I must, however, make clear what I mean by Judaism; I mean neither a race nor a people nor a recognized creed. I think of it as a tendency of the mind, as a psychological constitution which is a possibility for all mankind, but which has become actual in the most conspicuous fashion only amongst the Jews. Anti-Semitism itself will confirm my point of view. (Weininger, 1907, p. 303)

Weininger's is more than a *racist* anti-Semitism; for Weininger, 'Jewishness' is a metaphysical state into which anyone may fall. In his view, Jews have no soul or idea of immortality because Jewish ethics are founded in the Decalogue; Weininger interprets this to be an alien, outside source for ethics, what he terms in a Kantian vein a 'heteronomous code of ethics' (Weininger, 1907, p. 313). Weininger continues:

> To defeat Judaism, the Jew must first understand himself and war against himself. So far, the Jew has reached no further than to make

> and enjoy jokes against his own peculiarities. Unconsciously he respects the Aryan more than himself. Only steady resolution, united to the highest self-respect, can free the Jew from Jewishness. This resolution, be it ever so strong, ever so honourable, can only be understood and carried out by the individual, not by the group. Therefore the Jewish question can only be solved individually; every single Jew must try to solve it in his proper person...
>
> The Jew, indeed, who has overcome, the Jew who has become a Christian, has the fullest right to be regarded by the Aryan in his individual capacity, and no longer be condemned as belonging to a race above which his moral efforts have raised him. He may rest assured that no one will dispute his well-founded claim. The Aryan of good social standing always feels the need to respect the Jew; his Antisemitism being no joy, no amusement to him. (Weininger, 1907, p. 312–13)

Weininger, having internalized the tropes of anti-Semitism, develops a philosophy of anti-Semitism. Weininger's philosophy of anti-Semitism has an ethical dimension: work on oneself. Readers may find the pages of *Sex and Character* haunting. It is hard to imagine what Wittgenstein found salutary about Weininger's book.

It is interesting to observe that Wittgenstein uses the language of anti-Semitism in a way coherent with his own rather harsh self-criticism[10]; in this sense, Wittgenstein was Weiningerian. The paragraphs quoted above are consistent with Wittgenstein's remarks about 'the Jews' in his diaries. The fact that these remarks only arise in his diaries is also instructive; one cannot but wonder if part of Wittgenstein's work on himself may have, for a time, included his desire to rid himself of his 'Jewishness'. Yet, since Wittgenstein rejected Weininger in a letter to Moore (dated August 23, 1931) – the same year as most of these remarks – it seems unwarranted to interpret simple Weiningerian themes into the remarks from *Culture and Value*. Even so, in all instances where Wittgenstein refers to 'The Jew' or 'Jews', a reader may get the sense that Wittgenstein is referring to something he perceives in himself, in the name of his Jewishness, a blemish on his person that could not be mastered.

Even so, ultimately Wittgenstein may be more like Kraus than Weininger. When he uses anti-Semitic tropes, it is frequently ambiguous. At times, he seems to be critiquing the trope (see remark on Jews as tumor on the body of Europe). At other times, Wittgenstein seems to use anti-Semitic tropes to chide himself and his own intellectual abilities, one wonders perhaps to compel his mind to the genius he so longed to possess. Unlike Kraus, Wittgenstein's harshest critic was no doubt himself. He eventually came to reject much, perhaps all, of Weininger, but Weininger's resolute conception of philosophy as work on oneself remained. While Wittgenstein was troubled by his relationship to Judaism at least as late as his confessions of 1936 and his remarks in his 1937 diaries, I know of no other collected remark on 'the Jews' after this period.

These generalizing, stereotyping remarks are troubling, but are they anti-Semitic? Any answer to this question presupposes a definition of anti-Semitism. If anti-Semitism is akin to racism, then it may be helpful to investigate whether the conditions for racism are met in these remarks. According to Kwame Anthony Appiah, one precondition of racism is what he calls 'racialism', the view that

> [T]here are heritable characteristics, possessed by members of our species, that allow us to divide them into a small set of races, in such a way that all members of these races share certain traits and tendencies with each other that they do not share with members of any other race. (Appiah, 1990, pp. 4–5)

Racialism describes a way of thinking about human beings; it a name for the idea that individuals may be accurately described in terms of stereotypes of racial identity. Racism, according to Appiah, involves assigning moral value to the differences racialism sees. With racialism described as a prerequisite to racism, Appiah further divides racism into two kinds: intrinsic and extrinsic. Briefly, we may understand the difference as involving openness to evidence that would show racialism to be false. The extrinsic racist is one who is capable of replacing a racialist mindset with an anti-racist mindset; the intrinsic racist is not. According to Appiah's distinctions, Weininger seems to have been intrinsically racist with a twist; Weininger seems to view Jewishness as a metaphysical condition, which afflicts the Jews in the greatest degree, other 'races' to a lesser extent.

Because of the fragmentary nature of Wittgenstein's remarks on 'Jewishness' and 'the Jews', it is difficult to draw firm conclusions. There is some *prima facie* evidence in support of Wittgenstein's remarks on Jewish people as being racialist. Wittgenstein's remarks on the traits of Jewish people sometimes seem neither positive nor negative (for example, 'the Jew is a desert region', 'the only Jewish genius is the saint') and at other times carry negative connotations (for example, of Jews not being capable of originality and not understanding tragedy). Insofar as one remark seems to hold the Jewish people responsible for their own status of being a target of hatred, Wittgenstein seems to be applying a different moral standard to 'the Jews' than to other peoples. Otherwise, his remarks do not go as far as to claim that the Jewish people are less deserving of moral consideration than human beings generally. In 1948, a contrasting remark appears in a manuscript as is included in *Culture and Value*. Wittgenstein writes,

> If you cannot unravel a tangle, the most sensible thing you can do is to recognize this; & the most decent, to admit it. [Antisemitism.]
>
> What you should do to cure the evil is *not* clear. What is *not* permissible is clear from one case to another. (Wittgenstein, 1998, p. 85e)

David Stern reads this passage as indicating a late awareness both of the problematic nature of his anti-Semitism and of his own inability to unravel the language connected to it that ensnared his thinking. This seems a plausible reading to me. Furthermore, had Wittgenstein mastered the discourse over Judaism and anti-Semitism in the remarks from the 1930s, this late remark would be mysterious; in light of the self-hatred reading of these remarks, the 1948 quote makes sense.

In his biography of Wittgenstein, Monk includes a story of Wittgenstein writing to the British publisher and journalist Victor Gollancz shortly after the end of World War II. Gollancz had recently written the pamphlet *What Buchenwald Really Means* in which he criticizes the moral smugness of British journalists along with the collective guilt presupposed in the treatment of German citizens following the war. Wittgenstein commended Gollancz while offering some constructive criticisms for a more effective argument. In his correspondence, there is little to be gathered about Wittgenstein's response to the concentration camps (he refers to 'horror' in his letter), but Wittgenstein's primary concern seems to be support for correcting a tendency of moral smugness among the Allies and a projection of collective guilt onto the German people. Monk observes further that immediately following the end of the war, Wittgenstein fell into deep pessimism and even despair about humanity. Technological advances had allowed for 'the mechanical means of killing people', and this 'seemed to reinforce in him the certitude of a long-held conviction that mankind was headed for disaster' (Monk, 1990, p. 489). Monk writes 'His notebooks of the post-war years abound with reflections of this sort. A picture intruded upon him, he wrote, was of our civilization, "cheaply wrapped in cellophane, and isolated from everything great, from God, as it were"' (Monk, 1990, p. 489).

Wittgenstein's racialist remarks about 'the Jews' are troubling in part because they point to a more complex historical situation than readers might wish to recognize in a philosopher whose work can be so helpful for confronting unclarity and obtuseness. In remarks about Christianity, and in other remarks about indigenous religions (such as in the 'Remarks on Frazer's *Golden Bough*'), Wittgenstein is seeking clarity with respect to beliefs, doctrines, practices, and religious identities. His tone here is hermeneutical; yet there is no evidence of Wittgenstein showing this same empathy for the practices of Judaism.

2.5 Conclusion

How is Wittgensteinian philosophy of religion inspired by his primary writings to be reconciled with the interpretation of Wittgenstein's views on religion as found in his private and originally unpublished writings? It seems to me that there are two options: (1) reject the biographical Wittgenstein and develop a philosophy of religion drawn only from the philosophical works most prepared for publication by Wittgenstein himself, and (2) integrate a philosophical appropriation of Wittgenstein with a biographical study; the idea here being that Wittgenstein's philosophy and life have a dialectical relationship. I am arguing for the second approach in this book since it more fully grasps the dialectical style of Wittgenstein's philosophical writings.

Interpreting Wittgenstein's remarks on religions would appear then to be critically important for philosophers sensitive to the interconnections between philosophical practice and biography, yet given the weight of the issues connected to these remarks, such study seems potentially overwhelming. In her review of the James C. Klagge's edited volume *Wittgenstein: Philosophy and Biography*, Juliet Floyd writes of the ambiguity seen in studying Wittgenstein's biography philosophically:

> Philosophy was for him a way to expose the places where vanity, received authority, unclarity and lack of resolve blunted his powers of expression, making him dishonest with others and himself. His difficulties were thus the kind of difficulties we all face one by one as we inherit a language, and it is one of his great intellectual contributions to have made this struggle worthy of the name of philosophy. (Floyd, 2002)

Studying Wittgenstein's struggles with the language he inherited may grant contemporary philosophers inspired by his work an existential humility that may not otherwise appear in Wittgenstein's official philosophy. Taking a cue from Floyd's remark on philosophy as working to 'expose the places where vanity, received authority, unclarity and lack of resolve' blunt our powers, Chapter 7 of this book will address some potential new directions for philosophy of religion after Wittgenstein.

While Wittgenstein's tendency of thought may give contemporary readers pause, they show how stubborn a way of thinking may be. This is why I think we need to retain the dialectical features of Wittgenstein's philosophy if we are to see what it might have to say about contemporary philosophical problems regarding religions. Increasingly, communities and societies are characterized by diversities; learning how to live well amidst these diversities has become a critically important ethical problem. The critical self-examination highlighted by the dialectical approach in Wittgenstein's philosophy has benefits for those seeking to engage in cross-cultural and cosmopolitan conversation, not least in the propensity of Wittgenstein's philosophy to uproot stereotypical or clichéd forms of thought. But it is important to remember that this self-criticism goes two ways: philosophers should uproot their own biases about others as well as biases they have internalized from powerful others.

3

A History of Wittgenstein and the Philosophy of Religion

The association of Wittgensteinian philosophy of religion with fideism did not develop overnight. Today, this association proves quite strong, especially among philosophers who are not primarily Wittgenstein scholars. It is commonplace to find characterizations of fideism that identify Wittgensteinian philosophy of religion as exemplifying the category[1], just as it is common to see characterizations of Wittgensteinian philosophy of religion that invoke the category of fideism[2]. When Kai Nielsen first categorized Wittgensteinian philosophy of religion as fideistic (Nielsen, 1967), philosophy of religion influenced by Wittgenstein had been emerging in published and unpublished form for nearly a decade. By the time Nielsen used the term to classify what he saw as a movement, it seemed to many readers to name a real phenomenon in middle to late twentieth-century analytic philosophy of religion; thus the name 'Wittgensteinian fideism' remains with us to the present day.

Nielsen's classification has been contested for a long time by those it was meant to cover. This dynamic shows little sign of change, yet greater recognition of the academic inadequacy of the term should go some ways towards helping change the subject in Wittgensteinian philosophy of religion. What is clear is that a certain tendency in interpreting Wittgenstein on religion emerged during the 1950s, 1960s, and 1970s, and it is this tendency of interpreting Wittgenstein that is understood by critics to be Wittgensteinian fideism. It is unlikely that the interpretive distance between the disputants can be bridged, especially since they differ on the meaning of the very term of appraisal. However, tracing the development of critical categories used by both Wittgensteinian philosophers of religion and their critics suggests that such categories are neither inevitable, nor unavoidable. Insight into the development of the 'fideist' reading of Wittgenstein on religion may be helpful also in overcoming the sense of interpretive inevitability accompanying the long-standing characteristics of many other philosophers.

This chapter traces the development of what P. F. Bloemendaal calls 'The Wittgensteinian School of Philosophy of Religion' (Bloemendaal, 2006). In the book, *Grammars of Faith: A Critical Examination of D. Z. Phillips's Philosophy of Religion*, Bloemendaal studies the evolution of Wittgensteinian philosophy of religion from Wittgenstein to Norman Malcolm, Rush Rhees and Peter Winch and finally to Phillips, the main subject of Bloemendaal's book. While I find Bloemendaal's historical study helpful in many respects, I avoid using the name 'Wittgensteinian School of Philosophy of Religion', for it is not as if all philosophers of religion influenced by Wittgenstein were located at the same institution and wrote on the same topics in the same manner, with the same priorities. In this chapter, I trace the reception of Wittgenstein in the philosophy of religion in order to show how the association of Wittgensteinianism with fideism need not be a part of Wittgensteinian philosophy of religion.

3.1 Philosophy of religion during the first half of the twentieth century

At the beginning of the last century, while what would come to be known as analytic philosophy was still in its infancy, the philosophical traditions of idealism and pragmatism were still relatively strong in Britain and the United States respectively. Representative of the idealist tradition were J. E. McTaggart in Britain and Josiah Royce in the United States, while William James and Charles S. Peirce inspired the pragmatist movement. Idealism and pragmatism were philosophical movements that were not generally opposed as such towards either science or religion. Far from it, in fact, idealists and pragmatists saw themselves as providing the metaphysical or methodological grounding for the sciences and for the 'essence' of religion. Idealist and pragmatist philosophers sought to understand humanity within an evolutionary framework, but one that drew upon a certain abstract ideal of divinity at the limit of human understanding. F. H. Bradley's conception of the Absolute as resolving internal tensions in concepts like God, truth, and morality likewise reflected this updated vision of idealist philosophy as resolving the tensions present in phenomenal experience, be it understood as common sense or empirical in nature (Bradley, 1914).

While Peirce's pragmatism was both evolutionary and naturalistic, he maintained room for speculative theology through his 'neglected argument' for the reality of God (Peirce, 1908). Peirce's neglected argument consisted in the power of what he termed 'reverie', the free play of the mind. When allowed to wander freely, the mind might come to consider the existence of a divine being responsible for ordering the universe. It is not that this order is in itself sufficient to compel belief in a deity; rather, Peirce's idea is that belief in a deity (or some such divine principle) can help organize what one already knows about the world. James's pragmatism was more overtly open to religious ideas and experiences, but many of James's writings reflect an empiricism that a reading of 'The Will to Believe' (1896) or *The Varieties of Religious Experience* (1902) alone might not suggest.[3] Pragmatism may well have helped to lay the groundwork for the new realism while simultaneously sustaining the speculative philosophy that would become the target of that realism and of analytic philosophy. The pictures of the universe offered by idealist and pragmatist philosophers ran counter to the images developed by a new generation of thinkers who were less impressed by these remnants of teleology (such as the ideas of 'design' and 'providence' in the natural world, as seen in Russell's 'A Free Man's Worship'). Indeed, Russell and other realists sought a metaphysics that did not speculate about the nature or end of the cosmos but rather hung closely to the facts.

The nineteenth century was a golden age for philosophy of religion in no small part because it was a golden age for idealism. Post-Kantian Idealism grounded knowledge and morality in God or God's abstracted stand-in: the Absolute. Idealist philosophy in the nineteenth century took off from this point seeking to understand speculatively the nature of this God or Absolute; theologians influenced by the idealist philosophers sought to relate particular world religions through history – and especially Christianity – to this absolute. Idealism also provided a philosophical ground understood to deal adequately with skepticism through various sorts of transcendental depictions of the mind.

Pragmatism offered a different solution to the modern skeptical problem, one grounded not in metaphysics but in human action and behavior. Knowledge, morality, and religion were now to be understood through action and behavior. Science, experience, and utility would now collectively determine truth. Peirce's depiction of the states of belief and doubt as natural states of the mind seemed to anticipate the naturalization methods of doing philosophy that would become prominent a century later. In his classic early essay, 'The Fixation of Belief', Peirce describes doubt as an irritation that produces in people the desire to return to a state of belief; the methods people use to reestablish a state of belief vary considerably: tenacity, authority, *a priori* reasoning, and experience (Peirce, 1877). Peirce criticizes the first three and valorizes the last as being the proper method of philosopher and scientist alike. Pragmatism may well have prepared a path for the development of what would eventually be called analytic philosophy in spawning the more empirical pragmatism of C. I. Lewis and the new realism of Roy Wood Sellars (Kuklick, 2003).

Although the movement that began with Moore and Russell has come to be known as early analytic philosophy, Hans Sluga reminds us that the name 'first appeared relatively late, in the 1930s but came into general usage only twenty years later, after Wittgenstein's death' (Sluga, 1998, p. 100). Analytic philosophy began, in part, as a movement that was largely spawned by common sense and scientific realist reactions against nineteenth century and early twentieth century idealist philosophy. Perhaps the relatively low status of philosophy of religion in early and mid-twentieth century analytic philosophy can be attributed, in part, to the fact that a central element of idealist philosophy was philosophy of religion. Much of what Moore and Russell railed against in their writings was what they took to be an obscure spiritualism found in idealist philosophy. On the matter of unity in early philosophical analysis, Scott Soames writes in his two volume work *Philosophical Analysis in the Twentieth Century*:

> If analytic philosophy is not a unified set of doctrines adhered to by the broad range of philosophers, what is it? The short answer is that it is a certain historical tradition in which the early work of G. E. Moore, Bertrand Russell, and Ludwig Wittgenstein set the agenda for later philosophers, whose work formed the starting point for the philosophers who followed them. The work done today in analytic philosophy grows out of the work done yesterday, which in turn can often be traced back to its roots in the analytic philosophers of the early part of the twentieth-century. (Soames, 2002, p. xiii)

Soames identifies three overarching tendencies in early philosophical analysis[4]: (1) a concern for doing philosophy with 'clarity, rigor, and argumentation' (2002, p. xiii); (2) the aim of philosophy being 'truth and knowledge, as opposed to moral or spiritual improvement' (ibid., p. xiv); and (3) the sense that productive philosophical inquiry may be had through a 'piecemeal approach' to addressing philosophical problems (that is, through short, focused essays over grand philosophical tomes).

By the 1930s and 1940s, when logical positivism became ascendant in English-speaking philosophy, language involving supernatural entities became suspect insofar as it referred to beings whose existence could not be verified. Earlier in the century, Russell displayed a more or less tolerant attitude towards certain aspects of religiosity in his essay 'Mysticism and Logic', written during what he later considered to have been a more romantic time in his life.[5] Russell's later thought grew increasingly skeptical towards religions.

Moore and Russell agreed in the basic principles of the new philosophical movement they spearheaded, but their interests in doing so were different. Russell writes in *My Philosophical Development* (1959): 'Although we were in agreement ... I think that Moore was most concerned with the rejection of idealism, while I was most interested in the rejection of monism. The two were, however, closely connected' (Russell, 1993, p. 42). The realism of Russell, Moore, and others at Cambridge and Oxford, in overturning the idealist philosophies of their teachers was less engaged with philosophical questions about religion. This is not to say these philosophers were uninterested in religion, but typically such philosophical reflection was of secondary importance.

Philosophy of religion did not cease entirely to be a topic of inquiry among philosophers who were associated with the new realism. C. D. Broad reflected on religious claims using tools of philosophical analysis; although he was unconvinced by theistic arguments, he respected the truth claims of Christian theism enough to engage them philosophically. John Cook Wilson and John Baillie reflected on belief in God as springing from the intuitive presence of God within a common-sense realist philosophy; however, as Eugene Thomas Long writes in his extensive historical study *Twentieth-Century Western Philosophy of Religion 1900–2000*:

> Moore showed little interest in religion in his philosophical work, and Russell's attitude towards religious belief was similar to that of W. K. Clifford ... Russell had little sympathy for those who appealed to religious experience or reasons of the heart, rejected arguments for the existence of God on the grounds that theists were unable to provide sufficient evidence for belief in God, and in general was hostile to the role of religion in society. (Long, 2003, p. 138)

Broad maintained a sort of skeptical interest in philosophical questions regarding religion, yet like Russell, he found little in the way of evidential support for theistic belief.

One exception during this time to the tendency for philosophy of religion to thrive primarily within continental thought, or in increasingly marginalized movements such as pragmatism or process philosophy, lay in the work of F. R. Tennant. Tennant was a professor of theology at Cambridge where he came into contact with McTaggart, Russell, and

Broad. Broad later reviewed, rather positively, Tennant's two volume *Philosophical Theology* (1928) for *Mind* in 1929 and 1930. Under the new realist and analytic paradigms, Tennant would be admired for his philosophical rigor. About Tennant's rigor, Broad writes: 'The present deplorably low intellectual level of doctrinal teaching in both the Anglican and the Nonconformist churches in England is no doubt largely due to the very poor materials with which the theological colleges have to deal'. However, Broad is quick to add: 'but, if Dr. Tennant's work could be generally adopted as a text-book, much better bricks might be made even with this sadly unpromising straw' (Broad, 1929, p. 94). Broad is clearly impressed by the work Tennant has created even if he does not find the inference to the existence of a God compelling:

> If a system of speculative philosophy cannot be established by Dr. Tennant's method, I agree that it is still less likely to be established by any other. Dr. Tennant's method at least ensures those who use it against nonsense, enthusiasm, and credulity; it leads to a form of theism which is intellectually and morally respectable and in practice inoffensive; and, if one must try to explain the ultimate and formulate the ineffable, Dr. Tennant's type of conclusion is perhaps the least unintelligible explanation and the least misleading formulation available to us here and now. (Broad, 1930, pp. 483–4)

This is not glowing approval, but it is hard to imagine enthusiastic support at the time from the sectors of analytic philosophy and new realism. Broad judged Tennant to develop his theological arguments in a way that was recognizable as rigorous thought from the standpoint of Broad's realist philosophy.

Tennant's approach to the theistic proofs was novel for the time. After Kant, little credence was being placed in the traditional proofs (ontological, cosmological, and physico-teleological). Many nineteenth-century theologians sought to ground theology not on the traditional arguments and focused instead on developments of Kant's moral 'proof' and on the significance of religious feelings and experiences. Tennant saw problems with these nineteenth-century strategies and sought to offer a refurbished argument from design to the reasonableness to the idea of God:

> The empirically-minded theologian ... asks how the world, inclusive of man, is to be explained. He would let the Actual world tell its own story and offer its own suggestions: not silence it while abstractive speculation, setting out with presuppositions possibly irrelevant to

> Actuality, weaves a system of thought which may prove to conflict with facts. The explicanda which he investigates, and the results of his investigation, alone will determine the content or essence of the explicative idea of God to which he is led, as well as the grounds for belief that such an essence exists. (Tennant, 1928–30, p. 78)

Although considerably less ambitious than design arguments of the eighteenth or early nineteenth centuries[6], Tennant held that the design inference provided coherence otherwise lacking in a world-view. Tennant hoped to provide a new rational basis for theology, taking seriously the obstacles present in then recent philosophy and science.

In some of Russell's early texts such as 'A Free Man's Worship' (1903) and *The Problems of Philosophy* (1912), he deals with the problem of the self in an indifferent universe; the widely read *The Problems of Philosophy* conceives of the universe in terms of what is the self and what is not the self. Written for a broad audience, these texts offer clear arguments in favor of Russell's basic philosophical positions, such as, the use of scientific methodology in philosophy, the adoption of naturalistic metaphysics, and the use of a correspondence theory of truth. However, in the text he is also deeply concerned with what might be called 'the problem of life' (that is, how to live a good life and the role philosophical thinking plays in that life), and how philosophy might aid the solution of this problem.

Where Russell's philosophy differed most radically from that of the idealists or pragmatists was in philosophical method. Russell combined an enthusiasm for logic and the scientific method with liberal use of Ockham's Razor. In sources such as the essay 'On Denoting' (1903) and *The Philosophy of Logical Atomism* (1918), Russell held that it was through the logical analysis of our statements about the world that one could break down the world into its most basic parts. He rejected the doctrine of internal relations, a central feature of monistic metaphysics. Russell instead held that logically proper names (that is, denoting expressions) referred to particular entities in the world. It would be a stretch to say that Russell was primarily motivated in this philosophical endeavor by a desire to rid metaphysics of teleology; but that is one of the accomplishments of his philosophy.

Moore had a different approach in his break with idealism. His common-sense philosophy was highly critical of idealism. Consider his remarks in his 'Refutation of Idealism' (Moore, 1903). Moore's contempt is driven by a concern for clarity of expression and the use of common-sense language in philosophical reasoning. This approach is born of the idea that philosophy, when it abstracts too far from ordinary experiences, is apt to lead to confusion. Moore writes in his 'autobiography' (included in his volume from the Library of Living Philosophers series):

> Russell had invited me to tea in his rooms to meet McTaggart; and McTaggart, in the course of conversation had been led to express his well-known view that time is unreal. This must have seemed to me then (as it still does) a perfectly monstrous proposition, and I did my best to argue against it. I don't suppose I argued at all well; but I think I was persistent and found quite a lot of different things to say in answer to McTaggart. It must have been owing to what I said on such occasions as this that Russell came to think I had some aptitude for philosophy. And I think this example is typical of what (if I am not mistaken) has always been, with me, the main stimulus to philosophise. I do not think that the world or the sciences would ever have suggested to me philosophical problems. What has suggested philosophical problems to me is things which other philosophers have said about the world or the sciences. (Moore, 1942, pp. 13–14)

This last sentence could well be something that Wittgenstein would have said. When Moore dismisses idealism for tending towards meaningless assertions, he is not merely rejecting a competing paradigm but helping define the very program of philosophy with which he would later come to be identified.

Moore, with his defense of common sense, and Russell, with his advocacy of logical atomism, were both inspired by a kind of philosophical humanism. Both trusted the cognitive powers of the human mind to know the nature of the world. Moore begins the 'The Refutation of Idealism' thus: 'Modern Idealism, if it asserts any general conclusion about the universe at all, asserts that it is spiritual' (Moore, 1959, p. 1). By spiritual, Moore does not mean merely that idealism is identical with some sort of religious worldview. Moore continues,

> When the whole universe is declared to be spiritual, it is meant not only that it is in some sense conscious, but that it has what we recognise in ourselves as the higher forms of consciousness. That it is intelligent; that it is purposeful; that it is not mechanical; all these different things are commonly asserted of it. In general, it may be said, this phrase 'reality is spiritual' excites and expresses the belief

> that the whole universe possesses all the qualities the possession of which is held to make us so superior to things which seem to be inanimate: at least, if it does not possess exactly those which we possess, it possesses not one only, but several others, which, by the same ethical standard, would be judged equal to or better than our own. When we say it is spiritual we mean to say that it has quite a different number of excellent qualities, different from any which we commonly attribute either to stars or planets or to cups and saucers. (Moore, 1959, pp. 1–2)

A view generally supported by idealists is that the world is fundamentally mental (or spiritual) rather than merely material. Idealist philosophers of religion contemplate this supposed essence of religion from which positive religions are derived. Thus nineteenth and twentieth century idealist philosophers of religion were at the center of the emerging field of religious studies. As with many modern philosophical systems, idealism may be thought of as a response to the skeptical crisis. Kant's resolution to the skeptical crisis is to turn over philosophical attention to the conditions of human experience and knowledge (of space, time, and the empirical world) asking regressively, 'How is this knowledge possible?' rather than asking whether that which is believed is possible. This faith (moral faith, epistemological faith) became a matter of increased interest among subsequent philosophers.

Despite the fact that idealism developed as a response to the problem of skepticism, for Moore, idealism and skepticism are similar to one another. Moore notes that both reject the reality our sense impressions might lead us to believe in. He took it that in leaving common sense, idealism ultimately creates conceptual room for skepticism. In the case of idealism, genuine knowledge is possible; however, it is knowledge of the spiritual reality behind appearances. With respect to skepticism, the method of doubting appearances moves from being epistemological method to metaphysical proposition.

Yet Moore's stated reasons for rejecting these two philosophical directions in favor of common sense are that neither idealism nor skepticism makes sense once one has become aware of the consequences of these views. Moore criticizes the arguments advocated by many idealists to the effect that 'esse est percipere': to be is to be perceived. This line of thought is attributed to Berkeley but can be seen in the thought of other idealists (for example, Bradley) and skeptics (for example, Hume). Moore directs his attention to it because he takes it to be central to the various idealist philosophies. Moore writes, 'The trivial proposition which I propose to dispute is this: that esse is percipi. This is a very ambiguous proposition, but in some sense or other, it has been very widely held' (Moore, 1959, p. 5). He continues,

> It is said that since whatever is, is experienced, and since some things are which are not experienced by the individual, these must at least form part of some experience. Or again that, since an object necessarily implies a subject, and since the whole world must be an object, we must conceive it to belong to some subject or subjects, in the same sense in which whatever is the object of our experience belongs to us. (Moore, 1959, p. 6)

The sorts of arguments criticized by Moore preclude the analysis of wholes into parts. Since the very existence of discrete entities depends upon there being epistemic agents who are perceiving the objects as distinct. It does not make sense to speak of there being discrete entities when using proper philosophical language, according to Moore's idealist. However, this type of idealist argument is undercut by Moore's 'refutation'. Moore distinguishes between the object perceived and the object as object of perception. This is not so much an argument as it is the expression of a commonsense intuition about metaphysics. It is also a classic example of conceptual analysis, a method that would come to be associated with analytic philosophy.

At this point, a reader might stop and ask if Moore is being fair to idealists. After all, idealists are not the nihilists that Moore makes them out to be. That Moore is not being charitable seems fairly plain from the following passage:

> Many philosophers...when they admit a distinction, yet (following the lead of Hegel) boldly assert their right, in a slightly more obscure form of words, also to deny it. The principle of organic unities, like that of combined analysis and synthesis, is mainly used to defend the practice of holding both of two contradictory propositions, wherever this may be convenient. In this, as in other matters, Hegel's main service to philosophy has consisted in giving a name to and erecting into a principle, a type of fallacy to which experience had shown philosophers, along with the rest of mankind, to be addicted. No wonder that he has his followers and admirers. (Moore, 1959, p. 15–16)

Moore is correct to criticize the rational legitimization of a fallacy. It also may be that some idealists with whom Moore was acquainted were flippant in their affirmation of contradictory propositions. However, whether successful or not, it is important to note that idealist philosophers who deny certain logical principles are not simply committing mistakes; they understand principles such as that of non-contradiction. Instead, they may be reaching for some way of appreciating a certain ontological nuance for which they feel ill-equipped despite their command of philosophical discourse. Successful or not, many idealists seek philosophically to account for a profundity of experience or intuition of the sublime. Nineteenth-century philosophers of religion often strove to articulate that which they understood to exceed the very possibility of articulation: the divine source or 'ground of being' (to borrow Paul Tillich's phrase). However, Moore is not interested in assertions of ontology or of intellectual goals that lay outside of one's actual philosophical work. What interests him primarily are the actual arguments deployed by philosophers.

Philosophy of religion in the middle of the twentieth century continued to develop within what would come to be called continental philosophy and theology, only rarely directly engaging analytic philosophy. In the first volume of Tillich's *Systematic Theology* (1951), one finds just such a rare occasion:

> Since theology claims to be true, it must discuss the meaning of the term 'truth,' the nature of revealed truth, and its relation to other forms of truth. In the absence of such a discussion, the theological claim can be dismissed by a simple semantic device, often used by naturalists and positivists. According to them, the use of the term 'truth' is restricted to empirically verifiable statements. The predicate 'true' should be reserved either for analytic sentences or for experimentally confirmed propositions. (Tillich, 1951, p. 100)

Tillich's response to the problem presented by the naturalists and positivists for metaphysics is a variation on the common quip that the verifiability criterion of meaning cannot itself be verified:

> The way in which philosophical systems have been accepted, experienced, and verified points to a method of verification beyond rationalism and pragmatism ... Their verification is their efficacy in the life-process of mankind ... Nevertheless, even this way of verification is threatened by the possibility of final meaninglessness. (Tillich, 1951, p. 105)

Tillich is here discussing the method by which a philosophical system, or perhaps a conception of what philosophy is, is determined by thinkers. Tillich considers verificationism to be an instance of a human drive to control knowledge. While Tillich thinks it is possible to hold such a view consistently, he does not think that such a view leads towards the living of a fully meaningful life. Tillich's conception of truth is one that goes beyond being a mere property of propositions. From the perspective of an analytic philosopher, it might look as though Tillich wishes to reify truth as 'being itself' and return to the very monism Russell sought release from; the ultimately indivisible unity of being itself puts Tillich squarely within the tradition of post-Kantian idealism. In Tillich's time and indeed up until today, lines distinguishing philosophy of religion and philosophical theology have not always been clear. Perhaps this lack of clear demarcation between the two disciplines is another reason for confusion surrounding the place of philosophy of religion within analytic philosophy.

3.2 Philosophy of religion influenced by Wittgenstein

3.2.1 The influence of the *Tractatus*

Although Wittgenstein's *Tractatus* seems to express ideas similar to those of Russell, especially as regards truth and meaning, it also provocatively makes reference to 'the mystical'. It clearly articulates a division between facts and values; value-language might be, strictly speaking, meaningless, but Wittgenstein's evident regard for morality, aesthetics, and religion seems to suggest a non-referential way of thinking about these matters. Language referring to or implying gods, souls, spirits, or an afterlife may be nonsense, but it may also indicate a natural human desire to reach beyond the limits of what can be said. Substantial interest in the *Tractatus* itself as a primary source for the philosophy of religion would have to wait until the 1970s and later, when interest in Wittgensteinian philosophy of religion was strong and when readings exploring the 'ethical' or 'therapeutic' dimensions of the text gained greater currency.

When the *Tractatus* was published, it gained a considerable following among the scientists, philosophers, and mathematicians of Vienna. Readers such as Rudolf Carnap and Moritz Schlick found in the *Tractatus* an exploration of the philosophy of logic which could complement their philosophical reflection on scientific practice. During the first few decades after its publication, the *Tractatus* was not typically seen as a text friendly to the philosophy of religion. Insofar as the text was embraced by members of the Vienna Circle, it was seen to signal a stark division between meaningful language (that is, language expressing truths about the natural world) and nonsense (that is, language purporting to express truths about values or metaphysical entities). That it made short work of the grand metaphysical systems of nineteenth century philosophy was for the good. This philosophy could help clear the way for a truly scientific philosophy.

The Vienna Circle took inspiration from Wittgenstein's rejection of the idea that metaphysics is meaningful discourse. For example, Rudolf Carnap evinces this attitude towards religious language in his 1932 essay, 'The Elimination of Metaphysics through Logical Analysis of Language':

> In its metaphysical use ... the word 'God' refers to something beyond experience. The word is deliberately divested of its reference to a physical being or to a spiritual being that is immanent in the physical. And as it is not given a new meaning, it becomes meaningless. To be sure, it often looks as though the word 'God' had a meaning even in metaphysics. But the definitions which are set up prove on closer inspection to be pseudo-definitions. (Carnap, 1959, p. 66)

Carnap held religion to be suspicious because it employed terms which when treated metaphysically were meaningless and when treated empirically were false.

Emerging here among the early readers of the *Tractatus* was a nascent view about value-language that would come to be called 'non-cognitivism'. In the picture of language offered by Wittgenstein in the *Tractatus*, meaningful language is representational because there are states of affairs for genuine propositions to correspond to. Moral language, however, is not representational; there is nothing moral in the world for putative moral propositions to correspond to. Therefore, moral language is not 'cognitive' (that is, it does not participate in a correspondence relation with the world or particular facts in it). As Carnap described in the essay quoted above, religious language may appear to be representational, putatively referring to supernatural entities, but it is unsuccessful as the existence of such entities is unverifiable. One can judge, as did Moore in his *Principia Ethica* that moral language is primitive and that efforts at semantic reduction cannot succeed because moral language and language about nature are of a wholly different order. To mistake this distinction led to what Moore termed the 'naturalistic fallacy'. Another kind of non-cognitivism is what came to be known as emotivism. Rather than interpreting value-language as being semantically primitive, such language is interpreted as having expressed a subjective attitude about some state of affairs. Thus 'torture is never morally acceptable', could be rendered as I have a negative subjective attitude regarding torture.

Note that while Moore's non-cognitivism remains anti-reductionist, emotivism – as in A. J. Ayer's view of moral and religious language – is precisely that. Emotivists of Ayer's variety hold that value-language does not refer and that it does not have meaning in its own right. Instead, this class of language is used to express subjective states.

Ayer's *Language, Truth and Logic* (1936) presents what is probably the best known example of emotivism. To the members of the Vienna Circle, metaphysics had far too often precluded empirical philosophy; doing away with metaphysics opened the door to truly scientific philosophy. Along with Ayer, Richard B. Braithwaite is important when considering mid-century approaches to the philosophy of religious language. While Ayer himself did not hold religious ideas in high regard, Braithwaite attempted to construct an empiricist account of religious language, based upon the views on language and meaning put forth by the positivists. In his essay 'An Empiricist's View of the Nature of Religious Belief' (1955), Braithwaite argued for an expressivist interpretation of religious language. The idea was that statements involving religious terms, while appearing to refer to facts, actually express subjective attitudes. Braithwaite held that expressions involving religious language were in essence expressions of commitment to a way of life. The implication is that Ayer's emotivism is reductionistic while Braithewaite's expressivism is descriptive. What each of these non-cognitive approaches to value-laden language share is an aversion towards treating these uses of language as being propositionally meaningful.

While Wittgenstein's *Tractatus* helped fuel the verificationist movement in analytic philosophy,[7] his later output inspired humanistic and religious critics of verificationism. After the emergence of Wittgenstein's later philosophy, philosophers of religion were increasingly interested in using it to analyze religious expressions, beliefs, and practices; in this way, Wittgenstein was assimilated into so-called Ordinary Language Philosophy. While differences are apparent now, they were not yet so then. Both Wittgenstein and ordinary language philosophers were concerned with studying everyday expressions and locating their meaning in social contexts, but that is where the similarity ended. Ordinary language philosophy took as its aim the development of a robust theory of meaning that took seriously the many different forms of expression (locutionary, illocutionary, perlocutionary, etc.); Wittgenstein's aim was to respond to philosophical confusion about meanings with clarificatory distinctions and dichotomies. His approach to philosophy was decidedly minimal and pessimistic about theory-building. Due to Wittgenstein's influence on and association with Russell and the Vienna Circle, the *Tractatus* was viewed as being insensitive to religious language (due to its treatment of religious language as nonsense). The later philosophy of *Philosophical Investigations* was widely understood to be sensitive to the diversity of uses of language.

3.2.2 The influence of Wittgenstein's later philosophy

In the third quarter of the twentieth century, some students of Wittgenstein's found in his later thought a new avenue for approaching philosophy of religion within analytic philosophy. Eugene Thomas Long writes about Wittgenstein's work and its bearing on philosophy of religion: 'Wittgenstein does not fully develop the implications of his view for religious discourse, but he does make a number of scattered remarks about religious belief and language which have helped generate an approach to religious meaning and truth known as Wittgensteinianism' (Long, 2003, p. 272). It is misleading to speak of Wittgenstein having a philosophy of religion, for this was not a major area of his philosophical work. It is also potentially misleading to say that Wittgenstein's scattered remarks generated the Wittgensteinian approach to philosophy of religion. I take it that the works Long has in mind were published in the late 1960s and later; however, Wittgensteinian philosophy of religion begins to emerge by the late 1950s and early 1960s. I would contend that it is more to the reception of *Philosophical Investigations* than to the reception of the 'Remarks on Frazer's *Golden Bough*' or the 'Lectures of Religious Belief' that we should look in tracing the beginnings of Wittgensteinian philosophy of religion.

As I indicated earlier in the chapter, scholars should be careful with expressions like 'Wittgensteinianism' and 'The Wittgensteinian School of Philosophy of Religion'. Various points of engagement with Wittgenstein's philosophy connect the figures placed underneath these characterizations. In what follows, I will use the name 'Wittgensteinian philosophy of religion' merely as an umbrella term to refer to approaches to philosophy of religion that self-consciously draw on Wittgenstein's thought; I do not presuppose any ideas or methods common to all instances of Wittgensteinian philosophy of religion. Key among the students that helped develop the earliest expressions of Wittgensteinian philosophy of religion were Norman Malcolm and Rush Rhees; two other important philosophers during this period who came into contact with Wittgenstein or his work through Malcolm and Rhees were O. K. Bouwsma and Peter Winch. Perhaps the most influential Wittgensteinian philosopher of religion has been D. Z. Phillips, who worked closely with both Rhees and Winch. Bloemendaal traces historically the development of Phillips' thought and, in so doing, the thought of Rhees, Winch, and Malcolm (Bloemendaal, 2006). The thought of these early Wittgensteinian thinkers helped frame much of how the first two generations of Wittgenstein scholars – and indeed many other thinkers – thought about philosophy of religion after Wittgenstein.

The first philosopher to publish work in a Wittgensteinian vein in philosophy of religion seems to have been Malcolm, and his subsequent publications have exerted much influence on how Wittgensteinian philosophy of religion developed. Bouwsma, a professor of Malcolm's, recommended Malcolm go to Cambridge to study with Moore. While at Cambridge, Malcolm came into contact with Wittgenstein and the two remained friends until Wittgenstein's death. Through Moore and Malcolm, Bouwsma became acquainted with Wittgenstein's work and, eventually, with Wittgenstein himself (Hacker, 1996, p. 147). Malcolm's 1960 essay 'Anselm's Ontological Arguments' exemplifies this early appropriation of Wittgenstein's thought. According to Bloemendaal, Malcolm makes two critical moves in this essay. First of all, Malcolm directs special attention to the use of 'religious language' (Bloemendaal, 2006, p. 117). Second, in perhaps his most influential move, Malcolm treats religions as language-games (Bloemendaal, 2006, p. 118). This is, indeed, one of the prevailing ideas associated with Wittgensteinian philosophy of religion. The strong identification of religions (or another set of practices) with language-games presupposes that religions are far more rule-governed groupings of behaviors than they are.[8] This is not to say that religions are not rule-governed institutions; some forms of religiosity look like that. It is just that not all religious people participate in those forms of religiosity. Bloemendaal refers to Joseph Incandella's criticism of much Wittgensteinian philosophy of religion and its supposed positivist bent:

> Not only does Malcolm's revision of the ontological argument deprive the unbeliever of the possibility of denying God's existence, what is more, he cannot be said truly to understand the argument that accomplishes that feat. Even if Malcolm may not have intended his remarks to be taken in this way, it should not surprise us that critics have found them to imply some form of fideism. (Bloemendaal, 2006, p. 199)

Bloemendaal summarizes: 'Like Wittgenstein, Malcolm urges us to pay attention to the natural use of our language. Where he goes beyond Wittgenstein is in awarding religious belief the status of a distinct and logically autonomous language-game or form of life' (Bloemendaal,

2006, p. 120). It is this latter elaboration of Malcolm's that leaves him open to charges of fideism, according to Bloemendaal.

Bloemendaal also explores the thought of Rhees, identifying three themes in his 'elaboration' of Wittgenstein's thought on religion. The first theme is the methodological point that philosophical problems are conceptual problems (Bloemendaal, 2006, p. 106). The second is that religion is a form of life and that this form of life has an absolute relationship to the religious person's worldview. With this in mind, religious language functions confessionally, as opposed to speculatively (Bloemendaal, 2006, p. 106–7). Note how this non-referential interpretation of religious language cedes the point of the verificationists but contends that referentiality is only one way in which language can be meaningful. Rhees's move here anticipates the questions later scholars would raise over whether Wittgensteinian philosophy of religion is in some sense non-cognitivist or anti-realist with respect to religious language. For Rhees, the most important role of religious language is found in this confessional use. The third theme Bloemendaal identifies in Rhees's work is an appeal to the thought of a group of Christian 'mystical' thinkers whose work Rhees understood to be akin to Wittgenstein's: Kierkegaard, Weil, Tolstoy, and Eckhart. Related to this mystical theme is Rhees's tendency to oppose natural theology[9] (Bloemendaal, 2006, p. 109–10). Like Wittgenstein, Rhees wrote much but published little during his life. However, his work on Wittgenstein was deeply influential on his student, D. Z. Phillips, who published extensively during his lifetime.

Rhees also influenced Winch in his work on Wittgenstein and religion, while they were colleagues at the University of Wales at Swansea. Winch's book *The Idea of a Social Science and Its Relation to Philosophy* (1958) was written in a Wittgensteinian vein and indeed predates Malcolm's first essay by two years; a reasonable case could be made for Winch's work being the first instance of Wittgensteinian philosophy of religion (broadly understood to include philosophical critique of anthropology of religion). Winch held that the social sciences ought to be thought of as conceptual rather than empirical sciences. Bloemendaal writes that Winch's thought holds that '[s]ociology is philosophy in disguise' (Bloemendaal, 2006, p. 111). Bloemendaal continues:

> Winch rejects a monolithic account of human institutions and practices in favor of 'an infinitely extendable number of distinctive modes of social life, each of which can be evaluated only on its own terms ... There is, in other words, no single account of truth, meaning,

> rationality, or, indeed, reality, to which all human institutions implicitly do or must conform. (Bloemendaal, 2006, p. 112–13)

In *The Idea of a Social Science*, Winch holds that criteria of identity – such as those used by a social scientist – are relative to a mode of human behavior. Winch is here talking about institutions of social scientific as well as academic inquiry.

Furthermore, Winch argues that sociological investigation of religious phenomena must on occasion ask religious questions when seeking to identify particular instances of a general phenomenon:

> I do not wish to maintain that we must stop at the unreflective kind of understanding of which I gave as an instance the engineer's understanding of the activities of his colleagues. But I do want to say that any more reflective understanding must necessarily presuppose, if it is to count as genuine understanding at all, the participant's unreflective understanding. (Winch, 1990, p. 89)

We see here a familiar theme in Wittgensteinian studies of religions or cultures: the appreciation for the distinctive ways in which particular institutions operate, including the institutions of those performing the investigation. The task then of philosophy is to describe rather than prescribe standards of rationality.

While this approach is laudable insofar as it redirects the attention of the sociologist or philosopher of religion to the faithful description the actual practices of the people under study, it can be taken to extremes. Bloemendaal observes, 'As Winch would later admit, it is difficult to avoid the impression that *The Idea of a Social Science* presents social practices, traditions and institutions as more or less isolated and self-contained, each going its own, fairly autonomous, way – a necessary ingredient, one might say, for a fideist philosophy' (Bloemendaal, 2006, p. 115). Of course, Winch was putting forth a philosophical critique of social science, not a theology or an apologetic of religious faith. The fact that it seemed plausible to ascribe fideism to philosophies and not just to theologies indicates that by 1960, the meaning of the term 'fideism' had migrated from being a term of classification and dispute in Christian theological circles to being a name for a secular philosophical error. Wayne Proudfoot and others would come to describe this intellectual maneuver a 'protective strategy'; while not necessarily motivated by theological commitments, a protective strategy might be used by an overly romantic scholar who wants to preserve ways of life that might be criticized by academic or scientific inquiry. Nevertheless, Winch's inclusion of religious points of view in the process of understanding social practices was read by some, including Kai Nielsen, to be close enough to the genre of apologetics to merit the fideist classification.

Many factors combined in the production of the idea of a 'school' of Wittgensteinian philosophy of religion. For example, consider the presence of Rhees, Winch, and Phillips, among others, on the faculty of the University of Wales, Swansea and Phillips' role as literary executor to Rhees and Winch. The publishing of Nielsen's article 'Wittgensteinian Fideism' did much to solidify the impression. Nielsen was not criticizing Wittgenstein's philosophy so much as the philosophy of religion of some of his interpreters. Nielsen begins his essay, 'Wittgenstein did not write on the philosophy of religion' (Nielsen and Phillips, 2005, p. 21) and continues:

> There is no text that I can turn to for an extended statement of this position, but certain remarks made by Winch, Hughes, Malcolm, Geach, Cavell, Cameron and Coburn can either serve as partial statements of this position, or can be easily used in service of such a statement. Some of their contentions will serve as targets for my argumentation, for as much as I admire Wittgenstein, it seems to me that the fideistic conclusions drawn by these philosophers from his thought are often absurd. This leads me back to an inspection of their arguments and the premisses in these arguments. (Nielsen and Phillips, 2005, p. 21)

Nielsen directs his criticism to philosophers of religion who have appropriated Wittgenstein's thought for their own projects. That such a grouping (not yet including Phillips, who goes unmentioned in the article) was already in existence indicates at the very least a common recognition of resources in Wittgenstein's thought for a new avenue for philosophy of religion in a philosophical milieu still haunted by verificationism.

Although increasingly less authoritative in analytic philosophy following W. V. O. Quine's 'Two Dogmas of Empiricism' (1951), verificationism retained what might be called an afterlife in philosophy of religion much the way skepticism has an afterlife in analytic epistemology despite the fact that radical global skeptics and doctrinaire verificationists are rather difficult to find. Philosophers of religion in the 1960s and 1970s sought to think their way out of older philosophical paradigms. Nielsen writes,

> These philosophers call attention to the linguistic regularities concerning 'God' that Ziff notes, but beyond anything Ziff claims

> they stress that religious concepts can only be understood if we have an insider's grasp of the form of life of which they are an integral part. As Malcolm puts it, the very genesis of the concept of God grows out of a certain 'storm in the soul'. Only within a certain form of life could we have the idea of an 'unbearably heavy conscience' from which arises the Judaeo-Christian concept of God and of a 'forgiveness that is beyond all measure'. (Nielsen and Phillips, 2005, p. 21)

Wittgenstein's writings seemed to many to provide such a resource; however, some naturalist philosophers of religion were troubled by how a simplistic equation of religions with language-games and/or forms of life isolated religious discourse from public disputation or correction.

As we will come to see, the idea of being epistemically and semantically located inside of a form of life is central to Nielsen's understanding of Wittgensteinian fideism. However, other themes too are associated with the view. Discerning a pattern among the writings of various philosophers of religion, Nielsen articulates eight theses he associates with 'Wittgensteinian fideism':

1. The forms of language are the forms of life.
2. What is given are the forms of life.
3. Ordinary language is all right as it is.
4. A philosopher's task is not to evaluate or criticize language or the forms of life, but to describe them where necessary and to the extent necessary to break philosophical perplexity concerning their operation.
5. The different modes of discourse which are distinctive forms of life all have a logic of their own.
6. Forms of life taken as a whole are not amenable to criticism; each mode of discourse is in order as it is, for each has its own criteria and each sets its own norms of intelligibility, reality and rationality.
7. These general, dispute-engendering concepts, i.e. intelligibility, reality, and rationality are systematically ambiguous; their exact meaning can only be determined in the context of a determinate way of life.
8. There is no Archimedean point in terms of which a philosopher (or for that matter anyone else) can relevantly criticize whole modes of discourse or, what comes to the same thing, ways of life, for each mode of discourse has its own specific criteria of rationality/irrationality, intelligibility/unintelligibility, and reality/unreality. (Nielsen and Phillips, 2005, p. 22)

Discerning the relationships among these theses is not straightforward, but Nielsen's list provided his contemporaries with some means for identifying when a view was or was not an instance of Wittgensteinian fideism; however, because the relationships among the theses are unclear, it is likewise unclear how many of the criteria must be satisfied in order for a view to be considered to be an instance of Wittgensteinian fideism.

The articulation of these criticisms both put Wittgensteinian philosophy of religion on the defense and also served to help determine what Wittgensteinian philosophy of religion was understood by the larger philosophical community to be, in part because of the need for philosophers to define themselves against the characterization offered by Nielsen. Theses 1, 2, 4, and 5 all use the phrase 'form of life', and theses 7 and 8 uses the expression 'way of life'. Theses 4–8 each place emphasis on the context sensitivity of not just meaning but also rationality. Part of what is apparently rejected by Wittgensteinian fideists is the so-called 'God's-Eye-View'[10] of the world. The putative irrelevance, inadequacy, and impossibility of criticism of religious forms of life is indicated in theses 4, 6, and 8 respectively. Together, these theses seem to call out for criticism the view that Nielsen sees in so much Wittgensteinian philosophy of religion – a view that he considered to be the most important rational alternative to scientific naturalism – that religions, conceived of as forms of life, are immune to external criticism and that criticism only makes sense from inside a form of life.

Aside from Winch's *The Idea of a Social Science*, Phillips's first book, *The Concept of Prayer* (1965), was the first book-length work in philosophy of religion to be inspired by Wittgenstein's writings. Unlike Winch's book, it is uncontroversially a work of philosophy of religion. In the book, Phillips argues that being a religious believer consists in having internalized religious language, by means of which one may commune with God (that is, through prayer). To understand the meaning of religious language is to understand its place within the language-game of that religion. Understanding religious language involved in prayer then must involve the practice of prayer in which the language has its home. Traces of Winch's view of understanding and Rhees' ideas of religious language functioning confessionally rather than speculatively may be found in Phillips' writings, especially from this period. Prayer is not metaphysics or epistemology and should not be understood as either. Following the publication of this book, Phillips came to be associated with the Wittgensteinian fideists, and then, in the 1970s, to be the principal exemplar of the philosophical type.

In his introduction to *Belief, Change, and Forms of Life* (1986), Phillips rejects the label 'fideism' as an accurate characterization of his work. He writes, remarking on some comments made by Anthony Kenny:

> Unfortunately, it cannot be denied that a philosophy by innuendo has grown up by which it is hinted, rather than argued, that what Wittgenstein is said to have said about religion and ritual is not closely related to the rest of his work. It has been suggested also that those influenced by him in the philosophy of religion have imposed alien features on Wittgenstein's work, and made use of certain of his terms, such as 'language-games', in ways of which he would not have approved. (Phillips, 1986, p. 1)

Indeed, this cuts right to the core of Nielsen's critique of Wittgensteinian philosophy of religion. The strong emphasis on language-games and forms of life as determining the use of language (and religious language in particular) contributes to the sorts of 'absurd' characteristics Nielsen sought to refute in his essay. While Nielsen took himself to be arguing against a position he took himself to neutrally describe, Phillips understood Nielsen and Kenny and others to be accusing Wittgensteinian philosophers of religion of some sort of intellectual crime:

> It is hard to see how these charges can be sustained. If we look at some other areas of philosophy, we shall find a continuity between many of Wittgenstein's emphases there and those we find in his comments on religion and ritual. For example, logic, for Wittgenstein, is not an a priori realm which is, in some sense or other, prior to all experience. Distinctions between sense and nonsense have their life in activities and ways of living we share with one another. (Phillips, 1986, p. 1)

Not only does Phillips reject the criticism, but he argues that the accusation is itself poorly thought out. Phillips argues that in fact, language-games and forms of life permeate other areas of philosophy influenced by Wittgenstein. To criticize Wittgensteinian philosophy of religion for such an emphasis is off the mark.

No doubt Phillips is accurate in noting the ubiquity of 'language-game' in mainstream Wittgensteinian philosophy, but this does not mean that the development of Wittgenstein's idea has been done in a satisfactory way. Just because philosophers of religion lean as heavily on terms such as 'language-game' and 'form of life' as do philosophers in other philosophical subdisciplines does not mean that broad use of the expressions is warranted. After all, Wittgenstein used the terms in highly context-sensitive places in his corpus. However tempting, generalizing uses of a philosopher's terms without extensive textual support runs the risk of creating a new philosophy that shows traces of influence without a demonstrated lineage; thus early Wittgensteinian philosophy of religion distorts Wittgenstein and other ways in which his philosophy may be incorporated into philosophy of religion. Cora Diamond notes interestingly that while Malcolm followed the traditional 'two Wittgensteins' view, Winch did not (Diamond, 2005). This serves as a reminder that early Wittgensteinian philosophy of religion was not uniform. Such a fact should not surprise us, but the way in which partisans in this intellectual skirmish express themselves might lead one to believe otherwise; both Nielsen and Phillips have displayed a tendency to generalize about what Wittgensteinian philosophers of religion do and do not say (with Phillips denying that which Nielsen ascribes to the group).

For some time, Phillips had hoped to avoid discussing Wittgensteinian fideism. He thought the idea was an unscholarly caricature. When Phillips eventually addresses the criticisms in *Belief, Change, and Forms of Life*, he attempts to throw the burden of proof back on the critic for uncharitable and unscholarly interpretation. Phillips writes,

> Those influenced by Wittgenstein who have attempted to throw light on the nature of religious beliefs have been accused of wanting to shield religious belief against criticism. This alleged anti-intellectualism and conservatism has been given the name 'fideism', a term which, unfortunately, seems here to stay. (Phillips, 1986, p. 4)

I agree wholeheartedly with Phillips's skepticism about the hermeneutic adequacy of these theses. Nielsen left them hanging in the air, without providing textual evidence to support his interpretation.

3.3 Criticisms of Wittgensteinian philosophy of religion

3.3.1 Alvin Plantinga and analytic philosophy of religion

Although Nielsen was the first to criticize Wittgensteinian philosophy of religion, he was not the only philosopher at the time to be troubled by this new movement. Before long, critics from a variety of sectors in philosophy began to offer criticism of the movement. Religious critics also had their points of contention. Even the then famously atheistic[11] Anthony Flew noted this possibility in his very negative review of Phillips's *The Concept of Prayer* (Flew, 1967). Alvin Plantinga's early philosophy is a good example of protestant Christian criticism of Wittgensteinian philosophy of religion. In his early book, *God and Other Minds* (1967), Plantinga is highly critical of what he takes to be 'the Wittgensteinian view' of the nature of consciousness. In the book, Plantinga notes that since Wittgenstein's comments are not entirely clear, he will take those of Norman Malcolm to represent the Wittgensteinian view. Plantinga wants to show that belief in God is a properly basic belief; that is, it is a belief that does not stand in need of justification, is not epistemically blameworthy for its lacking justification, and may be used in the formation of other more complex beliefs.

Plantinga's book was an important early foray into another avenue philosophy of religion would take within analytic philosophy in the middle to late twentieth century: Reformed Epistemology. Basically put, Reformed Epistemology is the class of epistemological theories that seek to establish the reasonableness of Christian theistic belief on the basis of its rational parity with other putative foundational beliefs naturalist critics are likely to hold, such as beliefs about the existence of the external world or of other minds. Consistency would thus require that naturalist critics of religious belief likewise criticize their own basic beliefs. Plantinga understands Malcolm's Wittgenstein to criticize the view that human beings infer the existence of other minds by means of analogy with one's own consciousness. Because this is an important step in the development of Plantinga's argument, he rejects what he understands to be the Wittgensteinian view.

This move of Plantinga's is ironic given that Wittgenstein's corpus might well have had something to offer Plantinga in his argument. In *Culture and Value*, a remark of Wittgenstein's is collected that might have interested Plantinga had it been widely available when Plantinga wrote his book: 'If someone can believe in God with complete certainty, why not in Other Minds?' (Wittgenstein, 1998, p. 73e). How best to understand this remark is not immediately clear, a matter that Plantinga would likely have taken to heart, but it does suggest an appreciation for the idea that there may be epistemic parity between belief in the existence of a God and belief in the existence of other minds. It also seems to suggest the peculiarity of being 'completely certain' about such a common-sense belief. Who besides philosophers and those with mental illness disputes the existence of other minds? That this remark was written down in 1948 also suggests that the idea was near the period in Wittgenstein's thinking to the composition of the remarks that would be collected in *On Certainty*.[12] Plantinga, in developing his defense of religious belief nevertheless sought a different path around the problems skepticism poses for philosophy of religion. Plantinga chose the common-sense thought of Thomas Reid over what he called the 'ordinary language philosophy' of Wittgenstein. Furthermore, Plantinga's conception of philosophy of religion is closer to apologetic philosophical theology than Wittgensteinian approaches to philosophy of religion, which have tended to be more hermeneutical in spirit.

Evangelical Christian philosophers have often had difficulty with Wittgensteinian philosophy of religion due to their perception that the approach slides into relativism or at least anti-realism about meaning and truth, metaphysical stances that are untenable given their doctrinal epistemic, metaphysical and moral commitments. Evangelical Christian philosophers have typically sought realist interpretations of doctrinal statements and faith commitments and thus have been wary of the tendencies of Wittgensteinian philosophers of religion to focus on the practical manifestation, rather than the propositional content, of religious belief. This propensity towards metaphysical realism also explains the appeal of Reformed Epistemology, with its defense of the rational parity of belief in the existence of God with other basic beliefs, among Evangelical Christian philosophers.

Despite falling under criticisms from some secular and orthodox religious philosophers, Wittgensteinian philosophers of religion like Phillips insisted that they had been misunderstood, that the emphases placed on their thought by their critics distorted the nature of the philosophical enterprise in which they engaged. Thus, despite occasions of encounter and engagement, Wittgensteinian philosophy of religion developed a reputation for insularity.

3.3.2 Naturalist criticisms of Wittgensteinian philosophy of religion

Nielsen has continued his criticisms of Wittgensteinian fideism over the years, and other naturalist scholars joined in. Wayne Proudfoot, who has been previously mentioned, is known principally for his naturalist, contextualist interpretations of mysticism and religious experience. He criticizes Phillips' philosophy of religion as an example of an apologetic or 'protective' strategy (Proudfoot, 1985, p. 200). Proudfoot contends that Wittgensteinian approaches, such as the view put forward by Phillips, typically hold that only those possessing a common language and form of life can be said to understand one another. In such a setting, religious experiences, integrally part of such 'forms of life', cannot be exhaustively explained by external, naturalist critics. Proudfoot takes these Wittgensteinian approaches to understanding religious life to be part of a long-standing tradition since Friedrich Schleiermacher of explaining religious experiences in terms of inaccessible, private feelings (Proudfoot, 1985, p. 210).

Proudfoot's singling out Wittgensteinian philosophers on religious experience might seem a bit odd. After all, Wittgenstein did not write much about 'experience', religious or otherwise. Like many of his contemporaries and followers, he was preoccupied with problems of language; Wittgensteinian philosophy of religion has likewise reflected this preoccupation with language. Nevertheless, when elaborating on just what makes life distinctive when practiced according to a religion, it is commonplace to say that one experiences the world differently. Whether this amounts to what Proudfoot has in mind with respect to religious experiences is another matter; Proudfoot likely has in mind extraordinary religious experiences (for example, of a mystical or ecstatic sort).

In Proudfoot's book, he argues that some philosophers use protective strategies in order to stave off non-religious explanations for religious experiences. He writes of the long-standing influence of Schleiermacher[13] in studies of religious experience:

> Schleiermacher's approach continues to inform much contemporary religious thought and philosophy of religion, even among those who think of themselves as having broken with that tradition. If they disagree with the claim for the autonomy of religious experience viewed as a sense of the infinite or the feeling of absolute dependence, they employ similar arguments to defend the irreducible character of religious experience construed as the experience of the sacred, or as limit experience, or of religious language, practice, or doctrine. In each of these cases, despite considerable differences, the autonomy of the religious life is defended in order to preclude inquiry and to stave off demands for justification from some perspective outside of that life. The result is a combination of genuine insights into the ways in which religion ought to be studied and protective strategies that serve apologetic purposes. (Proudfoot, 1986, p. xv)

In order to explain a religious experience, according to Proudfoot, one must include the subject's own description of the event as well as the attendant beliefs the subject must have in order to understand the experience as a religious experience; however, the scholar of religions need not then adopt those religious beliefs in order to understand the experience in question.

Phillips is among those figures whose philosophical work comes under Proudfoot's scrutiny. Phillips has written repeatedly on the concept of explanation, and it is this to which Proudfoot is primarily responding. In particular, Proudfoot directs his attention to Phillips' book *Religion without Explanation* (1976), the book he would later re-write as *Religion and the Hermeneutics of Contemplation* (2001). Throughout his analysis of Phillips' defense of religious ways of life from naturalistic explanation, Proudfoot emphasizes Phillips' resistance to treating religious language as being referential in nature. This he understands to be a part of Phillips' agenda of protecting religious discourses from naturalistic explanation. Proudfoot writes:

> Phillips recognizes that religious experience is constituted by concepts and beliefs, and he urges attention to the grammar of those concepts. He argues that the rules of that grammar must govern any account of the experience. If questions are raised about the validity of beliefs assumed by the subject in his identification of the experience, one has imported issues from outside the religious form of life and ipso facto shown that one does not understand that life. Both positions [Phillips's and Schleiermacher's] assume that religious experience and belief can be understood and assessed only from the inside. (Proudfoot, 1986, p. 212)

Proudfoot notes Phillips's understanding of religious forms of life being rigorously rule-governed.

Proudfoot's former student Matthew Bagger also criticizes what he sees as a protective strategy among Wittgensteinian philosophers of religion. In particular, he criticizes those who use Wittgensteinian ideas to set religious discourse off from secular discourse, rendering it immune from external critique. In his book, Bagger criticizes primarily the Reformed Epistemology of William Alston, which takes some inspiration from Wittgenstein's writings (*On Certainty* in particular). There are clear differences between early Wittgensteinian approaches to religious epistemology and reformed, but where there is similarity is in recognizing the relative autonomy of religious beliefs (that is, that they participate in a different region of the epistemic lives than do beliefs about states of affairs in the natural world). Bagger compares Alston to Malcolm and Phillips:

> In this regard his interpretation of Wittgenstein resembles the regrettable alternate language-game approach championed by Malcolm and Phillips. Alston's effort to insulate religious belief-forming mechanisms as much as possible from their more mundane counterparts recalls Malcolm's desire to protect religious forms of life from external critique. (Bagger, 1999, pp. 117–18)

Bagger draws upon a distinction made by Bernard Williams between Right and Left Wittgensteinians (Williams, 1992). The distinction concerns how broad the 'we' is construed with respect to participation in a linguistic community. Right Wittgensteinians identify particular cultural or epistemic practices and treat meanings as settled and determined by those practices. In this sense, Right Wittgensteinians emphasize the rule-governed nature of 'religious language-games'. Left Wittgensteinians by way of contrast construe the community of language users much more broadly and do not claim that an unbridgeable semantic gulf lies between those who participate in a social practice and those who do not. While both agree that language – or religion – is constituted largely through social cooperation, they disagree on how permeable the boundaries between and among communities are.

3.3.3 Criticism of Wittgensteinian philosophy of religion by scholars of Wittgenstein

Lastly, there are those philosophers who, as scholars of Wittgenstein's work, criticize what they take to be excesses in Wittgensteinian philosophy of religion. Such critics may vary in the particulars of their criticisms, but all agree that more faithful readings of Wittgenstein do not support certain themes in Wittgensteinian philosophy of religion. Most commonly, Wittgenstein scholars take issue with the strong equation of religions with language-games or forms of life. Key among these critics would be Hilary Putnam, Cora Diamond, Patrick Sherry and Brian Clack.

Cora Diamond is critical of readings of Wittgenstein that imply the privacy of experience or thought. In particular, one can see this as regards religious puzzles, such as Anselm's argument. For example, consider the following passages from the essay 'Riddles and Anselm's Riddle':

> What difference it makes, that 'this language-game is played,' depends on the game. Set theory is 'played,' too. But Wittgenstein wanted to show that it was not what we had taken it for – and he thought that our interest in it would be very different once we saw that. I am not suggesting that that is what Anselm's talk of God is like, but that there is no support in Wittgenstein for the idea that if a form of words has a place in some activity, that form of words is not expressive of deep confusion. ('Mathematics is ridden through and through with the pernicious idioms of set theory.' –PR, p. 211.) He spoke in connection with set theory of the glitter of the concepts. The 'glitter' of the concepts here is even more dazzling: what after all are we talking

> about but that than which nothing more dazzling can be conceived? (Diamond, 1995, pp. 286–7)
>
> The questioning expressed in great riddles is anyone's; the possibility of such questions belong to language itself and not to any particular language-game. (Diamond, 1995, p. 287)

In this regard, Diamond is also a critic of Malcolm. In Malcolm's influential early essay on Anselm, he had offered a Wittgenstein-inspired defense of the ontological argument. Among other things, this argument had provided some foundation for Wittgensteinian fideism by providing a case where an argument for the existence of God could not be properly understood if one did not accept the premise of God's existence outright. Against this view, Diamond contended that there is nothing private about Anselm's puzzle, that it is a puzzle for anyone who encounters it, not just the religious believer. The consequence of Diamond's interpretation of Anselm and Wittgenstein is that incommensurability cannot be said to apply especially to religious or any other kind of language; use of the concept of incommensurability may be an attempt to capture the gulf between believer and atheist, but it does not capture the phenomenon for which it aims.

In the collections of lectures, *Renewing Philosophy* (1992) and *Pragmatism* (1995), Hilary Putnam criticizes what he understands to be a standard reading of Wittgenstein on religious belief. In *Renewing Philosophy*, Putnam challenges the reading of simple incommensurability into religious disagreement (Putnam, 1992, p. 150–1). He writes in a passage on Wittgenstein's 'Lectures on Religious Belief':

> Wittgenstein is often charged with simple-mindedly equating use and meaning. Yet here he imagines an interlocutor who plays the role of the stock 'Wittgenstein' and proposes to say that the words 'I believe in a Last Judgment' have a different meaning in the two uses (one is, of course, completely imaginary), and the real Wittgenstein reminds the stock 'Wittgenstein' that we don't use the word 'meaning' that way, that is, that the difference in these two uses is not something that we would ordinarily call a difference in meaning. (Putnam, 1992, p. 151)

This is not to say that a gulf does not lie between the atheist and the believer, but the gulf is not one of semantics. Instead, Putnam suggests that the gulf may be, in part, understood through broad differences in social practice, a theme to which I will return in Chapter 6.

In *Pragmatism*, Putnam continues his criticism of what he takes to be conventional readings of Wittgenstein on religion. Readings which stress above all else the incommensurability of language-games Putnam associates with Malcolm's interpretation of Wittgenstein. However, Putnam also points out that Malcolm's Wittgenstein is also the Wittgenstein of Richard Rorty. Against Malcolm and Rorty, Putnam wishes to maintain that there are better and worse language-games – in short, that they may be criticized – and that language-games represent particular capacities of language or human reason; they do not represent the whole of either.

Patrick Sherry's *Religion, Truth, and Language-Games* (1977) provides a good corrective against tendencies to use expressions like 'the Christian language-game' and 'the religious form of life'. Sherry seeks in this text to overcome the tendency to read Wittgenstein's bearing on the philosophy of religion as anti-realist; Sherry argues 'that one can both derive benefit from [Wittgenstein's] philosophy and do justice to a propositional conception of religious truth' (Sherry, 1977, p. 1). In critically assessing the contributions of Malcolm, Winch, Phillips, and others, Sherry seeks to identify tendencies in Wittgensteinian philosophy of religion (an expression he eschews) as well as to set aside what is not ultimately useful for understanding religions or assessing the doctrinal truth-claims associated with them.

Brian Clack accuses Phillips not just of fideism but of dismissing magic and related rituals as mere superstition. Clack's 'Wittgenstein and Magic' offered a critique of what he took to be a superficial (yet conventional) reading of the 'Remarks on Frazer's *Golden Bough*'; namely, the so-called expressivist reading of ritual. Against the intellectualist theory of Frazer – a theory that held magical and religious rituals to be in essence folk science – Wittgenstein is understood by expressivists to think that magical and religious rituals express practitioners' commitments to their form of life. Clack argues that not only do the Remarks on Frazer not support the expressivist reading, but such a reading would be incompatible with the principal features of Wittgenstein's later philosophy (although he notes that such an expressivist view could perhaps have been reconciled with the Tractarian Wittgenstein). Instead, Clack thinks,

> [W]ith its emphasis on deed over deliberation, the Remarks on Frazer form an early and crucial part of Wittgenstein's late attack on the calculating, rational, Cartesian self. Just as it is 'humiliating to have to appear like an empty tube which is simply inflated by a mind' (CV, p. 11), so it is debasing and implausible for human beings to be presented as merely reasoning entities, whose actions are consistently

> the result of deliberation and calculation. Human life is more intense and colourful than that: it is ruled by passion, by instinct, by motivations we can barely grasp. As a result, our life here is strange and disconcerting. Hence why Wittgenstein's reflections on magical practice ultimately reach their bedrock with haunting thoughts about 'man and his past... the strangeness of what I see in myself and in others, what I have seen and have heard' (RF, p. 18). (Clack, 2001, p. 26)

Phillips responded in 'Wittgenstein, Wittgensteinianism and Magic: a Philosophical Tragedy?' (Phillips, 2003) arguing that Clack had effectively constructed a straw argument as no one holds the views Clack attributes to the 'orthodox' interpretation. Clack in turn responds to Phillips by offering examples of the sort of interpretation he critiques. While he does offer several examples, it is notable that none are recent or high-profile. All are instead offered by non-Wittgensteinian philosophers of religion, seemingly conceding Phillips's criticism that Clack is committing a 'sleight of hand'. Eventually, Clack accuses Phillips of defending the sort of expressivism Clack critiqued.

Catholic philosopher Terrence W. Tilley has also criticized Phillips in an exchange in the *Journal of the American Academy of Religion* for Phillips' distinction between religion and superstition.[14] Consider the following critique from Tilley:

> Phillips follows Wittgenstein in construing religious practice as ingredient in a form of life and religious expression as a language game played in that form of life. In doing that Phillips refuses to conform to the warped practice that is modern philosophy of religion. But just as in the Varieties James may have romantically canonized 'original' individuals and religious 'geniuses,' and distinguished them from the herd, so also does Phillips focus on the geniuses and separate them from the herd. They are the folk whom he, working to show to his logical positivist opponents that religion is not meaningless, holds up as impressive exemplars. These exemplars may indeed be impressive even to sceptics. But that does not make these geniuses to be actual exemplars of religious belief and practice but exceptions to the ordinary practice of ordinary believers. Hence, much of 'the herd's' religious practices must be confused, unimpressive, or 'superstitious.' This is where Phillips begins to go amiss. (Tilley, 2000b, p. 352)

What Clack and Tilley object to is what they see as anti-realism about religious expressions in Phillips' account of the genuine nature of religious expressions (that is, the confessional use originally outlined in *The Concept of Prayer*). In addition, they criticize Phillips' separation of magic and religion. Phillips wishes to deter superstitious 'misreadings' of religion, but Tilley observes that these too are among the phenomena of religion.

3.4 Conclusion

In this chapter, I have traced the reception of Wittgenstein's philosophy in analytic philosophy of religion. The ideas in Wittgenstein's thought that have been most influential in the philosophy of religion are clearly those associated with 'meaning as use', 'language-games', and 'forms of life'. These ideas were of interest to philosophers of religion in the mid to late twentieth century because of the influence of verificationist tendencies in theories of meaning and austere naturalistic metaphysical pictures. Many critics have detected an intellectually evasive or protective trend in Wittgensteinian philosophy of religion, and interpretations of Wittgenstein that suggest or propose a strong identification of language-games with religions clearly ought to be left behind.

The preoccupation of philosophers with these themes has constrained other possible lines of research into what Wittgenstein might bring to the philosophy of religion; meanwhile, debates over the application of 'Wittgensteinian fideism' have typically perpetuated the influence of these very same themes in readings of Wittgenstein. In an effort to get past this, to change the subject, I have tried in this chapter to show how these themes became prominent and how some recent philosophers have sought to move beyond them. In doing this, I am laying the groundwork for a different way of reading Wittgenstein on religion. The philosophical problems of the 1950s and early 1960s concerned the nature and meaning of various kinds of language (metaphysical, scientific, moral, and religious) That scholars would find some inspiration in Wittgenstein's thought for a way forward for philosophy of religion within analytic philosophy should not be surprising. The overly strong identification of religions with language-games or forms of life was probably some sort of attempt to articulate this viability. That the identification came to be associated with fideism reflects, among other things, the comparatively shallow view of religious thought held by many analytic philosophers in the 1960s. The persistence of concern over the possibility of fideism suggests that contemporary philosophy of religion is not settled on how to approach the issue of the epistemic status of religious belief.

4
The Traditions of Fideism

Since Kai Nielsen's widely read essay 'Wittgensteinian Fideism' was first published in 1967, philosophy of religion influenced by Wittgenstein has often been associated with fideism (Nielsen, 1967). One need not search far to see how extensive this association is, and it has affected what philosophers understand fideism to be. Definitions and explorations of fideism since 1967 rarely fail to mention Wittgenstein's thought on religion. While much has been published on whether or not Wittgenstein or Wittgensteinian philosophers are in fact fideists (McGovern and Szabados, 2002), comparatively little has been written on fideism itself.[1]

The diverse and sometimes conflicting individual definitions of fideism call out for some philosophical housekeeping if the term is to be useful academically. This preliminary investigation into the genealogy of fideism shows that the meaning of the term is not at all clear in either philosophical or theological discourse. Because of this confusion, academic investigations into the fideism of, for example, Wittgenstein, Kierkegaard, or philosophers influenced by them are often disconnected from the historical origins of the term. The goal of this chapter is to suggest some ways towards clearing up this confusion and identifying the uses of the term that are fruitful in academic discourse. Taking a cue from Wittgenstein,[2] I propose that it is best to see how the term was actually used in its original context and to construct extensions of the term carefully from this original use. Otherwise, the danger is that scholarly use of 'fideism' may degrade into instances of 'language gone on holiday' and if confusion is to be avoided, use of the term must be well grounded.[3] While some scholars might conclude that the term should be avoided altogether, I argue that confusion over the meaning of the term may be resolved when references to fideism are contextually grounded.

4.1 The confusion around use of the term 'fideism'

One need not venture far into theological and philosophical discourse about fideism to get the sense that often the term is not defined clearly. Philosophers and theologians use the word to pick out any of a number of views dealing with tension between commitments to faith, reason, and tradition. This may lead some readers to wonder with Richard Amesbury whether the term can be used properly (Amesbury, 2007, 2012). The causes of this confusion over the meaning of 'fideism' are many; while it is not the goal of this essay to list them all, the following are some contributing factors.

4.1.1 'Fideism' is commonly used pejoratively

A survey of philosophical and theological writing over the last century shows that 'fideism' is sometimes, although not always, understood to be a term of reproach. This is shown as much in dictionary and encyclopedia articles as it is in essays and books. 'Fideism' often goes undefined in scholarly literature, its meaning apparently presumed to be clear. However, when it is defined, it is defined in various ways. The following excerpts represent some of this variety:

(1) Fideists hold that religious belief is based on faith rather than reason. Extreme fideists maintain that it is contrary to reason; moderate fideists argue that what must first be accepted on faith may subsequently find rational support. (Quinn, 2005)

(2) A contrasting view [to evidentialism] is *fideism*, best understood as the claim that one's fundamental religious convictions are not subject to independent rational assessment. A reason often given for this is that devotion to God should be one's 'ultimate concern,' and to subject faith to the judgment of reason is to place reason above God and make of it an idol. Proponents of fideism include Tertullian, Kierkegaard, Karl Barth, and some Wittgensteinians. (Hasker, 1995)

(3) Fideism is the view that truth in religion is ultimately based on faith rather than on reasoning or evidence. This claim has been presented in many forms by theologians from St. Paul to contemporary neo-orthodox, antirationalist writers, usually as a way of asserting that the fundamental tenets of religion cannot be established by proofs or by empirical evidence but must be accepted on faith. (Popkin, 1967)

(4) It should be noted that neither the Wittgensteinians nor the Reformed epistemologists espouse the view that the rationality of

faith is irrelevant to whether or not it is acceptable to embrace it. That position has traditionally gone under the name of 'fideism', and such thinkers as Tertullian, William of Ockham, Pierre Bayle, Søren Kierkegaard, and Leo Shestov have regularly been classified as fideists. However, when one digs into the thought of the five thinkers mentioned on the topic of faith and reason, one not only finds it to be in each case subtle, and the various positions taken diverse, one also becomes less and less convinced of the propriety of describing any of them as a defender of irrationality in matters of faith. (Wolterstorff, 1998)

(5) Philosophical defenders of faith have commonly tried to show that it is not at odds with reason: that it is internally consistent, that it accords with scientific knowledge, or even, more positively, that some of its tenets can be established independently by philosophical reasoning. Fideists reject this mode of apologetic argument, and maintain, in contrast, that faith does not need the support of reason, and should not seek it. (Penelhum, 1997)

(6) 'Fideism' is the name given to that school of thought – to which Tertullian himself is frequently said to have subscribed – which answers that faith is in some sense independent of – if not outright adversarial toward – reason. In contrast to the more rationalistic tradition of natural theology, with its arguments for the existence of God, fideism holds that reason is unnecessary and inappropriate for the exercise and justification of religious belief. (Amesbury, 2007)

In these excerpts, three types of definitions are offered for 'fideism'. The first, shared by (1) and (3) is that fideism is the view that religious belief or truth in religion is based on faith rather than reason. Note that both indicate a division between moderate and extreme fideists. The second type of definition is found in (2): fideism is defined as 'the claim that one's fundamental religious convictions are not subject to independent rational assessment'. Definitions (5) and (6) share this conception. This portrait of fideism focuses not so much on what fideism is (for example, a view that religious belief is based on faith rather than reason) as what fideism is not (a view that religious belief is subject to independent rational critique). This manner of definition by exclusion from a normative conception of rationality is also found in (4): 'the view that the rationality of faith is irrelevant to whether or not it is acceptable to embrace it'. However, note how careful the author of (4), Nicholas Wolterstorff, is in mentioning the usefulness of this irrationalist category of fideism. While he mentions many of those philosophers frequently associated with fideism, he goes on to observe that after careful scrutiny, the 'irrationalist' category of fideism fails to adequately describe their thought. Wolterstorff's observation on the futility of this conception of fideism anticipates the argument of the first section of this chapter: fideism, when used pejoratively, is not very useful in academic discourse.[4]

In theological discourse, fideism is generally considered to be a negative term of appraisal. This is the case in both essays and dictionary articles, although dictionary articles, by their very nature, attempt generally to be more balanced. Here are some representative definitions of 'fideism' from theological sources:

(7) A philosophical and theological doctrine or attitude that minimizes the capacity of the human intellect to attain certitude and assigns faith as a criterion of the fundamental truths. Thus, God's existence, the immortality of the soul, principles of morality, the fact of divine revelation, and the credibility of Christianity cannot be proved by reason alone, but must be accepted on authority. The term fideism (from the Latin *fides*, faith) was used for the first time by Eugène Ménégoz, *Reflexions sur l'evangile du salut* (Paris 1789 [*sic*]), and then it was applied to traditionalism and other theories of similar strain. (Matczak, 1967)

(8) A view which assumes that knowledge originates in a fundamental act of faith, independent of rational presuppositions. Though the term in this form dates only from about 1885 when it was associated with and adapted by French theologians, the standpoint represented by it had several times been officially condemned during the pontificate of Gregory XVI (1831–46). (Douglas, 1978)

(9) The word was coined in the nineteenth century, probably by A. Sabatier and his modernist circle of Protestants in Paris, to denote the view that (as Kant has demonstrated) reason could not prove the truths of religion and that therefore believers could rely upon faith, which was a kind of religious experiencing. Dogmas were only the symbolic expression of religious feelings; this view stands in the general succession from Schleiermacher (and Ritschl). 'Fideism' has continued to be used especially by theologians of the Thomist tradition as a pejorative term for subjectivist theories which are based upon religious experience and which undervalue reason in theology. 'Wittgensteinian fideism' is the term that has been applied to the work of some theologians and philosophers of religion who claim that every form of life, including religion,

develops its own autonomous language-game, and that it is neither necessary nor possible for it to be justified by anything outside of itself. (Richardson and MacQuarrie, 1983)

(10) A theological term coined at the turn of the century by Protestant modernists in Paris (Ménégoz, Sabatier) to describe their own thought, but since used pejoratively to attack various strands of Christian 'irrationalism.' Fideists, following Kant (who argued that reason cannot prove religious truth), are said to base their understanding of the Christian faith upon religious experience alone, understanding reason to be incapable of establishing either faith's certitude or credibility. Among others, Luther, Kierkegaard, Van Til, Schleiermacher, and Barth have been accused of fideism. The term, however, is used too imprecisely to be of much value. Certainly none of these theologians would deny the use of reason altogether. If helpful at all, the term functions to describe an excessive emphasis upon the subjective dimensions of Christianity. (Johnson, 1984)

(11) Fideism, as the word indicates, attributes to faith (*fides*) the principal role in religious knowledge, which, when taken to the extreme, however, leads it to question the very possibility of an authentic access to faith. Reacting to the exclusive rationalism of the Enlightenment, fideism is nevertheless dependent on certain fundamental presuppositions of the position that it challenges...

The best known representatives of this movement were, under the label of 'traditionalism,' L. de Bonald (1754–1840), and H.-F.-R. de Lamennais (1782–1854), and under the label of 'fideism,' Ph.-O. Gerbet (1798–1864), L.-E.-M. Bautain (1796–1867), and A. Bonnety (1798–1879). Their attacks against the Scholasticism of their time, which they regarded as rationalist, provoked controversies that focused essentially on the status of knowledge within the framework of a fundamental theology... The name 'fideism' was also claimed around this time be a group of French Protestants represented by A. Sabatier and E. Ménégoz, who applied the principles of Schleiermacher and adopted positions derived from the school of the history of religions. (Neufeld, 2005)

Most definitions in theological sources point to Eugène Ménégoz (1838–1921) and Auguste Sabatier (1839–1901), both Protestant

Theologians at the Sorbonne in the late nineteenth century, as the originators of the term (although, it is striking that the Catholic Encyclopedia (1909) points to no origination of the term, freely using it to describe theologians and philosophers throughout the history of Christianity). Religious experience is listed in (9) and (10) as being a source for religious truth separate from reason. Authority stands in as the alternate source in (7) and (11). The independence of religious belief from reason is stressed in (8). Each of these definitions takes a historical approach to understanding the term, and all but (8) indicate that the term was used by both Protestant and Catholic theologians in late nineteenth century France. While (7), (9), and (10) list Ménégoz and Sabatier as originators of the term, (11) remains agnostic on whether others used the term first. The pejorative use of the term is noted in definitions (9) and (10), and it is interesting to see skepticism expressed about the usefulness of the term at all in (10).

The philosophers above, on the whole, have been drawn to seek after the essential doctrine underlying various instances of fideism through intellectual history; the theologians above, on the whole, have been drawn to locate the lineage of the term and its subsequent use in theological discourse. An appreciation for the confusion over use of the term is evident in some of the theologians' definitions, but the philosophers mentioned above – with the exception of Amesbury and Wolterstorff – do not seem to register this. Nevertheless, the term is used in philosophical and theological discourse *without* context more often than not. The meaning of the term is presumed to be understood between author and audience.

A recent example of this presumption is found in probably the most widely read text to mention fideism explicitly, Pope John Paul II's 1998 encyclical *Fides et Ratio*. The document echoes many of the ideas presented in the nineteenth century in the documents of the First Vatican Council (1869–70) and the 1879 encyclical, *Aeterni Patris*. The Pope admits as much in the encyclical (John Paul II, 1998, §52). 'Fideism' is treated as a word with an unproblematic meaning, as in the following passages from *Fides et Ratio* where John Paul II interprets *Dei Filius* from the First Vatican Council:

> Against the temptations of fideism, however, it was necessary to stress the unity of truth and thus the positive contribution which rational knowledge can and must make to faith's knowledge: 'Even if faith is superior to reason there can never be a true divergence between faith and reason, since the same God who reveals the mysteries and bestows the gift of faith has also placed in the human spirit the light of reason. This God could not deny himself, nor could the truth ever contradict the truth'. (John Paul II, 1998, §53)

> One currently widespread symptom of this fideistic tendency is a 'biblicism' which tends to make the reading and exegesis of Sacred Scripture the sole criterion of truth. (John Paul II, 1998, §55)

> Other modes of latent fideism appear in the scant consideration accorded to speculative theology, and in disdain for the classical philosophy from which the terms of both the understanding of faith and the actual formulation of dogma have been drawn. (John Paul II, 1998, §55)

Fideism is understood by John Paul II to be the excessive reliance on faith in determining religious truth – as compared with the favored method of the Catholic Magisterium: faith and reason working in concert. While the pope may have held that the 'original' fideism of the nineteenth century had been adequately dealt with in prior encyclicals, these twentieth century variants called for attention in a new encyclical. The biblicism the pope mentions is presumably the Fundamentalist movement in American Protestant Christianity. The antimetaphysical approach of much twentieth century philosophy and its subsequent influence on theology is presumably what is being criticized in the latter remark on latent fideism.

John Paul II places a number of different views under the banner of fideism. Fideist philosophies and theologies are to be corrected with a Catholic philosophy where faith and reason work in partnership. What these fideist views have in common is a divergence from the Catholic ideal of the relationship between faith and reason. Neither this encyclical, nor the first ever to use the word 'fideism', *Pascendi Dominici Gregis* of 1907, mentions the historical origin of the term and neither shows any reluctance in using the term critically. In contexts such as this, the meaning of 'fideism' is presumed to be understood – and to be understood as a term of reproach.

4.1.2 Scholarship on fideism is largely ahistorical

The second problem surrounding scholarship on fideism is that the work on it tends to be ahistorical. Accusations of fideism rarely show signs of awareness of the historical origins of the term. Instead, critics depict fideism as a position that could be occupied by thinkers of varying historical periods and cultural or religious contexts. Fideism is thus treated by some scholars as a general category in religious and philosophical thought; however, because of its common pejorative use, serious questions arise about whether fideism can be regarded as a general category.

Occasionally in scholarly literature, one will find references to thinkers far removed from modern philosophy labeled as fideists. Tertullian (c.150 – c. 230 CE), the early Church Father from North Africa, is one such example. On the face of it, it is not hard to see why. After all, he wrote of a stark opposition between Christian faith and Greek philosophy. In particular, Tertullian wrote extensive critical works attacking what he took to be the biased and/or ignorant depiction of Christianity among pagan intellectuals. In the *Apology*, Tertullian presents an attack not on the natural reason of the philosophers, per se, but instead, on the intellectual integrity of the pagan philosophers of his day (Tertullian, 1931, pp. 201–2). It is not reason that he abandons but trust in the sincere pursuit of truth that philosophers are supposed to value above all else. It is the virtue of pagan philosophers that Tertullian criticizes. His criticism could be taken as being compatible with the stated aims of philosophy – a search for truth over opinion and virtue over vice.

Those who classify Tertullian as a fideist typically point to the expression '*credo quia absurdum*' ('I believe because it is absurd') as indicative of the view that faith is based in absurdity and runs counter to reason. Scholars now often indicate that this is a misquotation of Tertullian; the phrase in question should be '*credibile est, quia ineptum est*' ('It is credible because it is inept') (Dunn, 2004, p. 31). Commenting on this point, Eric Osborn argues that Tertullian's use of paradox is an integral part of his apologetic argument:

> If God, who is wholly other, is joined to mortal man in a way which is not inept, then either God is no longer God or man is no longer man, and there is no true incarnation. Truth on this issue can only be achieved by ineptitude. Tertullian does not universalize his claim; most ineptitude is false. This argument is put into paradox, to imitate Paul and to make it more striking and provocative. Paradoxes are useful because they are wonderful and against common opinion. (Osborn, 1997, p. 58)

To think of Tertullian as a fideist is for Osborn to ignore both the genre Tertullian wrote in and the place of a conclusion in an argument. Tertullian sought to articulate a Christology that explained how God could save imperfect human beings; according to Osborn, the paradoxical description of this incarnated God was meant as a correction of Marcion's Christology, which denied the incarnation. But to Tertullian and others without the humility of God in the incarnation, the God in question did not seem capable of saving imperfect humanity. Although from a distance, Tertullian's thought may appear to be an uncontroversial case of fideism, a contextually situated reading of his work suggests that the term does not fit well.

4.1.3 The historical origins of 'fideism' are complex

The third problem stems from the complex origins of 'fideism' within nineteenth century Christian theology. When the term is defined in a historically sensitive way, it may not be robust enough to survive being detached from its context. Contemporary confusion over the meaning of 'fideism' also stems in part from the various uses of the term in the late nineteenth and early twentieth centuries. Perhaps the most surprising feature of the history of the term 'fideism' is that there seem to be two discrete points of origin for the term. In the nineteenth century, Protestant and Catholic theologians used the word to name post-Kantian theological approaches, but that in itself is not enough to warrant supposing that these two theological communities meant precisely the same thing by the word at the time. Furthermore, early Catholic use of the term to criticize modernist tendencies in theology was soon to be eclipsed by the pejorative meaning condemning traditionalist approaches in early- to mid-nineteenth century theology.

4.2 Popkin and Penelhum on 'skeptical fideism'

While not a lot of work has been done on the nature and history of fideism, the work of two historians of philosophy, Richard H. Popkin and Terence Penelhum, stands out in terms of influence. Popkin's groundbreaking study of the origins of modern skepticism, *The History of Scepticism: From Erasmus to Descartes* was first published in 1960. This book also included historically grounded exploration of what Popkin termed 'skeptical fideism': the appropriation of ancient skeptical arguments in the service of Christian apologetics. During the sixteenth and seventeenth centuries, as ancient skeptical arguments became more widely known, these arguments were appropriated into the intellectual debates of the day: debates that circled around the proper method of enquiry into the natural world and the proper method for determining truth about religious matters. Over the four decades following the publishing of *The History of Scepticism*, Popkin expanded his book through additional studies of early-modern philosophy.

Briefly, the narrative that Popkin, Penelhum, and others produced goes as follows. In 1562, a Latin translation of the Sextus' *Hypotyposes* (Outlines of Pyrrhonism) was printed and became widely available. During this time, skeptical arguments were swept up into polemical discourse between Catholics and Protestants. The debate between Catholics and Protestants largely concerned the proper criterion or criteria for religious truth, what they called 'the rule of faith'. Popkin writes, 'The problem of finding a criterion of truth, first raised in theological disputes, was then later raised with regard to natural knowledge, leading to *la crise pyrrhonienne* of the early sixteenth century' (Popkin, 2003, p. 3). While Catholics maintained, as always, that the proper rule of faith lay with the legal traditions and authoritative instruction of the Magisterium, Protestants held that the rule of faith ought to be what the individual believer discovers upon reading Scripture under the guidance of the Holy Spirit. While Protestant polemicists criticized Catholicism as just so much Pyrrhonism, no doubt aided by the writings of Erasmus, Catholics criticized the Protestants for in effect allowing anything and everything to be true, thus amounting to Pyrrhonism as well. 'Pyrrhonism' became a term of reproach; and yet, there were some moderate philosophers who sought after something like a Christian Pyrrhonism in the hopes of arriving at a peaceful, reasonable solution to the intractable and growing conflict between Catholic and Protestant powers. An example of this use of Pyrrhonism in supporting the Catholic religion can be seen in the thought of Michel de Montaigne. Montaigne's *An Apology for Raymond Sebond* is rightly remembered as a classic instance of skeptical arguments being put forward in defense of religious belief and practice. It is to members of the group of moderating figures that Popkin affixes the title 'skeptical fideists'.

Penelhum shares Popkin's association of the origins of skeptical fideism with the retrieval of ancient skeptical texts in the early modern period.[5] Yet, Penelhum's classification scheme is more strictly philosophical than historical. In *God and Skepticism*, Penelhum argues that there are two dominant strands of fideistic thought: conformist and evangelical fideism. Penelhum is in general agreement with Popkin that early-modern skepticism initially emerged as a movement *within* religious thought, before it became the familiar philosophical bogeyman of twentieth century philosophy. Penelhum understands fideism to be the 'recurrent theme in religious thought' that 'faith and reason are so disparate that faith is not undermined, but strengthened, if we judge that reason can give it no support' (Penelhum, 1983, p. ix). Penelhum focuses his attention on the class of fideists who use skeptical argument in the service of this end, the group Popkin termed 'skeptical fideists'. As previously mentioned, Penelhum further distinguishes two kinds of skeptical fideism. Penelhum writes, 'The attempt to represent Christian faith as analogous to the Pyrrhonian conformity to appearances I shall call Conformist Skeptical Fideism' (Penelhum, 1983, p. 15). He continues,

> Skeptical Fideism, however, has taken another, and in general much more influential, form. Its proponents have recognized that

> Skeptical belieflessness and Christian faith are indeed the polar opposites they seem. But they have nevertheless seen Skepticism as a tradition which has, unintentionally, served the cause of faith by exposing the inability of human reason to provide grounds for the commitment faith embodies... I shall call this position Evangelical Skeptical Fideism, or Evangelical Fideism for short. (Penelhum, 1983, pp. 15–16)

He understands Erasmus, Montaigne, and Bayle to represent conformist skeptical fideism and Pascal and Kierkegaard to represent evangelical skeptical fideism.

Technically speaking, both Protestant and Catholic thought could reflect conformist or evangelical expressions of skeptical fideism; however, the tendency according to Penelhum is for Catholic fideists to espouse conformism to tradition and for Protestant fideists to strive for theological purity. The reasons for this tendency are not difficult to imagine, given the rules of faith each group favors. Popkin's work on the history of skepticism, and the religious uses of it, helps spell out the interests Catholics have had apologetically in defending tradition from first Protestant, then Enlightenment challenges. Likewise, Protestants have had apologetic interests in establishing or shoring up the *sola fide* criterion of religious truth established by Luther and further worked out by Calvin. These overarching needs may indicate the tendencies found in Catholic and Protestant thought. Penelhum subsequently uses this distinction to explore contemporary philosophy of religion.[6]

The work of Popkin and Penelhum stands in contrast to much work on fideism that is not concerned with the history of ideas, and for this their work is rightly esteemed. However, neither Popkin nor Penelhum explores the comparably recent origin of the term and the problems this circumstance presents for using the term outside this context. In the course of about one hundred and fifty years, the meaning of the term has migrated considerably. In the first edition of *The History of Scepticism*, Popkin acknowledges the varying uses of the term between Protestant and Catholic thinkers (Popkin, 1960, p. xv). Protestants occasionally use the term to describe their own views, whereas Catholics treat fideism as a charge to be avoided. Popkin and Penelhum use the term merely to classify figures in early-modern thought, but the question remains over whether the term can be excerpted from its original context of use and applied to this novel setting (despite the wide influence of Popkin's treatment of these matters).

4.3 A genealogy of 'fideism'

The *Oxford English Dictionary* identifies French as the original language of the word and places its first appearance in English in 1885. Many sources identify the Lutheran theologian Eugène Ménégoz as the one who first coins '*fidéisme*' in his *Reflexions sur L'évangile du salut* (1879) (Ménégoz, 1900–21, I, p. 36). However, while variants of the term are not found among the documents of the First Vatican Council (1869–70), and are not widely used among Catholic philosophers until the 1880s, the term appears on occasion in theological periodicals as early as the 1850s.[7] The earliest source I have found is from the Catholic periodical *L'Ami de la Religion* in 1854 in which the Abbé Robitaille uses the term to classify the thought of Lamennais. (L'Abbé Robitaille, 1854). However, I suspect this early use of the term may not have been widely influential because no dictionaries or encyclopedia I know of place the origin of the term before 1879. Catholic philosopher Léon Ollé-Laprune (1839–1898) uses the word in his *De La Certitude Morale* (1880) to refer to what he took to be a distressing overreliance on moral faith in establishing the existence of God in Kantian and post-Kantian idealism (Ollé-Laprune, 1880, pp. 226–7). Neither Ménégoz nor Ollé-Laprune gives any indication of awareness of the term's having already been in use. Both authors appear to take themselves to be coining or otherwise appropriating the term (in both cases, placing it in italics). It is a testament to how cut off from one another Protestant and Catholic theologians in France were that Ménégoz did not discover the Catholic use of the word until three decades later when the 1907 encyclical *Pascendi Dominici Gregis* was written (Ménégoz, 1900–21, II, pp. 494–9). A key difference between neo-Thomist philosophers and theologians on the one hand and the Protestant faculty at Paris on the other is that these Protestants used the term '*fidéisme*' to describe their own theology; the neo-Thomists used it to classify the thought of others who relied 'dangerously' on faith alone in establishing God's existence.

4.3.1 The symbolo-fideism of Ménégoz and Sabatier

In 1879, when the French Protestant theologian Eugène Ménégoz chose the term '*fidéisme*' to express the Lutheran principle of *sola fide*, he most likely had no idea the range of applications to which the word would be put in the following decades. As mentioned previously, the French Protestant faculty at Paris, where Ménégoz was a central figure, sought to articulate a standpoint between orthodox Lutheranism and the agnosticism of positivist philosophy of science. During the nineteenth century,

French culture had been reeling from the Revolution and the overturning of long established order; theologians of both Protestant and Catholic affiliations sought to reframe the truth-claims of Christianity in order to find some footing in the new secular society. Within a few decades after its appearance in French, the term 'fideism' appears in English and other European languages and enters more fully into Catholic and Protestant theological conversation. Eventually, it would find a place in philosophical discourse.

Far from being anti-modern and opposed to Enlightenment thinkers, the Protestant theologians of the École de Paris, Sabatier, and Ménégoz, sought to articulate a path for Christianity after the Enlightenment, the rise of modern science and the development of the historical-critical method of biblical criticism. Rather than being a theology that sought to reinforce the importance of religious dogma or tradition over science, their theology sought to articulate a narrow path between what they took to be the two dogmatisms of orthodox religion and positivist science. Sabatier grounded religion in a primordial religious feeling – itself reminiscent of Schleiermacher's feeling of absolute dependence; he understood individual religious expressions (whether orthodox or heterodox) to be approximations of the primordial feelings of fear and hope. Their theology was sometimes called 'symbolo-fideism'[8] to indicate the contributions of Sabatier's reflections on religious symbols and Ménégoz's emphasis on salvation by faith independent of belief.

In their writings from the late nineteenth and early twentieth centuries, Ménégoz and Sabatier together sought to establish and defend the theological movement of symbolo-fideism. In the decades following the publication of the *Reflexions sur l'évangile du salut*, Ménégoz wrote short pieces for local theological periodicals. These essays include a commentary on the Epistle to the Hebrews (1894) and a study of the significance of miracle reports in biblical texts. In both cases, Ménégoz sought to expand on his view that salvation lies in the simple act of faith rather than in assenting to specific doctrines. Ménégoz held that this view of faith and salvation had a biblical basis and that the orthodox forms of Christianity were often distortions of these original biblical notions. Through the 1890s and 1900s, Ménégoz wrote many occasional pieces for Protestant periodicals, often responding to his more orthodox critics. Émile Doumergue (1844–1937) is representative of these critics in that he held that fideism was an intermediate step from the liberalism of post-Kantian theology to the agnosticism of modern secular society. Ménégoz was at pains to distinguish his fideism from modernism and liberalism, which sought to deny either grace or religious tradition a critical role in faith and diminished the very nature of the salvation to which a Christian may aspire.

In a series of lectures given in 1906, Ménégoz looks back on this movement and describes the type of theology that he thinks is needed:

> Amidst the religious crisis which is now spreading throughout the Christian Church, it is necessary to guard against some of the confusions of our fathers, which had but little danger for them, but which now, with the progress of modern culture, may become serious obstacles to the spread of the Gospel. These confusions are specially visible in the idea of the Holy Bible as the word of God, and in the official teaching of the Church regarded as an authentic interpretation of divine revelation. (Ménégoz, 1908, p. 7)

The religious crisis to which Ménégoz refers is that brought on by the Enlightenment in general and the thought of Kant and Darwin in particular. He writes of the influence of philosophy on Christianity:

> Kantism, certainly, is not itself absolute truth, I do not believe it to be eternal any more than the Platonic philosophy. But to-day we are surrounded by its influence, and our theology is bound also to feel it. It has to adapt itself, as our ancestors adapted their ideas to the principles of Platonism...To the philosophy of Kant, continued by the Neo-Kantians, has been added the powerful influence of Darwin's principles of evolution...The champions of orthodoxy clearly see the danger, they are terrified; they tremble, they make unheard-of efforts to support the cracked edifice, threatened with ruin. (Ménégoz, 1908, p. 35–7)

The result of Enlightenment thought was the slow ebb of confidence in the traditional theistic proofs and the very project of natural theology. Both the symbolo-fideists and the orthodox Lutherans they opposed can be thought of as responding to the crisis brought on by the decreased credibility of the traditional theistic arguments.

In response to the then new historical criticism of the Bible brought on by the Enlightenment, Ménégoz suggests historicizing the very representations of faith: 'The faith of the believer can only be expressed in the language of his time, and this expression is subject to the conception of the world which forms the spiritual atmosphere in which he lives' (Ménégoz, 1908, p. 7–8). This principle applies as much to the writers of the Bible as to any contemporary theologian. Ménégoz continues:

> [W]e must distinguish between faith itself, which is the essence of religious life, and the contingent and transitory form in which that faith is clothed at any given time in its history. The substance is, as to its nature, always identical with itself; the form is variable and subject to the laws of evolution. (Ménégoz, 1908, p.8)

Ménégoz does not shy away from the critique of theology received from the Enlightenment or the natural sciences. Instead, he believes that Christian faith must adapt to the new environment in which it finds itself: an environment where scientific rationality is increasingly the paradigm of rationality in general, an environment in which the traditional rational ground of faith no longer seemed to provide the security it once did. Ménégoz holds that the key to dealing with this crisis is to focus on the protestant principle of *sola fide*.

It is also here that the work of Auguste Sabatier on religious symbols is most relevant. Sabatier retains Ménégoz's observation of an intractable opposition between the sciences on the one hand and morality and religion on the other:

> Our century, from the beginning, has had two great passions which still inflame and agitate its closing years. It has driven abreast the twofold worship of the scientific method and of the moral ideal; but, so far from being able to unite them, it has pushed them to a point where they seem to contradict and exclude each other. Every serious soul feels itself to be inwardly divided; it would fain conciliate its most generous aspirations, the two last motives for living and acting that still remain to it. Where but in a renovated conception of religion will this needed reconciliation be found? (Sabatier, 1902, p. xii)

Sabatier's goal is to attempt to articulate a philosophy of religion (or perhaps 'philosophical theology' in contemporary parlance) that occupies and forges a middle path between the two dogmas. Sabatier writes:

> Our young people, it seems to me, are pushing bravely forward, marching between two high walls: on the one side modern science with its rigorous methods which it is no longer possible to ignore or avoid; on the other the dogmas and the customs of the religious institutions in which they were reared, and to which they would, but cannot, sincerely return. The sages who have led them hitherto point to the *impasse* they have reached, and bid them take a part, – either for science against religion, or for religion against science. They hesitate,

> with reason, in face of this alarming alternative. Must we then choose between pious ignorance and bare knowledge? Must we either continue to live a moral life belied by science, or set up a theory of things which our consciences condemn? Is there no issue to the dark and narrow valley which our anxious youth traverse? I think there is. I think I have caught glimpses of a steep and narrow path that leads to wide and shining table-lands above. (Sabatier, 1902, p. xiv–xv)

Investigating this contemporary crisis, Sabatier, like Schleiermacher before him, locates the origin of religion in a primordial feeling. However, writing as he does, after not just Kant but also Darwin, Sabatier depicts humanity in an evolutionary framework. In Sabatier's case, the primordial feelings of fear and hope are the beginnings of religiosity (Sabatier, 1902, pp. 12–13). Alone, fear is incomplete, destructive, but mixed with hope, the sentiment provides the desire for help and the feeling of comfort that religions seek to reinforce and cultivate. Together, these feelings are according to Sabatier the foundation upon which all forms of religion are built. On the basis of this understanding of the function of religion, Sabatier, like Ménégoz, separates the propositional aspect of religious faith from the core of faith. Sabatier even goes so far as to indicate the possibility of pious heresy, where the emotion underlying the unorthodox expression of belief lays closer to this original feeling than the 'mechanical devotion' of the orthodox.[9]

In shoring up this picture of religious faith, Sabatier criticizes natural religion. This might be expected of a fideist, but Sabatier's critique is nuanced:

> I now understand why 'natural religion' is not a religion at all. It deprives man of prayer; it leaves God and man at a distance from each other. No intimate commerce, no interior dialogue, no exchange between them, no action of God in man, no return of man to God. At bottom, this pretend religion is nothing but philosophy. (Sabatier, 1902, p. 30)

Sabatier objects to the picture of God entailed by natural religion: a God that is not religiously available (for prayer, for intercession, etc.). However, the following remark on evolution and teleology shows that Sabatier's thinking on natural religion was complex:

> Cosmic evolution proceeds always from that which is poorer to that which is richer, from the simple to the complex, from the

> homogenous to the heterogenous, from dead matter to living matter, from physical to mental life. At each stage Nature surpasses itself by a mysterious creation that resembles a true miracle in relation to an interior stage. What then shall we conclude from these observations except that in Nature there is a hidden force, an incommensurable 'potential energy' an ever open, never exhausted fount of apparitions at once magnificent and unexpected? How can such a universe escape the teleological interpretation of religious faith? (Sabatier, 1902, p. 84)

How are we to reconcile these two movements in Sabatier's thought? Note in the first that he criticizes natural religion primarily for *religious* reasons, while his recommendation of teleology in evolution is naturalistic and promotes a sense of wonder (and possibly some sort of 'primordial' religious feeling). When natural religion stands in the way of piety, it is rejected; when it may assist piety, it is endorsed. Sabatier's nuanced view of natural religion is all the more surprising given the association between fideism and a rejection of natural theology.

The influence of Sabatier's symbolism is evident in Ménégoz's historicism with respect to the Bible as well as to Christians of various eras. This historicism applies as much to the writers of the Bible as it does to Christians of various other historical periods (Ménégoz, 1908, pp. 8–9). Ménégoz reflects on the separation between the epistemic presuppositions of contemporary Christian believers and those of ancient Jews, Christians and pagans. He uses historical criticism to establish and support his positive interpretation of Christian faith. According to Ménégoz, when the Bible is ossified into a timeless expression of the Christian faith, it brings the believer into direct conflict with modern science and historical criticism. However, according to Ménégoz and Sabatier, this is unnecessary and destructive to authentic Christian faith. In order to move past the contemporary cultural and intellectual crisis and survive, they counseled that the faith should seek its essence behind the historical changes, an essence they held to lie in *sola fide*.

In depicting the faith alone that is to be the essence of religion (and Christianity supremely) – fideism – Ménégoz first circumscribes the region in which it lies by delimiting the regions in which the essence of faith does not lie: ancient metaphysics, ancient sacred texts, science, and philosophy. Christian faith also does not lie in any particular historical expression of itself: it lies in the experience of transcendence that the believer has through contemporary religious symbols.

4.3.2 'Fideism' in nineteenth century Catholic theology

French Catholic theologians in the early nineteenth century found themselves disoriented following the Revolution. While priests were still on the payroll of the state, mutual animosity presaged the separation that was to come between Church and State in France. The Abbé Felicité de Lamennais sought in his early writings to forge a path for the Catholic Church in the increasingly secular state of France. Against the tendency of the Enlightenment towards faith in the powers of human intellect to grasp the fundamental truths of reality, Lamennais held that human reason alone was insufficient to rise to genuine knowledge of divine matters; indeed, faith in reason alone is what thinkers like Lamennais thought helped bring about the Revolution and its horrors.[10] Many theologians, both Catholic and Protestant, during the nineteenth century searched for ways to criticize the view of rationality associated with the Enlightenment, that genuine knowledge is grounded primarily in experience and the autonomous use of reason. Kantian modifications of empiricism made room for faith of a sort, but it was a faith deprived of transcendental rational grounding. While the traditionalists sought to defend Catholic tradition from Enlightenment critique, their efforts came under the critical eye of the Vatican and were implicitly rejected at the First Vatican Council (1869–70) in favor of a revival of the Thomist ideal of the fundamental compatibility of faith and reason. Historian of theology Gerald McCool writes about the traditionalists, 'The most direct way to undercut rationalism was to show that unaided human reason was intrinsically incapable of reaching any true or certain conclusions about religious or moral issues' (McCool, 1977, p. 18).

The nineteenth century French Catholic traditionalist theologians are often depicted in histories of theology as having been among the first fideists. Their traditionalist religious epistemologies ran counter to the compatibilist view of the relationship between faith and reason exemplified in Thomism. Indeed, an argument can be made that there was a chain of influence from the traditionalists to mid-late nineteenth century romantics to the turn of the century modernists, whose 'errors' were understood by Pope Pius X in *Pascendi Dominici Gregis*[11] to be roughly the same as those of the fideists: their views degenerated into agnosticism.

The traditionalists held that the Protestant rule of faith – not just *sola scriptura* but what it implied, the autonomy of the reasoning individual – is what led ultimately to the horrors of the French revolution. Only a renewed Catholic communitarian epistemology would reestablish humanity's connection to morality and justice. Felicité de Lamennais was more theologian than philosopher, and his thought went through many stages of fealty to and rebellion against the Catholic Magisterium during his life. Louis Bautain likewise went through various intellectual stages, and like Lamennais, he had trouble with Catholic authorities during his life. However, unlike Lamennais, he submitted to the authority of the Church and assented to certain prescribed propositions on the ultimate compatibility of faith and reason.

It is likely that the association between the traditionalists and fideism stems not from their reactionary attack on the Enlightenment so much as their being perceived by later generations as being precursors to the modernism that would threaten the hold the neo-Thomists had on Catholic thought at the turn of the twentieth century. Ollé-Laprune was influenced by Bautain despite Ollé-Laprune's repudiation of what he took to be overreliance on moral faith in theologies such as Bautain's. Ollé-Laprune sought to find a middle way between the ascendant neo-Thomists and the romantic theology of Bautain (Horton, 1926a, pp. 289–90).

The first Vatican Council, commonly regarded as having deemed fideism heretical, makes no mention of the word. The document produced by Vatican I, *Dei Filius*, identifies the Enlightenment critique of religion, perhaps embodied in the Biblical criticism inspired by the writings of Spinoza and Lessing, as the problem that brought about the need for the 'Dogmatic constitution on the catholic faith'. During the third session of the Council, on April 24, 1870, various parameters were applied to the nature of faith within the Catholic Magisterium:

> Indeed even the holy Bible itself, which [the Protestant reformers] at one time claimed to be the sole source and judge of the christian faith, is no longer held to be divine, but they begin to assimilate it to the inventions of myth...Thus they would establish what they call the rule of simple reason or nature. The abandonment and rejection of the christian religion, and the denial of God and his Christ, has plunged the minds of many into the abyss of pantheism, materialism and atheism, and the consequence is that they strive to destroy rational nature itself, to deny any criterion of what is right and just, and to overthrow the very foundations of human society. (Tanner, 1990, pp. 804–5)

Note how the document identifies the problem as stemming from the Reformation. The 'rule of faith' – or the epistemological method used to determine religious truth – of the Protestants, the individual reading of scripture, is held to have degraded into the 'rule of simple reason or nature.' By this, the Council is criticizing a philosophy that takes material reality as being the only proper kind of reality. This metaphysic prevents a supernaturalist reading of the Bible, leaving in its place the need for a historical-critical method that encourages a purely moralistic reading of scripture. While subsequent Catholic sources point to Vatican I as stating the classic rejection of fideism, the word appears nowhere in the canons of the Council. This lacuna supports the idea that the term was not widely used at the time.

A decade lay between Vatican I and the publication of Ollé-Laprune's *De La Certitude Morale*. During this decade the authority of neo-Thomism would increase, culminating in the encyclical *Aeterni Patris* (1879) in which the thought of Thomas is recommended for 'clearly distinguishing, as is fitting, reason from faith, while happily associating the one with the other' (Leo XIII, 1879, §18). Thomas is celebrated because he

> both preserved the rights and had regard for the dignity of [both faith and reason]; so much so, indeed, that reason, borne on the wings of Thomas to its human height, can scarcely rise higher, while faith could scarcely expect more or stronger aids from reason than those which she has already obtained through Thomas. (Leo XIII, 1879, §18)

Again, the word 'fideism' is found nowhere in the encyclical despite the obvious relevance of the letter to subsequent Catholic criticism of what would later be understood as fideism.

Gradually, through the twentieth century use of the term 'fideism' drifts from these nineteenth century contexts and is projected back through the history of ideas to refer to philosophers and theologians such as Kierkegaard, Montaigne, Pascal, Erasmus, and Tertullian. In each of these thinkers, embrace of Christian faith was coupled with a relative lack of trust in philosophy for discovering religious truth. The term was taken to be helpful for understanding the occasional opposition, for religious reasons, between theology and philosophy.

According to the twentieth century theologian, Walter Horton, Ménégoz and late nineteenth century Catholic critics of traditionalism coined the term separately[12] (Horton, 1926a, 1926b). If Horton is right, then there is additional reason to be skeptical about the term possessing a stable meaning, or a meaning stable enough to be philosophically useful beyond its use in pejorative criticism. It may be that no stable meaning for the term can be identified, but this does not mean that the term is not useful as a term of classification or comparison. It just means that use of the term must be qualified appropriately.

4.4 Historical context and the traditions of fideism

If 'fideism' were defined loosely as the idea that the truth about religious matters cannot be established by natural reason alone, then the vast majority of religious thought – among the many religions in the world – would be fideistic. 'Fideism' would lose its usefulness as a term of appraisal, being in extension little different than 'religious thought'. If 'fideism' were then used pejoratively, this would implicitly amount to a dismissal of religious thought. While some philosophical critics of religion might see little problem in such a rejection of the reasonableness of religious belief, among religious thinkers themselves – and sympathetic scholars – a variety of standpoints are available with respect to the relationships among faith, tradition, and reason.

Taking a cue from Wittgenstein's mature philosophy, I suggest seeking not a single definition of 'fideism' but instead looking to the variety of ways the word is used – that is, to the traditions in which the term has been used. This is not to say that there is nothing in common among some or all of the various traditions of fideism;[13] however, inattention to the details of local usage of the term has contributed to confusion over the meaning of 'fideism' and thus to its oscillation between being used neutrally as a term of classification and negatively as a term of reproach. Clarity that is gained from study of particular traditions of use may contribute to resolution of philosophical problems concerned with the alleged fideism of a philosopher or theologian. With this goal of perspicuity in mind, I identify six types of uses:[14]

(1) Symbolo-fideism[15]
(2) Criticism of Catholic traditionalism
(3) Criticism of biblicism
(4) Criticism of anti-metaphysical philosophy and theology
(5) Conformist skeptical fideism
(6) Evangelical skeptical fideism

The first four items represent uses of the term in actual religious discourses, while the last two represent categories used by historians of philosophy. The pejorative uses of fideism (2–4), while perhaps having their place within polemical discourse – be it theological or naturalistic – are best not used in academic discourse. These uses tend to minimize or ignore salient differences between different philosophies and theologies and thus create the impression of 'fideism' referring to a general category in the comparison of religions, theologies, and philosophies. This leaves three remaining options: the symbolo-fideism of Ménégoz and Sabatier, and Popkin's category of 'skeptical fideism', of which Penelhum identifies two types, conformist and evangelical.

However, Popkin's category 'skeptical fideism' can be criticized for grouping together figures from disparate periods under a common name. I hesitate to reject 'skepticial fideism' as being a species of fideism because Popkin's work has done much to convince analytic philosophers, the present author included, of the importance of rigorous historical research in philosophy and in resolving contemporary philosophical confusion, and use of the phrase 'skepticial fideism' is now commonplace in studies of early-modern skepticism and religious thought. That said, I do think that care should be observed regarding the use of 'skepticial fideism' in categorizing early-modern pious skepticism if one wishes to avoid confusion.

Resolving philosophical confusion, bringing language home from its sojourns, is no simple task. While languages retain traces of their histories, historical complexities can be forgotten in ordinary language use. It may not seem obvious to all after this preliminary study that the use of 'fideism' should be curtailed to contexts where its meaning is clearly grounded. After all, a locution such as 'Wittgensteinian fideism' is far more common in today's academic discourse than is the 'symbolo-fideism' of Ménégoz and Sabatier or the critical use of 'fideism' of Catholic opponents to traditionalism. Yet many uses of 'fideism' in academic discourse draw upon a vague idea in establishing the category of classification. Because of this lack of clarity, these labels are liable to create further philosophical problems even while resolving current ones. Scrupulously identifying the tradition of fideism that informs one's scholarly use of the term is one way to avoid introducing further confusion into one's analysis of a problem.[16]

5
On 'Fideism' as an Interpretive Category

The first instance of the term 'fideism' being used to interpret Wittgensteinian philosophy of religion is found in Kai Nielsen's much cited 1967 article, 'Wittgensteinian Fideism'. In articles and books on Wittgensteinian philosophy of religion since, authors often sense the need to rebut the 'charge'[1], yet while 'fideism' is used frequently as a pejorative, this is not always the case.[2] Sometimes, philosophers are just searching for a useful tool to help them, or their students, grasp a philosopher's thought and its bearing on the epistemic dimensions of religions. Building upon the genealogy from Chapter 4, it is the goal of this chapter to show why 'fideism' is not a very useful hermeneutical tool for approaching Wittgensteinian philosophy of religion. When the term is sufficiently grounded contextually, it may provide some helpful connections among the work of particular philosophers, but *fideism simpliciter* does not refer to a coherent position and thus invites misunderstandings. What Wittgensteinian fideism refers to is distant from what a contextually grounded exploration of fideism and Wittgenstein would show; thus use of the expression 'Wittgensteinian fideism' is likely to invite misunderstanding. It would thus be more accurate to choose different terminology for hermeneutical analysis.

The meaning of the term 'fideism' developed over the course of the twentieth century from its origins in nineteenth century French Christian theological polemics to its use by Nielsen and others in the latter half of the twentieth century to constitute supposedly a *general* type of theological or philosophical view. In an early essay, Kai Nielsen writes:

> To be a fideist is to believe that fundamental religious beliefs rest solely and completely on faith. Finite and sinful man cannot by the

> use of his unaided reason come to know God. Belief and unbelief are intellectually on a par, religious experience is unalterably ambiguous as to the reality of its object, and the existence of God can never be established by empirical investigation or philosophical demonstration...The believer must simply take the leap of faith without any intellectual assurance at all that he is leaping in the right direction. (Nielsen, 1963, p. 158)

By neglecting the history of use of the interpretive category, critics of particular philosophers and theologians have unwittingly introduced confusion into their interpretations. 'Fideism' is frequently left undefined or defined so broadly that it would seem to cover too broad a swath of philosophical and theological positions. Thus, labeling a position as fideistic may hypostasize prevailing conceptions of what is rational and what is not, neglecting that which is named as fideistic as being on the wrong side of that line. Before considering the case of Wittgenstein, it will be useful to explore the cases of two other supposed fideists who to some extent influenced Wittgenstein, but more importantly, were earlier cases of supposed fideists, Søren Kierkegaard and William James. While threads of late nineteenth century French Protestant symbolo-fideism may be traced in James's writings, connections with Kierkegaard and various traditions of fideism remain speculative and liable to introduce more misunderstanding than clarification. Only when James and Wittgenstein are considered in connection with the well-established uses of fideism may such points of connection be illuminating. In short, if there were to be an element of fideism to be found in Wittgenstein's thought on religion, it would be there because of the influence of James, rather than Kierkegaard. Furthermore, the sort of 'fideism' that, arguably, is found in James may well be unrecognizable to many contemporary readers given the shifting meanings of the word. For this reason, unless narrowly circumscribed, use of the term 'fideism' in interpreting Wittgenstein is likely to introduce more confusion than insight.

Both Kierkegaard and James are commonly labeled as fideists; yet, frequently one also finds rebuttals of the label by specialists on the philosophers. The label is challenged more frequently in the case of Kierkegaard than James. Indeed, much more has been written on the putative connection between Kierkegaard and fideism, and disputing the charge, than James; yet scholars of both contest the label. In philosophical dictionaries and encyclopedia, valuable sources for discovering the prevailing philosophical views and lore of their time, Kierkegaard is a paradigmatic fideist (Popkin, 1967; Penelhum, 1983). After all, did he not famously identify faith with subjective rather than objective truth through the pseudonymous voice of Johannes Climacus? Climacus's acceptance of Hume's challenge to the theistic proofs despite his advocacy of faith would seem to be a classic example of Evangelical skeptical fideism (pace Penelhum). James is also widely considered to advocate a fideistic view of religious belief in his essay 'The Will to Believe', based on his 1896 lectures at Yale and Brown. While the depth and intensity of James's supposed fideism is sometimes debated, it has long been thought that this essay embodies a form of fideism. In what follows, I will first examine James's thought in relation to the uses of 'fideism' and secondly Kierkegaard's. Last, I will consider the bearing of these figures on the assessment of Wittgenstein and fideism.

5.1 The Case of James

It may seem strange in a historical study of fideism and philosophy to examine James before Kierkegaard. Kierkegaard was born thirty years before James, and his contributions to philosophy were written fifty years before James's. Yet, James's influence was far greater at the turn of the twentieth century philosophy than Kierkegaard's; Kierkegaard's first wave of influence would wait until the 1920s. While the first reference I have found to a supposed connection between Kierkegaard and fideism is in 1936[3], James's thought was first classified as fideistic as early as 1912. In that year, Ralph Barton Perry, a former student of James's, observed that the Italian pragmatist Giovanni Papini alludes to 'fideism' being the attitude pragmatism takes to religious questions (Perry, 1912, p. 264). James himself a few years earlier wrote approvingly of the Italian pragmatist movement of which Papini was a part (James, 1906, pp. 337–41)[4]. Perry goes on to explicate James's pragmatic theory of truth:

> Ideas or beliefs are essentially instruments of meaning. They are good instruments in so far as they afford access to their objects, and the test of their goodness in this sense is to try them; that is, employ them as means of access. If they present to the mind what they have led the mind to expect, they are true. But ordinarily one does not use ideas merely to test them; one assumes their reliability and employs them in the affairs of life. And if they work here, they receive additional verification; for if they were not good substitutes for parts of the environment, they would not fit in with the rest of the environment. But ideas acquire still a third variety of value through their immediate

> agreeableness, or their power to important vigor to the agent. In other words, they possess a *sentimental* or *emotional* value. This sentimental value, unlike their operative value, does not confirm their primary value as representations or means of access to things. A highly agreeable or inspiring idea, or a belief that disposes the mind to peace and contentment, may be of all ideas the least fitted to prepare the mind for what is to befall it. In other words, such emotional value is irrelevant to truth-value, in the strict sense. But there are cases in which this emotional value may nevertheless be allowed to weigh and to determine the acceptance of belief. And religion is such a case. (Perry, 1912, pp. 265–6)

Appreciation for the potentially positive role sentiment can play in epistemology is a recurring theme in James. James has long been taken by some readers to embody fideism in his essay 'The Will to Believe'. In his philosophical career, James occasionally shows sympathy for religious ideas, and in this essay, this sympathy takes the form of a challenge to W. K. Clifford's evidential basis for all beliefs – emphasizing the importance of the will in matters of religion.

James's epistemic freedom of will was not careless; he argued for 'a defense of our right to adopt a believing attitude in religious matters, in spite of the fact that our merely logical intellect may not have been coerced' (James, 1896, p. 88). James did not hold that people may believe whatever they wish; but beyond the constraints placed on our beliefs by the 'logical intellect', the will could decide among 'live options'. James's freedom of the will concerned 'live' hypotheses, possibilities that are real to particular persons:

> If I ask you to believe in the Mahdi, the notion makes no electric connection with your nature – it refuses to scintillate with any credibility at all. As an hypothesis it is completely dead. To an Arab, however (even if he is not one of the Mahdi's followers), the hypothesis is among the mind's possibilities: it is alive. This shows that deadness and liveness in an hypothesis are not intrinsic properties, but relations to the individual thinker. (Ibid., p. 89)

In addition to the logical intellect, one's live options for religious belief are constrained by historical, social, and cultural forces. James seems to be advancing the view here that belief in the Mahdi is not a live option for his audience at Yale because in the United States in the late nineteenth century, the claims of Shi'ism did not connect in the right way to the minds of his audience. In contrast, James offers agnosticism and Christianity as plausible epistemic possibilities for his audience.

James observes that Clifford contended that believing by volition ran counter to human epistemic duty. James quotes Clifford: 'Belief is desecrated when given to unproved and unquestioned statements for the solace and private pleasure of the believer' and 'It is wrong always, everywhere, and for every one, to believe anything upon insufficient evidence' (Ibid, pp. 92–3). In his classic essay of 1877 'The Ethics of Belief', Clifford argues for a strong evidentialist standard in the forming of belief. More so, he argues that human beings have an intellectual duty to seek out evidence and the conclusions to which the evidence points. In the essay, Clifford argues that one has the right to believe only that which the evidence supports; when the person does not have sufficient evidence, then the person does not have the right to believe the idea. This is not to say that unconfirmed hypotheses do not have a place in our epistemic lives, but it is important to scrupulously distinguish between claims for which one has evidence from those for which one does not. Only those claims that are well-supported by the relevant evidence are genuine candidates for belief.

James concurs with much of what Clifford has written, but he disagrees with Clifford in the latter's hope to purify epistemic life of passional elements. James holds up as an example the case of scientists resisting possible avenues of inquiry (for example, the paranormal) because they can make no use of it. Indeed, in cases of the paranormal or supernatural, putative evidence would seem to be largely contested or at best inconclusive. James writes:

> Our passional nature, not only lawfully may, but must, decide an option between propositions, whenever it is a genuine option that cannot by its nature be decided on intellectual grounds; for to say, under such circumstances, 'Do not decide, but leave the question open,' is itself a passional decision – just like deciding yes or no – and is attended with the same risk of losing the truth. (James, 1896, p. 95)

The key idea here, that the passions have a role within our epistemic lives, is not a new one. It is found in numerous thinkers in early modern philosophy. James objected to the strict evidentialism reflected in Clifford's piece. It is not that James thought that in matters of religion or philosophical speculation, one may believe whatever one wishes, as some of his critics would characterize him. Instead, he thought that when the evidence alone does not decide between two viable hypotheses, that other factors, such as coherence with other beliefs and values, may be taken into account.

In the opening lecture of *Pragmatism* James distinguishes between the 'tender-minded' and 'tough-minded' among philosophers. Clifford would seem to fit clearly several of the traits of the tough minded: 'Empiricist (going by "facts"), Sensationalistic, Materialistic, Pessimistic, Irreligious, Fatalistic, Pluralistic, Sceptical' (James, 1978, p. 13). In contrast, the traits of the tender-minded include: 'Rationalistic (going by "principles"), Intellectualistic, Idealistic, Optimistic, Religious, Free-willist, Monistic, Dogmatical' (James, 1978, p. 13). James remarks that few of his audience would neatly fit one of these poles; instead, most philosophers find something of value in each pole, weaving together a combined philosophical view. Despite this, James observes 'Never were as many men of a decidedly empiricist proclivity in existence as there are at the present day. Our children, one might say, are almost born scientific. But our esteem has not neutralized in us all religiousness. It is itself almost religious. Our scientific temper is devout' (James, 1978, p. 14). Mindful of the tense debate between the tender and tough minded, especially concerning the intellectual viability of religion, James writes: 'I offer the oddly-named thing pragmatism as a philosophy that can satisfy both kinds of demand. It can remain religious like the rationalisms, but at the same time, like the empiricisms, it can preserve the richest intimacy with facts' (James, 1978, p. 23).

Caricatures of pragmatist theories of truth hold that what is true is just what is useful. But that is not quite right. Later in the same series of lectures, in 'Pragmatism's Conception of Truth', James writes:

> Truth, as any dictionary will tell you, is a property of certain of our ideas. It means their 'agreement,' as falsity means their disagreement, with 'reality.' Pragmatists and intellectualists both accept this definition as a matter of course. They begin to quarrel only after the question is raised as to what may precisely be meant by the term 'agreement,' and what by the term 'reality,' when reality is taken as something for our ideas to agree with. (James, 1978, p. 96)

James's pragmatism does not conceive of the relationship between knower and reality as 'static' (that is, stable, unchanging): 'The truth of an idea is not a stagnant property inherent in it. Truth *happens* to an idea. It *becomes* true, is *made* true by events' (James, 1978, p. 97). This shows how utility is an identifier of truth only once an exploration of the facts has been completed. James may not have endorsed a correspondence theory of truth, but his pragmatism was thoroughly empiricist.

The religion that James's sought to identify and support in his pragmatism was decidedly elitist. While he had respect for the idea of religious belief, and showed respect for the people whose religious narratives were explored in the *Varieties of Religious Experience*, he himself had long since abandoned an everyday religious faith. Furthermore, he held credulity to be a principal human vice.[5] The religious faith that was plausible for James was that which did not stand in strict contradiction with science, was culturally accessible and activated the passional dimensions of the moral and epistemic lives of human beings. As Robert C. Fuller observes in an article marking the centenary of 'The Will to Believe':

> Educated men and women increasingly believed the road to an almost limitless extension of human knowledge was paved by the scientific method and the kinds of positivistic or materialistic thinking processes with which science was commonly associated. James astutely recognized just how far these northwest winds had blown humanity off the kinds of paths most likely to satisfy the broadest possible range of human satisfactions. This is why he suggested that a narrow understanding of scientific reasoning breeds a mental weakness of its own. His 'will to believe' essays, then, sought to demonstrate that an over-reliance upon science, or any other construct of what he called 'theoretical reason,' prematurely truncates our quest for other kinds of truth that life might have to offer. (Fuller, 1996, p. 635)

Thus, James interest in religion is of a piece with his interest in a wide search for truth. He is concerned that narrowing our vision for possible truths may deprive human beings of true ideas that may be accessible only to minds capable of venturing belief beyond what the evidence supports.

James was hopeful about the idea of religion and hoped that a science of religion might one day help construct religious concepts that would pass scientific and philosophical scrutiny. Far from being a thinker who sought to defend religious beliefs from attacks on their plausibility from the ever expanding area of experience science explains, James wished to criticize ultimately to improve religious hypotheses. However, James's goal was not just to create intellectual space for religious belief. Instead, he sought to point out a feature of how human minds actually work.

This point is brought home in John E. Smith's introduction to a 1985 edition of *Varieties of Religious Experience*. Yet, before James's work could offer, as Smith puts it, a 'necessary corrective to the fideistic tendency manifested in religious thinking in recent decades,' (James, 1985, p. li) James's work would itself serve, in Perry's view, as an example of fideistic philosophy. Clearly, Perry and Smith, writing seventy years apart, had different understandings of James, the term of analysis, or both. Smith observes that this 'fideistic tendency' in late twentieth century religious thought 'has resulted in the encapsulation of religion within the walls of sheer faith, where it is divorced from any form of knowledge' (James, 1985, p. li). In the early decades of the twentieth century, before 'fideism' became a term of approbation in philosophy (as it was in Catholic theology), it was to some extent, a neutral term of classification and association. In 1916, French philosopher Alfred Fouillée compared Pragmatism's stance on religion to 'the fideism of Pascal': 'the heart has its reasons which the mind does not know; we must make good men desire religion to be true. It is proper to recall, however, that Pascal added, "and then show them that it is true."' (Fouillée, 1916, pp. 102–3)

While James does not use the term 'fideism' anywhere in 'The Will to Believe' or *The Varieties of Religious Experience,* he does mention positively the work of Auguste Sabatier, the French Protestant theologian, who with Eugene Ménégoz founded the movement of symbolo-fideism (James, 1985, pp. 464–5). James quotes Sabatier:

> Prayer in this wide sense is the very soul and essence of religion. 'Religion,' says a liberal French theologian, 'is an intercourse, a conscious and voluntary relation, entered into by a soul in distress with the mysterious power upon which it feels itself to depend, and upon which its fate is contingent. This intercourse with God is realized by prayer. Prayer is religion in act; that is, prayer is real religion.' (James, 1985, p. 464)

James continues, repeating Sabatier's criticism of reliance alone on natural religion to establish religious doctrines: 'It cuts man off from prayer. It leaves him and God in mutual remoteness, with no intimate commerce, no interior dialogue, no interchange, no action of God in man, no return of man to God' (James, 1985, p. 465). James then returns: 'It seems to me that the entire series of our lectures proves the truth of M. Sabatier's contention. The religious phenomenon, studied as an inner fact, and apart from ecclesiastical or theological complications, has shown itself to consist everywhere, and at all its stages, in the consciousness which individuals have of an intercourse between themselves and higher powers with which they feel themselves to be related' (James, 1985, p. 465).

Furthermore, James was deeply influenced by the French philosopher Charles Renouvier in 'The Will to Believe'.[6] Protestant philosophy of religion in France was in close conversation with American Pragmatism, and neutral classificatory associations of James with fideism can be found in the 1910s and developing steadily through the early twentieth century. Yet it is worth remembering that Fouillée mentions 'fideism' to be a word absent from the Oxford and Century dictionaries but 'is treated by the editors of the Catholic Encyclopedia as sufficiently significant to have an article devoted to it' (Fouillée, 1916, p. 102). This 1909 article makes no mention of Ménégoz, Sabatier or James; it mentions the Catholic traditionalists of the nineteenth century – radical defenders of Catholic tradition from the French Enlightenment – and those medieval and early modern theologians the author, G. Sauvage, takes to have exerted an influence on the traditionalists (Sauvage, 1909).

In several commentarial works, Perry connects James with fideism. Perry traces James's fideism to Renouvier's influence, placing special emphasis on Renouvier's view that volition plays a central role in the epistemic lives of human beings. Perry writes,

> Fideism, however, has to do with extra-theoretical motives which express man's 'active powers' and carry belief beyond the data of experience. There are two specific senses of it, both of which have already appeared in the early beginnings of James's thought: the fideism which goes beyond all possible facts, and thus supplements a necessary agnosticism; and the fideism which supplements an accidental ignorance. (Perry, 1935, p. 209)

Whether James's apparent fideism was received through Renouvier or through Sabatier, both James and Sabatier wrote for Renouvier's journal *La critique philosophique*; it is plausible that James was well-acquainted with French liberal protestant philosophy of religion[7] (Strenski, 2002, p. 151). I write 'apparent fideism' because James did not use the term in his writings. Nevertheless, it seems be reasonable to draw lines of connection among Renouvier, Sabatier and James, but by the 1930s, Perry wants to protect James from simplistic fideism (Perry, 1938, p. 71). Something seems to have shifted in philosophical discourse in the intervening decades regarding the meaning of the term.

More recent assessments and interpretations of James have likewise sought to distinguish James from undesirable forms of fideism. Fuller writes:

> As a committed empiricist, James counters the rationalist objections to religious belief with his wry observation that 'objective evidence and certitude are doubtless very fine ideals to play with, but where on this moonlit and dream-visited planet are they found?' (Fuller, 1996, p. 634)

Fuller sees in James a thinker who sought to chart a middle path between 'naïve credulity' and 'agnostic skepticism', one that allows for the viability of certain forms of religious belief. This feature of James's thought secures his relevance to the academy one hundred years on.

The negative connotation of fideism arises also in Richard M. Gale's work on James, especially in *The Divided Self of William James*. Contemplating an interpretive dilemma for the James of the *Varieties of Religious Experience*, Gale observes that James appears to endorse the veracity of mystical traditions from both the 'dualistic' West and the 'monistic' East (Gale, 1999, p. 325). Gale sees two options for James, endorse the view that mystical experiences do not grant any 'new facts' or accept 'language-game fideism', the view that 'each of these reality-claims is warranted relative to the criteria for epistemic warrant or acceptability built into the special doxastic practice or language-game within which it occurs' (Gale, 1999, p. 326). Gale does not seem to think that the latter option is attractive since, '[l]anguage-game fideism is nothing but Ontological Relativism dressed up in fashionable new Wittgensteinian clothing' (Gale, 1999, p. 326). Instead, Gale argues that James, or a Jamesian, needs to accept a give and take between the mystical (or unity-craving) and the promethian (or desire-maximizing) parts of the self rather than strive for a higher unity of the two. Instead, Gale argues:

> The clash between his mystical self and these other selves [scientific and moralistic] will turn out to be the deeper and more intractable division within James. For whereas his pragmatism could serve as a reconciler but not as a unifier between his scientific and moralistic selves by showing that they both employed concepts to gain a promethean power to control their environment, with truth being based on how successfully they did this, it is of no avail in resolving this clash. For the mystical stance requires overcoming this promethean self. (Gale, 2004, p. 2)

For Gale, fideism is a tempting but unsatisfactory response to the clash between the 'divided selves' of James. Instead of insisting on unity, awareness that human beings are divided and must oscillate among their different selves is Gale's recommended 'solution'. In a sense, Gale detects a dialectic in James's pragmatism, but unlike Socrates's or Wittgenstein's, James's dialectic is not so much productive as inevitable. A divided self in Wittgenstein is also inevitable, but it always reaches for greater clarity; it is a productive dialectic. It is notable to find fideism unambiguously used as a pejorative, something with which no self-respecting philosopher would wish to be associated.

John Bishop is one of few contemporary philosophers who embrace the term fideism, albeit with extensive qualifications. Through the book *Believing by Faith: An Essay in the Epistemology and Ethics of Religious Belief*, Bishop articulates a form of justifiable 'faith venture' that he understands to undergird religious beliefs of a wide variety. Bishop links his epistemological and ethical project with James's fideism as it appears in 'The Will to Believe' (Bishop, 2007, p. 3). Similar to James, Bishop does not seek to support a particular kind of religious belief, simply a belief that is plausible (that is, is consistent with the available evidential support). In line with this form of fideism, and standing in contrast with forms of fideism associated with irrationalism, Bishop's defense of a form of fideism seeks to identify and support faith ventures for which one may be otherwise justified; this justification is 'supra-evidential', meaning that these are faith ventures that go beyond – but not against – what the evidence supports.

Human cognition is not merely a matter of collecting data but of integrating experiences into the life of a human being. Not just any hypothesis is plausible to any human being at any time. As Fuller notes of Peter Berger, plausibility is something that shifts with socialization (Fuller, 1996, p. 638). This expansion of the notion of 'live option' while not developed by James is implicit in his thought. What James shows about religious belief would likewise be true about much of human cognition. It may be that his disagreement with Clifford is more a matter of emphasis than a true clash of epistemic criteria. Nevertheless, due to James's rejection of evidentialism alone and his endorsement of the will in the formation of belief he has come to be labeled a fideist. Given the dominant associations today and in recent decades between fideism and rational insularity, it is no wonder that James's empiricism makes him seem an unlikely candidate for fideism. It is only when readers overlook this dimension of his corpus and attend only to 'The Will to Believe' that they may get the sense that James wished to place religious beliefs beyond reason;

to the contrary, religious beliefs are viable for the Jamesian only after one has thoroughly investigated what reason has to say about the beliefs in question.

5.2 The Case of Kierkegaard

When philosophers make lists of supposed fideists, Kierkegaard's name is often found high on the list.[8] However, there is good reason to proceed carefully here. In addition to these problems related to fideism, there are also problems of interpreting a philosopher who frequently wrote pseudonymously. The technical nature of contemporary philosophy can seem to be at odds with the tone of Kierkegaard's writing. Kierkegaard writes, in the pseudonymous voice of Johannes Climacus, in the Preface to *Philosophical Fragments*: 'Heaven ... prevent a kind and well-disposed reader from unabashedly looking to see if there is anything in the pamphlet he can use' (Kierkegaard, 1985, p. 7). Already, the reader is challenged to approach Kierkegaard's text on its own terms. Following Gadamer, successful reading involves a meeting of writer and reader, a bridging of horizons, but just what that means here is far from obvious. Any hermeneutically responsible assessment of the relationship between Kierkegaard and fideism will need to take seriously the rhetorical dimensions of Kierkegaard's texts.

Although Kierkegaard espoused no theory of knowledge as they are discussed in contemporary philosophy, his meditations on learning in *Philosophical Fragments* and truth in the *Concluding Unscientific Postscript to Philosophical Fragments* seem like good sources for approaching his views on the natures of faith and knowledge and of their putative relation to ascriptions of fideism. For the purposes of this short study, I limit my discussion of Kierkegaard's thought to these two sources; however, a thorough treatment of the relationship between fideism and Kierkegaard's thought would need to draw on texts from his larger corpus and other authorial personas.

Kierkegaard begins the *Philosophical Fragments* reflecting on Socrates' question: can the truth be learned? Socrates functions as a midwife in helping his interlocutors arrive at the truth. Socrates will not *teach* knowledge to his interlocutors, but something may be *learned* through the dialectical process he instigates. Socrates himself has the character to admit that he knows nothing. However, Kierkegaard appreciates that the point of the intellectual quest is to arrive at knowledge of the eternal, knowledge that illuminates life.

Towards clarifying this learning process, he distinguishes between occasions and moments. While, an 'occasion' is simply an ordinary historical event; a 'moment' is an event that has 'decisive significance' (Kierkegaard, 1985, p. 13) for the student:

> A moment such as this is unique. To be sure, it is short and temporal, as the moment is; it is passing, as the moment is, past, as the moment is in the next moment, and yet it is decisive, and yet it is filled with the eternal. A moment such as this must have a special name. Let us call it: *the fullness of time*. (ibid., p. 18)

As editors Howard and Edna Hong note, the phrase 'the fullness of time' comes from Paul's letter to the Galatians (Kierkegaard, 1985, p. 281). Moments of decisive significance are rare; mostly people experience life as a series of mundane occasions.

If Socrates, the paradigmatic philosopher, is but a midwife to education, who or what gives birth to knowledge? Climacus's answer is 'the god'. The teacher, *qua* teacher, must teach the student from out of love. The student is to be approached in his or her finitude. No education, properly so-called, violates the will of the student (a decisive moment). Learning, in this Kierkegaardian sense, involves a choice on the part of the student. The moment is an *invitation* to response, rather than an event that happens to the student.

Kierkegaard argues that this love of truth entails that the teacher must take the form of servant. Love desires unity, and unity cannot happen between unequals: 'He [the god] will appear, therefore, as the equal of the lowliest of persons. But the lowliest of all is one who must serve others – consequently, the god will appear in the form of *a servant*' (Kierkegaard, 1985, p. 31). As Kierkegaard describes the phenomenology of learning, this god begins to look more and more like the god of Christianity (Perkins, 1990). As the god lowers itself to the level of humanity, the potential for encounter between the two is actualized.

Kierkegaard argues that humanity, like the god, by nature strives with passion. Although some people may turn from this passion, Kierkegaard maintains that it lies behind the drive to know:

> This, then, is the ultimate paradox of thought: to want to discover something that thought itself cannot think. This passion of thought is fundamentally present everywhere in thought, also in the single individual's thought insofar as he, thinking, is not merely himself. But because of habit we do not discover this. (Kierkegaard, 1985, p. 37)

Merely noticing the paradox is not to live with the passion of thought. It is *responding* to the paradox that decides everything. One may notice the paradox but be offended by its stubborn reluctance to be assimilated to what is already known, or what can be accounted for by means of logic. That the object of this desire, thinking that which cannot be thought, cannot be achieved, means that this passion will go unanswered, unrequited. To reject this passion, to be offended by the paradox, is to persist in untruth, which in *Philosophical Fragments* is 'sin'.

In the *Concluding Unscientific Postscript,* Kierkegaard returns to issues dealt with in the *Fragments* adding special emphasis to the problem of history for faith. The opposition reflected in the question that opens the *Postscript,* 'Can a historical point of departure be given for an eternal consciousness?' (Kierkegaard, 1992, p. 15), recalls the distinction from the *Fragments* between 'occasion' and 'moment'. Kierkegaard valorizes the personal encounter with truth over the aspiration to objective rationality. Simply knowing or assenting to historical or eternal truths (objective truths) brings one no closer to authentic faith according to him. Subjective truth has to do with appropriating the truth for oneself.

Kierkegaard introduces the idea of direct and indirect communication to explore the difference between subjective and objective truth. Direct communication conveys objective truth while indirect communication invites subjective truth. Kierkegaard writes, 'Ordinary communication between one human being and another is entirely immediate, because people ordinarily exist in immediacy' (Kierkegaard, 1992, p. 74). In ordinary life, people take the meanings of words to be self-evident. Only when misunderstandings become obvious is there impetus to examine what was said and what was not said. Direct communication presupposes the stability of subjectivity (in this case, of both speaker and hearer). In direct communication, subjectivity is assumed to be capable of being grasped. Kierkegaard observes that objective thinking forgets that the subject exists in history. In order for a speech act to function possibly as a moment, it must allow for the possibility that its hearer may receive it as merely an occasion. Otherwise, insofar as the speech act assumes an understood subjectivity on the part of the hearer, it forces the hearer into a particular meaning.

Indirect communication presents the hearer with a mystery and the inborn desire to know drives people to pursue what the mystery means. James Kellenberger writes about communication: 'It is regarding direct communication of objective truth that *ceteris paribus* we can reason "I told him, so he knows." This reasoning does not hold for indirect communication of subjectivity; for indirect communication does not communicate a mere proposition – not even a secret proposition' (Kellenberger, 1984, pp. 153–4). The primary goal of indirect communication in

Kierkegaard's view is not to transmit information, although it does that, so much as it is to invite response.

Also in the *Postscript*, Kierkegaard canvasses several different intuitions about objective truth.[9] For Kierkegaard's purposes, it does not matter which definition of objective truth one adopts. All shrink subjectivity and therefore diminish human beings. In this vein, Kierkegaard writes: 'That the knowing spirit is an existing spirit, and that every human being is such a spirit existing for himself, I cannot repeat often enough, because the fantastical disregard of this has been the cause of much confusion' (Kierkegaard, 1992, p. 189). Kierkegaard has identified a *desideratum* for an acceptable account of the nature of truth: the humanity of the subject must be accepted while also challenged to let itself be transformed through the acceptance of divine love.

The question of the usefulness of 'fideism' in reading Kierkegaard hinges then on the extent to which we identify points of connection with either non-pejorative traditions of fideism, such as skeptical fideism or symbolo-fideism.[10] Kierkegaard articulates a philosophy of Christianity that does not compromise the personal dimensions of the faith amidst then contemporary efforts to defend it from secular critique. In line with Penelhum's category of evangelical skeptical fideism, Kierkegaard is seeking to purify the faith of Christianity from what he takes to be foreign elements. Yet, his view does not undermine objective truth (his name for rational inquiry) so much as represent it as powerless to decide commitments – like faith – which are of fundamental importance.[11] Looking back to his discussion of indirect communication, asserting the propositional content of the expressions used is not the primary goal of the speech act; the point is to convey an invitation to the hearer to encounter the world in a certain way.

Why does subjective thinking appeal to indirect communication in the first place? I think the answer for Kierkegaard is the love that is valorized in Christianity. The teacher/god accepts the inquirer without condition. The invitation to the moment will take place with language with which the inquirer is familiar. A deep piety that honors and respects things and people just as they are is part of how Kierkegaard understands Christian love; yet, this love does not mean leaving people in their state of alienation and sin. Rather, it is the acknowledgement that love is served only when people are invited to choose genuinely for themselves to let themselves be transformed. This piety respecting the uniqueness of individuals hints at a kind of realism. The idea is that there is something real about people (or about God) that cannot be put into words directly. Subjective truth involves the intuition that there is something real beyond what is objectively describable, something ineffable. Rather than being in conflict with objective thinking, subjective truth is the fulfillment of it. In a sense, subjective truth can be thought of as being motivated by a deeply objective concern: to understand things as they are. Just as the encounter with God as subjective truth is an invitation and not a command, love is knowable through its fruits – not that it *will* be seen as love but that it is *possible* that it may be encountered as love. There is an analogy suggested here: just as one wishing to know God should not demand proofs of God's existence, one should not demand fruits as proof of love; yet it is possible that one might encounter the consequences of love as fruits of that love.[12] Together these moments in Kierkegaard's thought point to how the desire to see prepares one to encounter love and God.

In these matters, Kierkegaard displays *some* similarity to the Protestant symbolo-fideists. Sabatier's dichotomy between symbols and faith parallels Kierkegaard's distinction between direct and indirect communication, the idea that the faith that transforms – that matters – is subjective and personal, that dogmatic codifications of science, reason, or religion (that is, symbols) can stifle the spirit. Yet, this reader suspects Sabatier's enthusiastic embrace of evolutionary biology and Ménégoz's use of the historical critical method in investigating the scriptures would put them at some distance form Kierkegaard. Connections between Kierkegaard and skeptical fideism are less clear. While Kierkegaard makes use of the skepticism of Hume and Lessing towards dogmatism with respect to natural or revealed theology, it is not clear to me that these moments in Kierkegaard's thought are best thought of as espousing either skeptical or symbolo-fideism.[13] Perhaps Kierkegaard's use of skeptical fideistic arguments in the voice of Climacus conveys a quite different overall point of view.

Focusing upon the opposition, inspired by Christian faith, to a dogmatism of objective truth in Kierkegaard's thought can be helpful for relating his thought to the thought of other philosophers, and in some cases, comparison using the term 'fideism' may in fact be helpful as an *initial* category for framing one's understanding of his philosophy. However, if one misses the hermeneutical use to which Kierkegaard puts his skepticism and subjectivism, one might say the 'pastoral' use, then one may mistake his thought in the *Fragments* and *Postscript* as being irrational. Kierkegaard's does not seek to destroy objective reason; instead, he seeks to transcend it. Once we see how taking into account the purposes of a 'prototypical' fideist such as Kierkegaard is important for appreciating what he has in common with the traditions of fideism, the same care should be understood to apply even more so to those other philosophers who also are listed as fideists.

So, is it helpful to think of thinkers like Kierkegaard and James as fideists? As it stands, the term's use is too diffuse to find a coherent implicit definition. No doubt this is due in part to the pejorative uses of the term. It is difficult on the face of it to identify a common factor among the various theologians and philosophers described as fideists (in the nineteenth century alone – never mind in the history of religious thought), beyond the fact that they are all – or nearly all – Christians and reject the supremacy of reason alone in religious epistemology. Nevertheless, in the nineteenth century, two types of fideism may be observed in France: Protestant symbolo-fideism, with its emphasis on personal faith (*sola fide*) and Catholic traditionalism, with its paramount emphasis on fidelity to the traditions of the Church. There is good reason to be skeptical about the stability and reliability of the term. Nevertheless, there is *partial* affinity between Kierkegaard and James and the symbolo-fideism of Ménégoz and Sabatier.

5.3 The case of Wittgenstein

As we saw in Chapter 3, the associations between Wittgensteinian philosophy and fideism developed in the late 1960s and soon became fairly entrenched. Despite the efforts of numerous scholars of Wittgenstein, the association continues to persist.[14] James Franklin Harris in his survey *Analytic Philosophy of Religion* observes:

> In the second half of the twentieth century, fideism came to be identified with the later work of Ludwig Wittgenstein, and thus the appellation 'Wittgensteinian Fideism' has come into common usage – a designation embraced by some Wittgensteinians and rejected by others... It must be said at the outset that Wittgenstein himself did not explicitly develop a position of fideism, but then the later Wittgenstein did not explicitly develop many positions that are now regarded as Wittgensteinian. Thus, it has been left to his followers to construct the position by extrapolating from various loosely connected Wittgensteinian themes regarding language and language-games. It must also be said that there is a rather wide range of interpretations of Wittgenstein on this score by different Wittgensteinians. (Harris, 2002, p. 179)

Once Nielsen's essay, 'Wittgensteinian Fideism' was published in 1967, the label began to stick. Over the next two decades critics of Wittgensteinian thought on religion (be it in philosophy, theology, or religious studies) directed their attention to the language-game reading of religions and criticized it repeatedly. While Phillips apparently had at one point endorsed such a view, he changed his mind and clarified his view in 1970.[15] No matter. The reading and its criticism had connected with an audience and Phillips became the quintessential Wittgensteinian fideist.[16] Once the associations between Wittgensteinian philosophy of religion and fideism developed, it became a shorthand to refer to a general approach in the philosophy of religion, one that preserved the integrity of the meaning of religious language and the autonomy of religious epistemology at the cost of relativizing religions to discrete language-games or forms of life.

There is another way of thinking about the relationship between fideism and Wittgenstein, and James's philosophy provides the cue. Although Wittgenstein refers to James's *The Principles of Psychology* in his more overtly philosophical writings, Wittgenstein was personally drawn to *The Varieties of Religious Experience*. Ray Monk cites a letter Wittgenstein wrote to Russell in 1912 of *Varieties*:

> This book does me *a lot* of good. I don't mean to say that I will be a saint soon, but I am not sure that it does not improve me a little in a way in which I would like to improve *very much*: namely I think that it helps me to get rid of the *Sorge* [worry, anxiety] (in the sense in which Goethe used the word in the 2nd part of Faust). (Monk, 1990, p. 51)

Monk observes 'The *Sorge* that prevents one facing the world with equanimity is thus a matter of more immediate concern than any misfortune that may befall one through the actions of others' (Monk, 1990, p. 53).

It is difficult to measure the influence that James had on Wittgenstein. When Wittgenstein directly refers to James in his writings (such as in *Philosophical Investigations* or *Last Writings on the Philosophy of Psychology*), it is as an interlocutor whom Wittgenstein questions. Russell B. Goodman has written a careful study of the influence of James on Wittgenstein, noting that while Wittgenstein admired what he had read of James, Elizabeth Anscombe remarked in conversation with Goodman 'not only had Wittgenstein not read *Pragmatism*... but if he *had* read it, he would have hated it' (Goodman, 2002, p. ix). Goodman goes on to trace the reception of pragmatism within the philosophical setting of Cambridge in which Wittgenstein was a student and later a professor. It does not seem that Wittgenstein had a different view of pragmatism than the dim one offered by his Cambridge colleagues.[17]

Goodman goes on to argue for a symmetry between what Wittgenstein understood by the term 'pragmatism' and his own philosophy as expressed in his late work *On Certainty*. Two themes found among pragmatist philosophers and Wittgenstein's thought are 'a sense that not all empirical propositions, or beliefs, play the same role; and a sense of the interrelation of action and thought' (Goodman, 2002, p. 19). Yet just because there is some symmetry between pragmatism and Wittgenstein's late philosophy does not mean that the thread of fideism within Jamesian pragmatism is traceable also in Wittgenstein. The latter makes no reference to 'The Will to Believe' in his corpus and what proved influential from the *Varieties* may have been more the plurality of experiences James listed than a particular view about the justifiability or permissibility of certain faith-ventures.[18] Even so, Wittgenstein found the *Varieties* to do him good. One wonders if James's description of the 'sick-soul', itself a partly autobiographical diagnosis of humankind's fascination with religion, appealed to Wittgenstein and his own longing for spiritual safety and security.

Goodman focuses primarily on the philosophical inheritance Wittgenstein receives from James. Goodman observes, 'Wittgenstein's method, as many commentators have remarked, is not to refute but to "defuse," or render less potent, the preconceived pictures philosophers entertain about language and logic. One of his methods is simply to point to the diversity – to use James's word, the variety – of the phenomena' (Goodman, 2002, p. 51). The primary influence here is in terms of philosophical methodology, not in terms of James's diagnosis of what living a meaningful life amounts to or in terms of James's views on religion. Here I am inclined to agree with a point Goodman observes about what Wittgenstein thought made James a good philosopher: that James philosophized as a human being. In so far as philosophy for Wittgenstein would be work on oneself, that personal presence in his philosophical text made his work interesting to Wittgenstein. In addition to this methodological similarity, it is appropriate to mention the affinity James and Wittgenstein both had for what they took to be authentic religiosity. Insincerity and social conformity do not just exert a bad influence on religiosity, they are signs of a sort of confused or false religiosity. Consider this passage on reading the New Testament from *Culture and Value*:

> The spring that flows quietly & clearly in the Gospels seems to foam in Paul's Epistles. Or that is how it seems to me. Perhaps it is just my own impurity that reads muddiness into it; for why shouldn't this impurity be able to pollute what is clear? But for me it's as though I saw human passion, something like pride or anger, which does not square with

> the humility of the Gospels. It is as though he really is insisting here on his own person, & doing so moreover as a religious act, something which is foreign to the Gospel. I want to ask – & may this be no blasphemy – : 'What would Christ perhaps have said to Paul?'
>
> But a fair rejoinder to that would be: What business is that of yours? Look after making yourself more decent! In your present state, you are quite incapable of understanding what may be the truth here. In the Gospels – as it seems to me – everything is less pretentious, humbler, simpler. There you find huts; – with Paul a church. There all human beings are equal & God himself is a human being; with Paul there is already something like a hierarchy; honours, and official positions. – That is, as it were, what my NOSE tells me. (Wittgenstein, 1998, p. 35e)

Likewise, in a conversation late in his life with Bouwsma, Wittgenstein criticizes Reform Judaism for its modern adjustments (Bouwsma, 1986, p. 33). Wittgenstein was highly sensitive to factors that could compromise the sincerity he took to be at the core of religiosity.

There is reason to think that Wittgenstein was exposed to Kierkegaardian ideas very early in his philosophical and religious education. Schönbaumsfeld writes:

> During his childhood and adolescence his elder sister Margarete ('Gretl') served as his 'philosophical' mentor... Given that Kierkegaard was Gretl's favorite author and was generally very much in vogue in turn-of-the-century Vienna, it would be very surprising indeed if Gretl had not drawn her younger brother's attention to Kierkegaard's works. (Schönbaumsfeld, 2007, pp. 13–14)

Schönbaumsfeld also mentions that between 1913 and 1921 Ludwig von Ficker translated some writings of Kierkegaard's for von Ficker's journal, *Der Brenner*, a journal that Wittgenstein read (Schönbaumsfeld, 2007, p. 14). Furthermore, Schönbaumsfeld cites a 1917 letter from Hermine Wittgenstein to Ludwig regarding a number of Kierkegaard's texts that apparently Ludwig had requested be sent to him. From this evidence, it is clear that Wittgenstein was actively interested in Kierkegaard's writings from an early point in his philosophical development.

However, just what the influence of Kierkegaard on Wittgenstein is remains unclear. Wittgenstein never wrote more than the occasional remark referring to Kierkegaard. There are additional remarks that do not mention Kierkegaard but that seem to refer to ideas Wittgenstein may have been entertaining on having read Kierkegaard. Wittgenstein writes in 1937:

> Christianity is not based on a historical truth, but presents us with a (historical) narrative & says: now believe! But not believe this report with the belief that is appropriate to a historical report, – but rather: believe, through thick & thin & you can do this only as the outcome of a life. *Here you have a message! – don't treat it as you would another historical message!* Make a *quite different* place for it in your life. – There is no *paradox* about that! (Wittgenstein, 1998, p. 37e)

This passage is reminiscent of the *Concluding Unscientific Postscript* and in particular of the passage quoted above about the difference between a mere occasion and 'the moment' of decisive significance. As Wittgenstein has referred to Kierkegaard in a manuscript just a month earlier, it seems reasonable to infer that Wittgenstein was still working over in his mind ideas from the book. Wittgenstein continues:

> Queer as it sounds: the historical accounts of the Gospels might, in the historical sense, be demonstrably false, & yet belief would lose nothing through this: but *not* because it has to do with 'universal truths of reason'! rather, because historical proof (the historical proof-game) is irrelevant to belief. This message (the Gospels) is seized on by a human being believingly (that is, lovingly): *That* is the certainty of this 'taking-for-true', nothing *else*.
>
> The believer's relation to these messages is *neither* a relation to historical truth (probability) *nor yet* that to a doctrine consisting of 'truths of reason'. There is such a thing. – (We have quite different attitudes even to different species of what we call fiction!) (Wittgenstein, 1998, p. 37e)

The disentangling of the 'historical proof-game' from Christian belief is what makes some interpreters identify Kierkegaard as a kind of fideist, and the existence of remarks in Wittgenstein's corpus would seem to provide support for the view that Wittgenstein was either a fideist or at least friendly to fideism (as some interpreters understand the word), if not exactly a religious person himself. Even so, this text did not play a definitive role in the development of the fideistic reading of Wittgenstein. *That* reading was already in place in the decade before passages such as these became widely available to scholars (1977 in German and 1980 in English).

The passage in question focuses not just on what belief ought not to be based on – an account of history – but on what belief ought to be based on: a seizing out of love. Of course, this is a description of a modern form of Christian religiosity, one where sensibility is essential. Before the development of the historical-critical method to study Biblical texts, it is difficult to imagine someone reflecting skeptically upon Biblical accounts while maintaining a faith that would be untouched. In focusing on the critical role of emotion in religious beliefs, Wittgenstein joins James and Kierkegaard (as well as the symbolo-fideists) in working to develop a conception of religious belief after the Enlightenment.

If there is a thread of fideism in Wittgenstein's thought, its presence would be traceable through James and not Kierkegaard. The Evangelical skeptical fideism ascribed to Kierkegaard in the mid to late twentieth century is a distortion; that ascribed to James in the early twentieth century unveils dimensions of his thought that may be overlooked otherwise. Insofar as Wittgenstein had sympathy for Jamesian 'faith ventures', then his thought may be thought of as fideistic or friendly to fideism, but because the sense of fideism in question has been largely overshadowed and replaced by pejorative meanings, one would do well to proceed with care. It would not be unreasonable to avoid the word altogether if one does not carry along the historical meanings closely in mind.

This is not to say that only terms that are self-ascribed may be used in interpretation. No interpretation, only repetition, would be possible were that so. But when it is evident that a critical term may introduce confusion if not handled with care, then the burden is on the one proposing to use the term anyway to demonstrate its usefulness and suitability. This shows a criterion for hermeneutical utility: hermeneutically useful categories are those that reveal connections with other figures that draw one's attention back to the figure (and not just to the abstract categories).

As explored in Chapter 3, the associations between Wittgenstein and fideism did not develop immediately. It was not until the appearance of the first wave of Wittgensteinian philosophy of religion (and related topics) that this work was labeled as fideistic. Perhaps it was in part the sense that an intellectual gulf was widening between secular philosophical discourse and the newly revitalized discourses of philosophy of religion and philosophical theology, perhaps it was the concern among religious philosophers to rein in what they perceived to be extravagant versions of religious philosophy, or perhaps it was scholars of religions who were concerned that philosophy protective of religiosities, if apparently resuscitated by the Wittgensteinians, would provide philosophical cover for traditional forms of religiosity in the emerging field of religious studies, protective strategies that immunize religious experiences or beliefs from social-scientific explanations. Perhaps it was a confluence between secular naturalists and orthodox theists who held that belief in God, be it viable, should be grounded in reason. Philosophies that made room for extra-rational features (emotion, will, practice) in religious epistemology might be suspect if they seemed to lean too heavily on these extra-rational factors.

Despite the protests of Wittgensteinian philosophers of religion such as Phillips, the reading and the criticism persisted in the philosophical lore. While few would nowadays defend the language-game interpretation of religion, the view persists in philosophical and theological discourses among non-experts that the language-game interpretation of religion is the Wittgensteinian contribution to philosophy of religion, dampening interest in the prospects of new research into Wittgenstein in the area.

It is time for a reappraisal of the import of Wittgenstein for philosophy of religion. This has already been anticipated by the development of what Anat Biletzki termed the third, fourth, and fifth stations of Wittgenstein interpretation. This was seen dramatically in debates over the 'New Wittgenstein' in the 1990s and 2000s. Motivated in part by scrupulous study of original and newly available texts from Wittgenstein's corpus, interpretations from this period refrained from accepting received views of Wittgenstein's philosophy and instead examined the developing workings of ideas across manuscripts, typescripts, correspondence, lecture notes, and ultimately books. Reappraisals of Wittgenstein for philosophy of religion began in earnest in the late 1990s and early 2000s, with the publication of Brian Clack's criticisms of Phillips (despite Phillips' early reversal on the viability of the language-game conception of religions) and the revisionist criticisms of the language-game conception of religion by Richard Amesbury and Bela Szabados. More recently, books by Genia Schönbaumsfeld and Earl S. Fronda have challenged the lore regarding Wittgenstein and religion. Yet it is worth noting that as early as the middle 1980s, philosophers criticized the fideistic reading of Wittgenstein on religion.

If it is not hermeneutically useful to think of Wittgenstein, and thus Wittgensteinian philosophy of religion, as fideistic *simpliciter*, it might, on occasion, be helpful to make comparisons with particular traditions of fideism, so long as they direct attention to the philosopher. The term 'fideism', when left unqualified or uncontextualized, is hermeneutically inept. Even so, one could object that whatever the appropriate classificatory terminology, Wittgenstein's philosophy tends to epistemic isolationism among religious and cultural groups and between religious and scientific ways of thinking about beliefs; this isolation is just as rationally problematic as what had been meant by the term 'fideism'. If language-games really are distinct from each other, then religious and cultural language-games may be epistemically isolated. It will be the goal of the next chapter to argue against this reading of Wittgenstein for philosophy of religion.

6
Religions, Epistemic Isolation, and Social Trust

Over the last two decades, scholarship on Wittgenstein has progressed significantly. Wittgenstein's compelling life story has received thorough study across book-length biographies as well as essay collections. Volumes exploring Wittgenstein's connections with and possible contributions to areas as varied as political philosophy, feminist philosophy, literary theory, and ethics have joined more traditional studies of Wittgenstein's import for topics in logic and the philosophy of language. During this same period, disputes over how best to interpret Wittgenstein's varied philosophical corpus have persisted. So-called traditional and resolute readers have debated one another over how seriously to interpret Wittgenstein's famous remark near the conclusion of the *Tractatus Logico-Philosophicus*: '6.54: My propositions serve as elucidations in the following way: anyone who understands me eventually recognizes them as nonsensical, when he has used them – as steps – to climb up beyond them' (Wittgenstein, 2001, p. 88). One result of this dispute has been very close study of Wittgenstein's corpus, this during a time in which numerous texts from his *Nachlass* as well as other sources have become more widely available, either through electronic media or traditional publication. Because of these developments, it is a time ripe with potential for exploring the insights Wittgenstein's work might bring to problems in disparate areas of philosophy, including the philosophy of religion.

Yet critics of Wittgenstein in general, and Wittgensteinian philosophy of religion in particular, have been great in number. Naturalist philosophers Kai Nielsen and Wayne Proudfoot have found potential in Wittgensteinian philosophy of religion for evasive and protective accounts of religious discourse. Nielsen has this evasion of public critique in mind when he describes Wittgensteinian approaches as being fideistic. Christian philosophers such as Alvin Plantinga and Nicholas

Wolterstorff remain critical of Wittgensteinian philosophy for putatively isolating religious language-games from rational practices such as justification or truth-seeking and thus recapitulating the positivist isolation of religious and metaphysical language.[1] Yet criticism has come from other quarters as well. Eminent interpreters of Wittgenstein such as Cora Diamond and Hilary Putnam have been critical of prominent figures in the philosophy of religion who have drawn on Wittgenstein's ideas for their theoretical projects.

In this chapter, I contend that evasion (Nielsen's conception of fideism), epistemic isolation, or protective strategies are out of keeping with Wittgenstein's philosophy and thus that a philosophy of religion growing from Wittgenstein's writings should not reflect what many critics contend is a distinctive feature of the approach to philosophy of religion. Critics of some instances of Wittgensteinian philosophy of religion are right to warn against the temptation to isolate religious discourses from outside critique out of the otherwise laudable goal of doing justice to the particularity of those religious discourses; however, I do not read Wittgenstein as isolating religious language from public reason. Wittgensteinian philosophy of religion could question temptations to protect religious phenomena from criticism; this is where D. Z. Phillips's recent 'contemplative' conception of philosophy is potentially helpful. In what follows, first I will examine the criticisms leveled against Wittgensteinian philosophy of religion. Second, in order to counter the isolationist reading of Wittgenstein on religion, I will argue that a central theme in Wittgenstein's philosophy – the social aspects of linguistic meaning – is incompatible with the idea that religious discourses are epistemically isolated from other discourses. Third, I explore some resources in Wittgenstein's views on language for thinking about the interpretation of religious beliefs. In particular, I elaborate on the ideas of social trust and intellectual distance in contemplating interpretation.

6.1 The promise and the problem: Wittgenstein and contemporary philosophy of religion

As recounted in Chapter 3, significant problems for philosophy of religion in the English speaking world developed along with the growing influence of the movement that would come to be known as Logical Positivism. Emerging out of 1920s Vienna, the Logical Positivists were concerned above all with doing philosophy in a scientific way. For example, this meant that sentences gained their meaning through specifying how their truth or falsity might be shown empirically (that is, the verifiability criterion of meaning). By the 1930s and 1940s, when this movement was ascending in the English-speaking world of philosophy, language involving supernatural entities became suspect insofar as terms attempted to refer to beings whose existence could not be verified. Earlier in the century, Bertrand Russell displayed what was more or less a tolerant attitude towards certain aspects of religiosity in his essay 'Mysticism and Logic', written during what he later considered to have been a more romantic time in his life. Russell's later philosophy grew increasingly pessimistic about religious beliefs, attitudes, and intuitions, paralleling the starkly skeptical attitude taken by the positivists. The Logical Positivists rejected the idea that metaphysics could be meaningful discourse; such a position precluded the intelligibility of any language involving supernatural beings. This foreclosure on the possibility of meaningful discourse concerning supernatural beings had a devastating effect on philosophy of religion. It was during the time of ascendancy of this approach in philosophy, the second quarter of the twentieth century, that Wittgenstein wrote most of what little he did concerning religious phenomena.

In the third quarter of the twentieth century, philosophy of religion began to rebound. Partly, this was due to the criticisms of the strong claims of logical positivism. Wittgensteinian philosophy, ordinary language philosophy, and the return of analytic metaphysics all allowed for new developments within analytic philosophy that took elements of Christian theism seriously. Some of his students found in his later thought a new avenue for approaching philosophy of religion within analytic philosophy. Eugene Thomas Long writes of this way of thinking:

> Religious beliefs are neither reasonable nor unreasonable in the ordinary sense of those terms. Religious beliefs are unreasonable or superstitious only when religious persons confuse religious and scientific forms of belief. Religious belief for Wittgenstein is not a matter subject to empirical verification or falsification. It has more to do with pictures that regulate our lives. (Long, 2003, p. 272)

Against the background of positivist scrutiny of nonsense in religious language, it is easy to see why a new approach such as this would appeal to philosophers concerned with religion as an object for philosophical investigation. In the 1950s and 1960s, philosophers such as Norman Malcolm, Peter Winch and D. Z. Phillips, found in Wittgenstein's writings resources for thinking about how religious language could be meaningful. Wittgensteinian philosophy of religion during this period tended to analyze religious beliefs and practices mostly in terms of his notions of language-games and forms of life.

While 'language-game' [*Sprachspiel*] and 'form of life' [*Lebensform*] are certainly important expressions in Wittgenstein's philosophy, they have taken on a life of their own beyond Wittgenstein's corpus. Wittgenstein uses the expression 'language-game' as a way of conveying the fact that language operates in rule-governed social contexts. The idea of a language-game is intimately connected with Wittgenstein's idea that the meaning of an expression can be identified by its use. Unlike the expression 'language-game', which Wittgenstein uses extensively in his later period, 'form of life' appears only a few times in his corpus; however, 'form of life' also has taken on considerable elaboration in secondary literature. Roughly speaking, when Wittgenstein uses 'form of life' he does so to indicate 'the intertwining of culture, worldview and language' as Hans-Johann Glock puts it (Glock, 1996, p. 124).

In the approaches of Malcolm, Winch and the very early Phillips, religions are depicted as language-games, as rule-governed social practices involving languages that perform particular functions. This view is found explicitly in Malcolm: 'Religion is a form of life; it is language embedded in action – 'what Wittgenstein calls a "language-game." Science is another. Neither stands in need of justification, the one no more than the other' (Malcolm, 1977, p. 203). The connection between understanding and being inside a form of life is also found in Malcolm's earlier essay 'Anselm's Ontological Arguments' (1960). Winch does not link religions with language-games as such, but he does argue that religions have their own 'criteria of intelligibility' and the sciences have theirs (Winch, 1990, p. 100). P. F. Bloemendaal traces the development of the Wittgenstein school in philosophy of religion and in so doing observes that Phillips in his first book, *The Concept of Prayer* (1965), makes very little use of the expressions 'form of life' or 'language-game'; instead, Phillips shows the influence more of Winch than of Wittgenstein (Bloemendaal, 2006, p. 125). Yet, as Bloemendaal argues, *The Concept of Prayer* places too strong an emphasis on distinctiveness and autonomy of religious forms of discourse'; this emphasis in part helped set the stage for Nielsen and others to find in the word 'fideism' an expression that grasped, however falteringly, the epistemic isolation that seemed out of keeping with the spirit of philosophy (Bloemendaal, 2006, p. 146). When Nielsen's eight theses of Wittgensteinian Fideism emerged two years later, these themes from Malcolm and Winch were combined into a supposed philosophical movement, one that Nielsen considered to be a threat to secular reason.

The idea is that the meaning of the language associated with religious practices may be uncovered by examining how people use the language; for if the language has a use, then it also has a meaning (and people clearly use language in religious rituals and practices in all sorts of ways). Secular critics of religion, according to this philosophical narrative, miss out in their interpretations because they do not look for, or cannot see, these context-sensitive uses; instead, they weigh the meanings of religious expressions against the possible uses such expressions would have in an empirical study or against the background of critical theories, as if there were a universal measure for the meaningfulness of expressions.

Kai Nielsen criticized what he took to be a new approach in the philosophy of religion in his widely read 1967 essay 'Wittgensteinian Fideism'. In associating this Wittgensteinian philosophy of religion with the word 'fideism', Nielsen sought to highlight the irrational and evasive character of this stance towards understanding religion. The idea that religious language is understood by Wittgensteinians as being epistemically and semantically located inside of a religious form of life is central to Nielsen's understanding of Wittgensteinian fideism. The articulation of these criticisms both put Wittgensteinian philosophy of religion on the defense and also served to help determine what Wittgensteinian philosophy of religion was understood by the larger philosophical community to be, in part because of the need for philosophers to define themselves against the characterization offered by Nielsen. According to Nielsen, the problem with Wittgensteinian philosophy of religion is that it characterizes religions as being immune to external criticism.[2]

However, the eschewing of a universal epistemic or semantic standpoint, one from which beliefs or propositions could be empirically assessed for justifiability or meaningfulness, need not lead to the simple relativism or perspectivalism that religious and naturalistic realists so fear, nor need such abandoning of a universal standpoint be in the service of protecting religious discourse from outside critique. A dominant theme in Wittgenstein's mature philosophy runs counter to evasive and isolationist readings of his work. I take some inspiration from both Diamond[3] and Putnam[4] in reading Wittgenstein's philosophy as open, not evasive.

6.2 The social aspects of meaning

In what follows, I argue that given Wittgenstein's appreciation for the public aspects of meaning, as seen in the remarks on private languages in *Philosophical Investigations* and those on being trained in a language from *On Certainty*, the separations between and among religious and secular-naturalist points of view should not be thought to be unbridgeable. A segment of *Philosophical Investigations* that has come to be known as the private language argument is one of the most-discussed segments of the book. While not an 'argument', per se, the remarks in the 200s on the very idea of a private language have long been considered to be of great importance for understanding the philosophical force of the *Investigations*. While Cavell thinks that this section has received more attention than it deserves, Mulhall disagrees (Mulhall, 2007a, p. 12). Whether Cavell is right or not, given the great attention directed to this portion of *Philosophical Investigations*, Wittgenstein interpreters need to wrestle with this section of the text. What this segment of the text calls into question is the idea that naming and referring are private relations between words or symbols in a mind and subjective experiences, such as the experiences of the senses.

These remarks on the idea of a private language express an idea central to Wittgenstein's mature philosophy: the idea that language is fundamentally a social phenomenon. Wittgenstein distinguishes the idea of a purely private language from private uses of otherwise public languages (for example, monologues, writing) (Wittgenstein, 2003a). Wittgenstein does not offer an argument in the conventional sense, per se, because he does not really advance a conclusion. Instead, he questions the coherence of the idea of a purely private language. Mulhall writes,

> Giving voice to our inner life for our own purposes is a commonplace of our life with words. How, then, can any participant in that life find himself asking whether we can imagine such a thing, thereby implying that its very intelligibility is questionable, when it is a humdrum activity? (2007a, p. 17)

The remarks on private language embody Wittgenstein's overarching philosophical goal. He famously writes early in the text that 'philosophical problems arise when language goes on holiday' (Wittgenstein, 2003a, §38). Wittgenstein's philosophical goal is to describe the grammar of our language so as to dispel confused thinking, or to put it another way, to attain a transparent or perspicuous representation of the use of language. The grammar of 'language' is that it is the kind of phenomenon (if it can even be called a phenomenon) that is social; it exists between people rather than within one and within another. In the present context, Wittgenstein uses the word 'grammar' to indicate that some propositions deal with the meanings of words and the range of their uses. 'Sensations are private', is thus a grammatical remark, a statement about the application of language about sensations. Wittgenstein calls into question the intelligibility of the idea of a purely private language.

In remark 244, Wittgenstein introduces 'one possibility' for how to understand reports of pain vis-à-vis private states. Words associated with pain are expressions of that pain: 'the verbal expression of pain replaces crying and does not describe it' (Wittgenstein, 2003a, §244). Wittgenstein calls into question the intelligibility of the idea that sensations can be privately named. Expressions that 'sensations are private' seem like factual (and uncontroversial) statements, but Wittgenstein contends that such remarks are in fact grammatical (§245). In §249, Wittgenstein moves from contending that the very idea of private meanings is nonsense to the view that language is fundamentally social in nature. Wittgenstein explores the idea that pain-language is learned through socialization and maturation.

In the next grouping of remarks, Wittgenstein turns to the idea of statements about the privacy of pain being tautological. In §251, he discusses the impossibility of 'imagining the opposite' of a tautology. To clarify, Wittgenstein writes: 'Of course, here "I can't imagine the opposite" doesn't mean: my powers of imagination are unequal to the task. These words are a defense against something whose form makes it look like an empirical proposition, but which is really a grammatical one. (Wittgenstein, 2003a, §251). In sources from Wittgenstein's corpus such as the 'Lectures on Religious Belief' and the 'Remarks on Frazer's *Golden Bough*', Wittgenstein discusses how expressions of religious belief also look like empirical statements, yet Wittgenstein thinks this view is mistaken. Could this mean that religious beliefs are really just grammatical? There is evidence available through Wittgenstein's writings that seem to support this view. Consider for example this remark, collected in *Culture and Value*: 'It appears to me as though a religious belief could only be (something like) passionately committing oneself to a system of reference. Hence although it's belief, it is really a way of living, or a way of judging life. Passionately taking up this interpretation' (Wittgenstein, 1998, p. 73e). Some religious persons (or especially philosophers weighing religious beliefs) may treat religious beliefs as if they are grounded on evidence, but Wittgenstein thinks these people misconstrue the nature of religious beliefs.

In remark 253, Wittgenstein explores the ideas of sameness and identity. He writes, '"Another person can't have my pains." –Which are my pains? What counts as a criterion of identity here?' (Wittgenstein,

2003a, §253). Wittgenstein goes on to question the idea that criteria of sameness of identity of meaning (*Bedeutung*) are neutral or universal. He writes:

> I have seen a person in discussion on this subject strike himself on the breast and say: 'But surely another person can't have THIS pain!' –The answer to this is that one does not define a criterion of identity by emphatic stressing of the word 'this'. Rather, what the emphasis does is to suggest the case in which we are conversant with such a criterion of identity, but have to be reminded of it.

Criteria of identity are established by agreement. This is, perhaps, another way of saying that the meanings of words are established in social use.

Remarks 254 and 255 shift this discussion to the nature of philosophy itself. For Wittgenstein, the aim of philosophy is not to state 'a psychologically exact account of the temptation to use a particular kind of expression' (§254). In Wittgenstein's understanding of philosophy, neither what we are tempted to say, nor psychologically exact accounts of those temptations, are philosophy. Instead, these matters form the 'raw material' for 'philosophical treatment'. As Wittgenstein indicates in remark 255, 'The philosopher's treatment of a question is like the treatment of an illness.'

After the remarks on the nature of identity, Wittgenstein returns to the topic of private naming of sensations. He discusses the problem of verification and falsification. Wittgenstein writes: 'But in the present case I have no criterion of correctness. One would like to say: whatever is going to seem right to me is right. And that only means that here we can't talk about "right"' (§258). Without some sort of external standard to mark one's use of language against, there is no way to be confident that one's use of language is consistent. The meaning of words like 'right' and 'wrong' is determined through contrast, but where contrast is unreliable, use of words like 'right' and 'wrong' is pointless.

Lastly, Wittgenstein connects this discussion of private naming with his overarching conception of philosophy. Consider the following:

> Look at the blue of the sky and say to yourself 'How blue the sky is!' – When you do it spontaneously – without philosophical intentions – the idea never crosses your mind that this impression of colour belongs only to you. And you have no hesitation in exclaiming that

> to someone else. And if you point at anything as you say the words you point at the sky. (§275)

The idea that meanings might be private mental states does not enter into our ordinary (pre-philosophical) experience of sense-perception or description. What Wittgenstein has shown is that one way of framing the modern problem of skepticism depends upon the idea of private naming of aspects of one's phenomenal awareness. Wittgenstein wants to say that this way of depicting the relation between the epistemic agent and the world (not to mention other people) is unintelligible.

Skepticism about the existence of the world outside one's mind is typically traced back to Descartes or to the early-modern Pyrrhonian skeptical crisis.[5] While skepticism as such in the twentieth century typically lacked the existential import the problem had for the early-modern philosophers who resuscitated ancient skepticism, the conceptual possibility of skepticism about the existence of the world or about the relationship between language and the world has continued to perplex many philosophers. A satisfactory response to skeptics lends a feeling of completeness to a philosophical project and is therefore much desired in the discourse at large.

While there have been a great many attempts since Descartes to refute various forms of skepticism, Wittgenstein has been widely regarded as having offered one of the more important critiques of language-world skepticism in the twentieth century. In particular, his investigation of linguistic meaning in social relationships, rather than in world-independent minds, suggests that there is no ontological barrier to be crossed between referring expressions and objects referred to in the world. Specifically, among other things, the remarks on pain and private languages subvert the dualistic view of the mind that gives rise to many modern skeptical problems. This *reductio* of this form of skepticism is a classic example of Wittgenstein's philosophical method, and thus, I agree with Mulhall that this is not an over-studied section of *Philosophical Investigations*. In these remarks, Wittgenstein deflates the philosophical problem by showing the incoherence of one element of its conception. Yet, the remarks on pain and private languages should not be taken to refute skepticism *simpliciter*, as if there were such a unitary philosophical problem called 'skepticism'; Richard Popkin among others has effectively reminded scholars that there are numerous skepticisms, depending on the ontologies in question and the aims (scientific, religious) to which philosophy may be put.

The treatment I have offered here of the remarks on private languages is different from that of Saul Kripke in *Wittgenstein on Rules and Private Language* (1982). He sees the private language argument as offering what he calls a skeptical solution to a skeptical paradox. I view Wittgenstein's remarks as calling into question the ground from which a skeptical paradox could be generated, but I am not clear on 'skeptical' being the best word to use here. Instead of being skeptical of the ground, Wittgenstein views references to it as nonsense (Mulhall). For Kripke, the problem Wittgenstein raises is that there is no way to know when an individual grasps the meaning of a word because rules governing meaning cover all uses of a word. The individual will have only used the word in question a finite number of times; it is always possible that a future use of the term will diverge from a given rule. The solution to this paradox comes from the checks brought in by participation in a community of language-users. Others who speak one's own language will challenge aberrant uses. This is fine so far as it goes, but as P. M. S. Hacker has noted, Kripke's Wittgenstein diverges somewhat from the historical Wittgenstein.[6] I read Wittgenstein not as embracing a kind of skepticism about meaning, but instead as calling into question a picture of meaning that itself leads to philosophical problems (problems Wittgenstein wants to avoid). Abandon the philosophical picture and one may avoid some philosophical problems. Furthermore, Wittgenstein advances the idea that language is social in nature. Kripke includes this idea as a check against potential skeptical scenarios, but Wittgenstein's interest in the social dynamics of language extends well beyond any concerns with grounding the meanings of terms when one cannot rely upon one's mind alone.

In the *Investigations*, Wittgenstein famously discusses the idea of the language-game and what it suggests for how philosophers should think about language. Wittgenstein wants to show the reader that a wide variety of social practices involve language and thus are candidates for philosophical study. Meaning is not merely a matter of the representation of objects or facts in the world but instead involves the wide array of uses to which people put words. Consider Wittgenstein's words on the plurality of forms of language use:

> [T]he term 'language-game' is meant to bring into prominence the fact that the speaking of language is part of an activity, or a form of life.
>
> Review the multiplicity of language-games in the following examples, and in others:
>
> Giving orders, and obeying them –

> Describing the appearance of an object, or giving its measurements –
> Constructing an object from a description (a drawing) –
> Reporting an event –
> Speculating about an event –
> Forming and testing an hypothesis –
> Presenting the results of an experiment in tables and diagrams –
> Making up a story; and reading it –
> Play-acting –
> Singing catches –
> Guessing riddles –
> Making a joke; telling it –
> Solving a problem in practical arithmetic –
> Translating from one language into another –
> Asking, thanking, cursing, greeting, praying. (§23)

The example Wittgenstein addresses in order to illustrate the social dimensions of language use is, perhaps, one of the most 'private' and basic of experiences: pain. Wittgenstein suggests that even this experience (including the words used to name or express it) is not privately developed. Instead, the most basic instances of pain-behavior are socially acquired. If even such personal experiences are not logically cut off from language, then it would seem to follow that religious experiences (and other phenomena) are not logically cut off from language either. If the *Philosophical Investigations* is the principal text of Wittgenstein's mature philosophy, then it would appear that Wittgenstein's philosophy ought not to be read as providing cover for intellectually evasive defenders of the viability of religiosities.

6.3 Wittgenstein on intellectual distance and trust

If 'private' experiences such as pain are actually infused with socially acquired behaviors, expressions, and expectations, then we should expect this social infusion all the more so with experiences having to do with religious phenomena and the language people use in describing experiences, practices, and truth-claims of their religions. The interpretations of religion seen in the early philosophies of religion of Malcolm, Winch, and Phillips are problematic because they lean too heavily on narrow readings of the notions of 'language-game' and 'form of life';

meanwhile, debates over the application of 'Wittgensteinian fideism' have perpetuated the influence of these very same themes in readings of Wittgenstein and philosophy of religion. A more nuanced understanding of the idea of a language-game shows that Wittgensteinian philosophy of religion need not be thought of as evasive or protective of religious discourse.

Early defenses of the viability of 'religious language' stemmed from the use of the idea of a language-game to parse these forms of language, the result being a depiction of the epistemic and semantic autonomy of religious language games. The problem with this sort of defense of religion is that it offers an overly narrow view of what a language-game is and therefore what a religion is. Religions are not language-games, but certain activities with language associated or involved with religions may well be. A form, or tradition, of prayer may be a language-game, but there are then many language-games of prayer. The performance of a ritual or liturgy may be a language-game, but then there are many language-games of ritual and liturgy. These language-games are not semantically or epistemically autonomous; that is what it means to say that we are speaking, listening, reading, or writing language. Intra-religious and religious-secular debates over belief and practice are commonplace. A declaration of autonomy is indicative of a lack of trust on the part of the speaker: 'you are not one I can or will speak with about these matters. You cannot speak on my behalf'.

Barriers to understanding language are, of course, all too common. Not sharing a language or a culture can impact the immediacy of interpretation. There are other obstacles to successful interpretation. Sometimes one just cannot 'get' what is right before one's eyes, a failure of imagination. A way of life one is investigating may appear opaque despite one's best efforts to understand it. In connection with problems of understanding, it is illuminating to consider the remarks on 'seeing-as' in the *Investigations*. The famous duck-rabbit and Necker cube examples show how certain aspects of seeing do not involve simply detecting visual data but significantly involve how the information is arranged (Wittgenstein, 2003a, pp. 165e–66e). Sometimes directions or hints may allow subjects to make the relevant perspectival shifts. But the images themselves are structurally ambiguous. Interpretation requires the appreciation of background or framing information. The capacity for perspectival shifting is critically important for the interpretation of religions. There may be more than one way of describing a phenomenon (for example, a ritual of consecrating images of the Buddha in Mahayana Buddhism; religious experts like nuns or monks, might use very different language than lay

Buddhists to describe what happens during the ceremony, let alone what a materialist Marxist would describe in such a ritual); the ability to appreciate multiple plausible interpretations of the practice will prepare the student or interpreter of religions to consider why one interpretation might be preferable to another.

In order to appreciate the multifarious interpretations of otherwise ambiguous arrays of symbols and gestures, it is helpful to consider an implicit dynamic of language use that receives little treatment by Wittgenstein, found explicitly in a just few scattered remarks: the concept of trust. Trust can provide the link by which one may take another's word on some matter. If someone I trust tells me there is something to see in, for example, a contemporary work of art, I may be more open to looking for what that might be. Furthermore, trust in the capacity of language itself to bridge disparate viewpoints is presupposed in any conversation that takes place across social boundaries. Trust may be present or lacking in a given circumstance; when trust is diminished or destroyed, understanding may be *de facto* impossible.

To elaborate on the idea of trust as a condition of understanding, it may be helpful to consider Wittgenstein's remarks on agreement (*Übereinstimmung*) in *Philosophical Investigations*. Just before Wittgenstein begins the section of the book in which he discusses pain and the idea of a private language, he comments on the relationships between truth, falsity and agreement in a form of life. Wittgenstein says that truth and falsity depend in some sense on agreement.

> 241. 'So you are saying the human agreement decides what is true and what is false?' – It is what human beings say that is true and false; and they agree in the language they use. That is not agreement in opinions but in form of life.
>
> 242. If language is to be a means of communication there must be agreement not only in definitions but also (queer as this may sound) in judgments. This seems to abolish logic, but does not do so. – It is one thing to describe methods of measurement, and another to obtain and state results of measurement. But what we call 'measuring' is partly determined by a certain constancy in results of measurement.

In these remarks 241–2, Wittgenstein is not saying that truth and falsity are secured by unanimity. A proposition is not true just because everyone in a community says it is. Instead, Wittgenstein is saying that the search for truth and falsity, and thus the use of these words, is secured by the shared form of life of those in the community. Standards of judgment including principles regarding establishing and revising beliefs, are likewise secured by the shared form of life.

Kripke sees these remarks reflecting, among other things, a dramatic shift in Wittgenstein's thinking; the shift is from a truth-conditional theory of meaning (as some readers find in the *Tractatus*) to an assertability-conditional theory of meaning (as some find in Wittgenstein's later philosophy). Kripke is not alone in this regard as other philosophers read Wittgenstein this way.[7] Against Kripke and others, I do not read these passages as offering an assertability-conditional theory of meaning. Aside from Wittgenstein's tendency to eschew theory-building in general, the *Philosophical Investigations* does not support an assertability-conditional theory of meaning. After all, Wittgenstein identifies meaning with use for 'for a large class of cases – though not for all' (§43).

What Wittgenstein has to say about truth and falsity anticipates recent work on deflationary theories of truth (for example, Quine's disquotationalism or Horwich's minimalism). In such theories, truth is not merely a property of a proposition (or sentence) but is also a linguistic device that allows for 'semantic assent', that is, abstracting one level above the discourse level of the proposition or sentence in question.[8] One can thus refer to sentences or propositions in nominalized phrases. For example, one may say, 'What Frege said is true' instead of having to repeat the sentence(s) in question that Frege actually used. Ultimately, it is not clear to me that Wittgenstein supports a deflationary theory of truth despite the fact that deflationary theories are consistent with what Wittgenstein has to say about truth.

What exactly sharing a form of life amounts to is not entirely clear. As previously mentioned, Wittgenstein did not use the expression frequently, and when he did, he left it undefined. Depending on context, it can refer to the broader social, environmental, or even biological contexts in which language is embedded. Sharing a form of life may well involve more than sharing assertability conditions (if all that assertability conditions are are agreed uses); it also can involve a shared engagement with the world.

In an article 'Language as Emerging from Instinctive Behaviour' from 1997, Rush Rhees writes of this element of agreement in Wittgenstein's philosophy. He writes, 'In Wittgenstein's use "Übereinstimmung" covers a considerable family. One of the most important uses comes when he speaks Übereinstimmung im Handeln (agreement in actions) or of Übereinstimmung in einer Lebensform (agreement in a form of life)' (Rhees, 1997, p. 8). A proposition is not true just because everyone in my community says it is. Instead, Wittgenstein is saying that the search for truth and falsity, and thus the use of these words, is secured by the shared form of life – including shared standards of judgment – of those in my community. Of course, in practice, the concepts people possess and the way they understand them varies from person to person, so even if a community shares a form of life, it does not mean that all of their standards of judgment will be *exactly* the same; it does however mean that they have a means for debating, clarifying, and perhaps changing standards of judgment. These forms of conversation are emblematic of the trust that I claim is implied within Wittgenstein's conception of language use. In order for a political community to be a genuine community, it must have some means for negotiating disagreements; if it lacks these means entirely, then it is a tyranny. A religious community may include disagreements, or not, on ethical, liturgical, or theological topics, but there will be traditional means for negotiating disagreements, resolving them or even dissolving or breaking with the community.

Stanley Cavell's reading of *Übereinstimmung* as 'attunement' is also helpful in seeking to understand the trust that is implicit in language use. Cavell writes of remarks 241–2:

> The idea of agreement here is not that of coming to or arriving at an agreement on a given occasion, but of being in agreement throughout, being in harmony, like pitches or tones, or clocks, or weighing scales, or columns of figures. That a group of human beings stimmen in their language überein says, so to speak, that they are mutually voiced with respect to it, mutually attuned top to bottom. (Cavell, 1979, p. 32)

In these metaphors, agreement presupposes common ways of measuring. Musical harmony requires a common key signature, and agreement between clocks requires a common means of measuring time as well as on what the time is in a particular place.

Having a shared conceptual framework does not guarantee shared beliefs within a community, but having a shared framework in which to carry on an investigation or a debate is a prerequisite for such intellectual activities. Rhees observes in connection with this point:

> Wittgenstein also speaks of 'the foundation of all judging' (OC: 614) and 'the ground on which I stand in making any judgements' [sic] (OC: 494)... He also says that the 'foundation of all judging' lies in the fact that certain propositions which have the form of empirical propositions are withdrawn from doubt, are beyond the reach of doubt. This does not mean that 'we are absolutely convinced of the

> truth of these propositions'; or: absolutely convinced of these facts. On the contrary. (Rhees, 1997, p. 9)

The view Rhees responds to in the piece previously quoted is that of Norman Malcolm. In a lecture, 'Wittgenstein: The Relation of Language to Instinctive Behaviour' delivered at Swansea in May 1981, Malcolm reflects on how learning a second language is not at all like learning a first, that language itself is founded on instinctual agreement (Malcolm, 1982). The agreement Wittgenstein mentions in 241–2 involves agreement in action, in judgment, and in a form of life. This agreement may or may not be consciously decided; perhaps in this way it is similar to the image of a social contract. It is this aspect of human collaborative endeavor, *Übereinstimmung,* that I wish to parse in terms of the idea of trust.[9]

To my knowledge, the word 'trust' (a translation from the German *vertrauen* and *glauben*) appears in Wittgenstein's works just a few times (once in *Culture and Value* and a handful of times in *On Certainty*). Yet since for Wittgenstein language is a social activity, the concept of trust lies implicit in his broader characterization of language use. Wittgenstein's remarks on trust in *On Certainty* typically have to do with training in a language or social practice. This is the trust involved in either collecting information (for example, the trust one has in the testimony of others) or in being trained in a way of life (for example, the trust a child has for a parent or teacher). Of course the two may overlap. Wittgenstein initially reflects that trust is an insufficient ground for philosophical certainty (Wittgenstein, 1972, §137). Yet despite the shakiness of this ground, it does govern much of our actual belief-formation:

> 159. As children we learn facts; for example, that every human being has a brain, and we take them on trust. I believe that there is an island, Australia, of such-and-such a shape, and so on and so on; I believe that I had great-grandparents, that the people who gave themselves out as my parents really were my parents, etc. This belief may never have been expressed; even the thought that it was so, never thought.
>
> 160. The child learns by believing the adult. Doubt comes after belief.

The picture Wittgenstein presents regarding linguistic training is familiar. Everyone is raised in ways of living, using language accordingly. Doubt is not initially a natural state of mind; rather doubt may arise out of puzzlement over what is first accepted on trust. Is there something natural about doubt in a mature mind? Insofar as one is likely to encounter and/or identify with numerous and potentially conflicting language-games as one grows older, the answer would tend to be 'yes'. I take it that this is what Malcolm intends by referring to the fundamental basis of language as being instinctual. In *On Certainty*, the image of trust between children and adults suggests that trust is initially a dispositional rather than intentional state. Human beings are trained in ways of living before they can formulate questions about why some belief or practice should be adopted or why some person should be trusted.

Descartes would concur with this picture of doubt in this respect in his *Meditations on First Philosophy*. Consider the opening meditation where Descartes reflects on the experience of the senses being deceived. Such deception or error would be notable only if it were the exception to the rule of the senses generally performing reliably. Peirce too would be in agreement, but rather more explicitly. For Peirce, doubt arises from an irritation in the mind. Belief is the rest state of the mind and doubt arises from friction between beliefs (Peirce, 1877). Yet for Peirce, too, doubt is a natural state, arising out of an inquisitive mind that has collected a variety of beliefs across a lifetime.

Wittgenstein describes trust as a prerequisite of language use: 'I really want to say that a language-game is only possible if one trusts something (I did not say "can trust something").' (Wittgenstein, 1972, §509) Note the internal dialectic in this passage. Wittgenstein lists his initial inclination only to correct it. It is not that the possibility of trust makes a language-game possible; rather, the actuality of trust makes a language-game possible. This seems to suggest that trust is a necessary but not sufficient condition for the possibility of a language-game. What sort of trust does Wittgenstein have in mind in this remark? It is not clear from the context. Surely, the trust must involve social trust (that is, in other people, their epistemic competence and good will), but Wittgenstein may also mean intellectual trust (that is, in one's own epistemic competence, in the intelligibility of the world, in the adequacy of one's language – in one's language holding up enough for one to go on).

In *On Certainty*, Wittgenstein writes mostly of the social trust that is presupposed in language instruction and use. In order for relativism or isolationism to be a possible outcome of Wittgenstein's picture of language, language-games would need to be in a deep sense private or separable from one another. In practice it may seem like this happens from time to time. Some religious movements may become so deeply distrustful of others that they effectively sever epistemic contact with the larger society. Certain forms of fundamentalist Christianity can be seen to operate in American society in this way. Social trust is contested in many European societies as immigrant communities occupy civic spaces along with previous generations of British, French, or German citizens; these fractured instances of social trust also are characterized by inter-religious and religious-secular dynamics of identification. When one says that these social and political tensions are due to religious and/or secular world views clashing, it could be said instead that the tensions are due to people finding it difficult to trust one another as political conversation partners. Wittgenstein writes of being trained in a way of life through one's upbringing and social context. Yet this training may not be final. One can be persuaded into or out of a way of life:

> 262. I can imagine a man who had grown up in quite special circumstances and been taught that the earth came into being 50 years ago, and therefore believed this. We might instruct him: the earth has long...etc. – We should be trying to give him our picture of the world.
>
> This would happen through a kind of persuasion.

Of course, one might well be unsuccessful in the attempt of persuasion. It depends, in part, on the respective standards of judgment people employ and whether there is necessary trust to bridge those standards.

In a remark from *On Certainty*, Wittgenstein uses the notion of 'intellectual distance' to describe the dramatic variance that can be discerned between one belief system and another. Wittgenstein writes:

> 107. Isn't this altogether like the way one can instruct a child to believe in a God, or that accordingly be able to produce apparently telling grounds for the one or the other?
>
> 108. 'But is there then no objective truth? Isn't it true, or false, that someone has been on the moon?' If we are thinking within our system [c.1949–51], then it is certain that no one has ever been on the moon. Not merely is nothing of the sort ever seriously reported to us by reasonable people, but our whole system of physics forbids us to believe it. For this demands answers to the questions 'How did he overcome the force of gravity?' 'How could he live without an atmosphere?' and a thousand others which could not be answered. But suppose that instead of all these answers we met the reply: 'We don't know how one gets to the moon, but those who get there know at once that they are there; and even you can't explain everything.' We should feel ourselves intellectually very distant from someone who said this.

Turning aside from the unintended irony in this remark brought on by the technological advances following Wittgenstein's death that allowed for travel to the moon and back, it is instructive to see Wittgenstein attending to the dramatic epistemic distances that are sometimes observed in human experience. Intellectual distance is the separation between standards of judgment between people or groups of people. If two people do not share a standard of judgment, then they are likely to have different impressions of what is plausible. Does this mean that epistemology is always relative to a culture or a social group? I think the question cannot be answered. Distant cultures might have different means of measuring time, but that does not mean that they live in different worlds. Conceptions of phenomena of the world found in the languages human beings form still must answer to the common world all people share. If the conceptions as a whole are not functional, then they would not survive.

Consider those who accept conspiracy theories, for example, those that hold that humans in fact never did walk on the moon. According to the principle of charity, an interpreter ought to conclude that most of the beliefs of these people should turn out to be true. They get about in the world relatively well. Their convictions might seem unbelievable to the general public who are otherwise satisfied with the official historical narrative that the space race resulted in humans traveling to and returning from the moon. The same could be said for those who believe in doctrines or rituals that lack plausibility or sensibility to others.

Encountering those who use different pictures or frames of reference is a real phenomenon; however, the nature of intellectual distance should not be exaggerated. Differences between ways of life, and the pictures that articulate relevant differences in judgment, entail practical barriers to understanding but not inherently unbridgeable gulfs; conversation and persuasion are possibilities. Nevertheless, practically speaking, it may feel impossible to bridge a gulf. The cost of trust, and thus of communication, may be too great to warrant the risk. This judgment is frequently made by political and religious partisans. It may be mutual or one-sided mistrust.

How best to understand the concept of social trust presents a problem, one that is being explored increasingly by moral philosophers and epistemologists. Is trust an intentional state? Is trust a disposition to act in a certain way? How is trust different from faith? Is trust different from confidence in social roles, and if so how so? What are the legitimate and illegitimate forms of trust when it comes to the role of testimony in social epistemology? In the work of Annette Baier among others, trust is a morally charged dimension of ordinary life.[10] Trust is an inevitable, if fraught, dynamic in social life. For these philosophers, practical reason plays an important role in the granting of trust. The granting of trust requires warrant just as being trusted, when warranted, entails obligations.

In two essays in particular, 'Trust and Anti-trust' and 'Whom Can Women Trust?', Baier discusses the idea of trusting another in some respects but not others. For example, I trust my dentist on certain medical matters, but I may not do so on aesthetic ones. Under Baier's conception, trust is a property of relationships, a property that may stand whether or not it is warranted. Human flourishing requires relationships with warranted trust, but trust is typically granted without warrant or sufficient warrant. In Baier's analysis, the paradigmatic case of trust without warrant is that between a parent and child. Baier does not think that all trusting requires warrant. After all, an attitude of vigilance or skepticism may stand in the way of building trust to begin with.

Here we see the normative dimension of Baier's discussion of trust. Some relationships contribute to one's flourishing, while others do not; critical, responsible thinking discerns the difference between the two. Baier is concerned with the place of trust in relationships, especially with regard to the goal of women's flourishing, while being mindful of both personal and institutional obstacles to such. In an essay from 2004, 'Demoralization, Trust, and the Virtues,' she writes:

> Since I have in other places defended an account of trust that sees it to lie in the attitude of the one who trusts to being in some respect in the power – sometimes but not always the voluntarily given power – of the trusted, and trustworthiness as the ability and willingness to use such power for the expected good, not the harm, of the one who trusts, I take the virtues to include good judgment about when to trust and willingness to meet such reasonable trust, but also to include many other qualities that affect such judgment and such willingness, all of them attitudes to mutual power and vulnerability. I take a climate of trust to be good to the extent that persons can safely trust others, including strangers, officials, makers of machines, builders, and those who issue licenses, control airports, and so on. (Baier, 2004, p. 187)

Baier's identification of the place of virtue in both trusting and being trusted is important here. Persons in both positions, as we are all sometimes in one position or the other, have their responsibilities. Yet as she also observes in her 1986 essay 'Trust and Anti-Trust', trust is not always granted, or held, responsibly, and sometimes justice calls for 'trust busting'. The absence of trust in civic life between political or religious actors does not mean trust *should* be established; it means the conditions for warranted trust may be lacking and it is to these conditions that those seeking to build social bridges should turn their attention.

In *The Claim of Reason*, Stanley Cavell contemplates risks of a related sort to those explored by Baier, risks involved in speaking for oneself. Speaking for oneself is risky at times simply because the good 'climate of trust' Baier envisions, where persons can safely trust others, is an ideal that our own communities may achieve to a greater or lesser extent. Cavell writes,

> To speak for yourself then means risking the rebuff – on some occasion, perhaps once for all – of those for whom you claimed to be speaking; and it means risking having to rebuff – on some occasion, perhaps once for all – those who claimed to be speaking for you. There are directions other than the political in which you will have to find your own voice – in religion, in friendship, in parenthood, in art – and to find your own work; and the political is likely to be heartbreaking or dangerous. (Cavell, 1979, p. 27)

Both Baier and Cavell see a good that is fundamental to flourishing as a human being in finding one's own voice and in cultivating trusting relationships that are conducive to mutual flourishing. For both Baier and Cavell, this mutual flourishing involves the cultivation of one's own autonomy so that one may trust responsibly as well as contribute to the edification of others with whom one is in trusting relationships. What Baier and Cavell hope for are social environments where an individual's flourishing may coexist, possibly even cooperate, with the flourishing of others, that a community's flourishing might involve the flourishing of the individuals composing it.

While Wittgenstein did not develop ideas on the ethics of trust, he was concerned with thinking scrupulously to the extent that one's mind was genuinely one's own, so that one was not unduly held captive by a picture.[11] Recognizing differences between claims made by people living according to a different way of life and one's own views as not merely contradictions but as instances of intellectual distance is one example of Wittgenstein's pursuit of perspicuity. Of course, sometimes the conflict between epistemic stances is best thought of as a contradiction, but if one misses the intellectual distances that sometimes work to produce the contradiction, then one has missed a great deal about the epistemic conflict in question.

It bears repeating that there are moments in Wittgenstein's writings where he refers to language-games changing, being created, or dying out. In these moments of possibility, trust or its lack is a key factor in what happens next. Trust may be lacking and cooperation can become increasingly difficult; this may lead to the death of a language-game. Because of a lack of trust, meanings for concepts may not be established or routinized in behavior. This dynamic can have important consequences when it comes to communication and interpretation across cultures, worldviews or religious ways of life. Lack of trust between secular critics of a religion and participants in the religion can obstruct interpretation or communication by denying the foundation upon which meaning or judgment is sustained. Thus, both religious and secular critics often find the other has fundamentally misunderstood what they had thought they were debating or discussing. Indeed, Phillips' and Nielsen's joint 2005 volume *Wittgensteinian Fideism?* displays repeatedly how determined professional philosophical critics and defenders of a view can misread each other. Shared histories of misunderstanding can become reasons for continuing to distrust, reasons that are difficult to counterbalance.

'Wittgensteinian fideism' is a problematic label because it is not clear what 'fideism' means except as a pejorative, but as such, it does not belong in academic discourse. Wittgensteinian isolationism might be better since it gets to the point, the epistemic isolation of religious communities from secular/public reason. But Wittgenstein turns out to be a poor choice for the isolationist about religions because the idea of the fundamental privacy of experiences is senseless in his view.

An appreciation for the dynamics of trust goes some ways towards dispelling the apparent relativism and epistemic isolationism some have thought implicit in Wittgenstein's treatment of meaning as use. Language-games do not have boundaries that are barriers preventing outsiders from understanding; rather, the boundaries between instances of language are practical. The players of a game may insist that only members of a particular gender, class, or ethnicity can play a game, but this is not a necessary feature of understanding the game, and besides, the rules of the game, under the right circumstances, may change. Since the agreement that undergirds language involves meanings and forms of judgment, within the space thus demarcated, dispute and disagreement over particular truths or how to implement epistemic or moral standards is common. Imagine that there is a concept one seeks to establish in social practice (for example, a particular form of prayer as being authentically Buddhist or an interpretation of a scripture as Christian). If trust is present, or can be established, then one may share standards of judgment with relevant others. One may then have an opportunity to establish one's version of a contested term as the preferred meaning. The meanings of contested concepts can also be established through political coercion, if one has the power to accomplish it, but the tyrant will *a forteriori* lose the ethical and epistemological goods that flow from warranted trust. However, if trust, or political coercion, is lacking, then the term will remain contested so long as sufficiently large communities of discourse remain partisans in favor of their local preferred meaning.

But note that conversion and resignation to conflict are not the only possible outcomes of intellectual dispute. Nielsen and Proudfoot would be right in thinking that Wittgensteinian philosophy of religion, especially as advocated by those like Malcolm who associate religions (however complexly) with language-games or forms of life, is antithetical to genuine intellectual engagement were it the case that conversion and resignation to conflict were the only possibilities. However, if the character of language-games or forms of life is grounded in the attunement of people with one another and their shared world, a dynamic that involves social trust, then boundaries between language-games or forms of life (if the metaphor of a boundary is apt here) ought to be thought of as being porous and even renegotiable.

What I take from the foregoing discussion of trust is that while it is, of course, by no means universal, it is universally experienced. For all of us at times rely on others – for both basic and profound matters. Human beings are social animals and our use of language is part of our social orientation. Mistrust can be warranted, and therefore the conditions for successful cooperation and interpretation might be lacking in a given situation. This is not to say that mistrust prevents any communication. But mistrust precludes to some extent the collaborative process of forming new concepts in connection with contested areas of life; it also precludes inter-cultural or inter-religious communication. Without requisite trust, there is no basis on which to form new concepts. The fine-tuning of interpretations can be itself a collaborative endeavor. It may well be that the circling around each other that is all too common between religionists and critics of religions is both symptomatic of a lack of trust and a reason for perpetuating that mistrust.

If language is like a city,[12] built up over many generations with neighborhoods constructed at different times for different purposes and with particular styles, then the city also has bridges that have been built or that have been dismantled. The presence or absence of bridges may make it easier or more difficult to travel around the city; they may make the job of a cartographer more or less difficult. This is the city to be mapped, one layered with history and reflecting the vicissitudes of that history.

It may seem like genuine engagement of ideas is impossible between defenders of Wittgensteinian philosophy of religion and critics of Wittgensteinian fideism, but this is at most a practical difficulty, for the language each camp uses is publicly available. The debates between Nielsen and Phillips over the very criteria of 'Wittgensteinian fideism' reflect the fact that neither one was able to speak on behalf of the other. Perhaps this dynamic just goes to show how difficult philosophical conversation can be; perhaps this difficulty too is something perspicuity should teach us.[13]

7
Wittgenstein's Ethic of Perspicuity and the Philosophy of Religion

Philosophy has been in crisis many times before. Sympathetic critics of philosophy have emerged throughout its history to set the field back on the right path or to provoke philosophers to consider their vocation. Today, in many colleges and universities in the United States and around the world, along with other liberal arts disciplines, philosophy is under increased scrutiny, not just from fellow philosophers who wish the best for it but from educational reformers who seek to transform higher education so that it is designed *primarily* to prepare students for employment in a competitive world. Philosophy, as with the other disciplines in the liberal arts, is at risk of being perceived as a non-essential feature of undergraduate education, except at the more elite institutions.[1] In contemplating the present dour circumstances facing philosophy, it is helpful to review earlier 'dark times'.

Nearly seventy years ago, Oxford philosopher H. H. Price argued that philosophy was in a different kind of crisis, a *moral* crisis. To an early critic such as Price of what was becoming known in the 1940s as analytic philosophy, it seemed evident that logical clarity alone was not enough as a suitable end for philosophy. While he agreed that no one has the right to tell anyone else what they ought to work on in their research, Price observed that the general public justifiably may expect more from a philosopher than analytic clarity about concepts. When Price delivered the address 'Clarity is not Enough' to the Joint Meeting of the Mind Association and the Aristotelian Society, only three months had passed since the end of World War II in Europe. Price thought it reasonable that the public might expect more from philosophers *as teachers*; he thought that the public might want some sort of comprehensive view of life.

To some contemporary philosophers, it might seem similarly unlikely that perspicuity could be a suitable end for philosophy. Wittgenstein's search for perspicuity might be fine *as a method* that lays the groundwork for the real business of philosophy: theory building and testing regarding topics in the central areas of philosophy such as metaphysics, epistemology and ethics. According to such a view, perspicuity could only ever be a penultimate end for philosophy, the seeking of clarity always being in service to more substantive goals. According to this perspective, the task of philosophy is to assess or offer theories that provide definitive answers to questions of the form 'what is X?' (where 'X' may be replaced with any central concept within the disciplines of metaphysics, epistemology, and ethics). Wittgenstein has been approached sometimes as a philosopher possessing theories about the topics he was interested in; the task for the interpreter, or for the disputant, then would be to identify these implicit theories and to assess the merit of them relative to their logical consistency and to contemporary theoretical projects. This much is evident in the historical reception of Wittgenstein in philosophy, theology, and religious studies.

As discussed in Chapter 1, the hermeneutic I use in reading Wittgenstein is what I call his ethic of perspicuity (the perspicuity reading). The aims of Chapters 1–6 were to articulate the perspicuity reading of Wittgenstein, to show the historical development (and idiosyncrasy) of standard picture readings of Wittgenstein on religion and to show the textual implausibility of these readings (for example, Wittgensteinian fideism or the view that religions are epistemically isolated language-games). The goals of the present chapter are (1) to compare the perspicuity reading with some other recent interpretations and (2) to speculate on new avenues for Wittgensteinian philosophy of religion.

7.1 Perspicuity, clarity, and contemplation

7.1.1 Wittgenstein and Price on clarity in philosophy

When Price criticized World War II era analytical philosophy in his lecture, he drew a distinction between what he termed 'analytic' and 'synoptic' clarity; the former was the target of his criticism while the latter he understood to be the proper aim of philosophy. The piecemeal approach of analytic philosophy, shunning the systematic philosophy of earlier eras, lacks a motivation or application transparent to the philosophical public and thus can lead to a crisis of relevance. He held that the public rightly might expect more from philosophers and observed the criticism that reluctance to address these sorts of practical concerns may have given rise to a climate where a war might happen. Leaving aside the causal thesis about the war, the admonition to philosophers to consider their teaching a vocation seems reasonable. Philosophers, at least of the analytic stripe, have not always been effective at showing the contemporary relevance of their work.

Where does Wittgenstein's philosophy lie with respect to Price's distinction between analytic and synoptic clarity? The short answer is that it does not fit easily the distinction. I do not think that Wittgenstein was simply after analytic clarity in his thought; he also used the word 'synoptic' when characterizing the perspicuity that he sought. Price's preferred end for philosophy, a comprehensive view of all that is known about the world, may or may not be something that is likely to be the outcome of Wittgensteinian philosophy. Wittgenstein's understanding of synoptic clarity is not the same as Price's. Wittgenstein's perspicuous representations may point to differences in meaning or application of concepts as much as they may point to common features. While the tendency, especially within Wittgenstein's mature thought, is to show differences, as can be seen from the 'Remarks on Frazer's *Golden Bough*', Wittgenstein did not take perspicuous representations to always indicate difference or distinctiveness. Commonalities between ancient or indigenous ritual practices and contemporary practices (like kissing a photo) show a recurring feature of human experience (Wittgenstein, 1993, p. 123).

It is appropriate to read both Price and Wittgenstein as critics of mid-twentieth century philosophy that aspires to be scientific in its analytical rigor but that lacks a sense of ethical commitment to the pursuit of wisdom; yet their prescriptions for what philosophy should be and do diverge. Price wishes to return to a form of systematic philosophy that was increasingly out of fashion in the English-speaking world of philosophy. Wittgenstein bemoans his lack of an appropriate audience and seeks to expose the pretensions of philosophers, and others, who have been so impressed by the developments in the sciences that they wish to make philosophy scientific. Price's preferred model for philosophy retains that scientific ambition, broad and encompassing though it may be. For Wittgenstein, the ethical commitment of philosophy goes right to the root of philosophical activity itself. In contrast with Price's conception of the philosopher as answering the classic philosophical questions of humankind, the philosopher, in Wittgenstein's view, must renounce ambitions that rise above the station of humanity; the local philosophical problems with which one finds oneself occupied are suitable for one's philosophical investigation and resolution. Wittgenstein was skeptical of the idea of essential philosophical problems. Authentic philosophical problems have a local, immediate quality. Thus, while Wittgenstein does not share the end for philosophy that Price does, he could concur with Price in criticizing the then current technical end for philosophy: analytic clarity as an end in itself. In short, one could propose a Wittgensteinian answer to Price: a clarity that flattens out differences or forces categories on the world is not the proper task for philosophy, but a clarity that transforms that which is opaque and confused to that which is transparent and perspicuous is not merely enough as an end for philosophy, it is the only end that is possibly achievable.

7.1.2 Mulhall and Phillips on the personal and the philosophical

Biletzki identifies five 'stations' or orientations in the secondary literature on Wittgenstein. The approaches linked with the last three of these concern us here in elaborating further on what perspicuity is as an end for philosophy. For the third station interpreters, perspicuity would be the discovery of the ineffability of the logic of our language, the idea being that the logic (or grammar, in Wittgenstein's mature thought) can only be shown in language use, not said. Regarding Wittgenstein's mature thought, it is not that this grammar cannot be described at all, far from it. Instead, any description of grammar must be understood as a description from within language, not from the standpoint of a universal metalanguage. P. M. S. Hacker is the philosopher most associated with this view, but variations on it can be found throughout the secondary literature on Wittgenstein.

This view can to some extent be ascribed to D. Z. Phillips; yet Phillips adds further a concern for how language hangs together (to use Wilfred Sellars's phrase). Phillips's 'contemplative philosophy' is not just analytical, in describing the grammar of religious language games, but it is also synoptic in seeking to identify how abstractive instances of language – language-games – are integrated together. In this second, synoptic philosophical activity, Phillips follows his teacher Rush Rhees's reading of Wittgenstein.

Stephen Mulhall is perhaps better represented in connection with the fourth and fifth stations, concerning the recognition of nonsense as nonsense and the ethical dimensions of that recognition. Furthermore, in following Cavell's reading of Wittgenstein, Mulhall emphasizes the way that Wittgenstein's philosophy aims at transforming the reader and his or her presuppositions about philosophy. Reading Wittgenstein is a reflective activity; in reading, one enters into a text and is challenged to continue reading in a way that is sympathetic to this dialectical process. 'Sympathy' does not here mean a lack of criticism; it is just to approach the text in its performative mood, rather than out of some preconception of what philosophy is, what its problems are.[2] Mulhall develops an approach he detects in Cavell's reading of Wittgenstein:

> Cavell is not proposing a view of philosophy as a set of texts rather than problems (a proposal requiring a suspiciously simple opposition between problems and texts), but rather opposing the presumption that philosophical problems can be thought to form a *given* set or list. The implication is that if we properly acknowledge the obvious fact that philosophers typically contribute to their subject by means of texts, then we will question the idea that we can define a distinctively philosophical problem by pointing to, or by enumerating, a given set of features. For Cavell, what a distinctively philosophical problem might be is itself a philosophical problem, and one of its most fundamental ones. (Mulhall, 2001, p. 7)

Cavell and Mulhall approach philosophical problems as arising in philosophical texts, not in some classic or given form. The same could be said for the genres in which philosophy is written. But what does it mean that the problems arise in philosophical texts? Mulhall reads Cavell as holding that the two, philosophical problems and texts, are internally related and that 'whether a text is one to which a philosophical response is appropriate, or (if you prefer) one that raises problems of a sort requiring a philosophical response, is not given or obvious, but is rather to be discovered through individual acts of what one might call philosophical criticism' (Mulhall, 2001, p. 8). This philosophical criticism bears a resemblance to Phillips's contemplative philosophy in that both require an involvement of the philosopher with the text, practices, beliefs, way of life, and so on being studied. A bracketing of one's own questions, if even for just a moment, is needed in order to listen for the distinctive features of one's object of study.

In being critical of Phillips's view in *Philosophy's Cool Place*, Mulhall first describes it as laying, in Phillips's description, between two poles: the cold conception of philosophy, 'that of saying only what can be said, and demonstrating to those who fail to respect this condition on speech that they have failed to give meaning to some portion of their putative utterance', (Mulhall, 2007b, p. 14) and the hot, that of running 'that distinctively philosophical passion [of doing justice to concepts] together with the passionate interest that every human being has in finding some way of inhabiting, making sense of, and hence participating in that unifying dialogue [that is language]' (Mulhall, 2007b,

p. 14). Contemplative philosophy, in Phillips's conception, builds on the scrupulousness of the cold conception of philosophy with Rhees's appreciation for the continuity of language over against a reified view of language-games as discrete entities.

Most germane to the present study is Phillips's associations of Cavell and James Conant with the 'hot' conceptions of philosophy. Replying to Mulhall, Phillips indicates he does not want to draw a strict line between the personal and the philosophical, only that 'the distinction is worth making... *at times*' (Phillips, 2007, p. 37). Phillips observes Conant's two categories to be avoided in biographical work on philosophers: 'reductivism', where 'the real explanation of a philosophical work is to be found in the personal details of the philosopher's life', and 'compartmentalism', where 'the philosophical and the personal are entirely separate from each other' (Phillips, 2007, pp. 37–8). Conant takes Phillips to be a compartmentalist, yet Phillips recognizes that philosophy can make demands on the enquirer, including ethical demands.

Still, Phillips wants to observe divergences between the philosophical and the personal in a few respects. While there are 'internal relations' between the philosophical and the personal, those could be overstated. Phillips, following Rhees, wants to observe that a certain sober character is needed for contemplative philosophy, and therefore, it is likely that this characteristic would appear elsewhere in a person's life (Phillips, 2007, p. 40). Yet, Phillips and Rhees also want to preserve the 'independence' of philosophical problems: 'Philosophy is not simply the means of removing obstacles in other fields, for example, the advancement of science, even if, on occasion, it succeeds in doing so' (Phillips, 2007, p. 40). On Phillips's and Rhees's view, philosophy clarifies concepts and the character required to do this well may appear in a person's life, but this does not make philosophy into a way of life (as with the ancients, as described in Pierre Hadot's historical work[3]). Phillips observes a distance between the clarifying work of a philosopher and the epistemological or moral conclusions the philosopher may draw about the phenomena.

Hot conceptions of philosophy would equate the philosophical and the personal, to use Phillips's parlance. The work of the philosopher would then be as much conceptual clarification as work on one's life. If Wittgenstein were a philosopher in Hadot's mould of the ancient practical philosopher, this would be so. Phillips insists a line must be observed between what philosophy is concerned with, the concepts and language we use, and the lives we lead. Yet in so far as our lives are lives with language, and language that may be conceptually confused, then philosophy has as its business the investigation of concepts that may range over what is found in university philosophy courses or well beyond those contexts.

I take it that Phillips's primary concern is to protect the philosophical from other commitments that might be present in a person's life. In this context, Phillips quotes Wittgenstein's claim from *Zettel*: '(The philosopher is not a citizen of any community of ideas. That is what makes him a philosopher.)' (Wittgenstein, 1967b, §455). This Phillips interprets as holding that the philosopher has no commitments to the truth, falsity, or value of the language under investigation. Stated so baldly, it is unlikely much of anyone could claim the title of philosopher, and maybe that is how it should be: to be a philosopher is an extraordinarily difficult undertaking. I would prefer to think of this as a hyperbolic statement, one that says that as a philosopher, one has no commitments (or one learns to bracket them). James Klagge writes of this remark, 'This suggests that exile is an appropriate status for a philosopher, discomforting though it may be. Perhaps the separation from a community is what allows the philosopher to gain the sort of synoptic overview of language necessary to see its ditches' (Klagge, 2011, p. 75). In Klagge's view, the remark highlights the extent to which exile was a resource for philosophy, that the kind of philosophy Wittgenstein was drawn to was a kind born of exile.

7.1.3 John Clayton and the clarification of defensible differences

A very different inheritance of Wittgenstein in the philosophy of religion may be found in John Clayton's *Religions, Reasons and Gods*. Clayton advances the thesis that philosophy of religion would benefit from greater attention to the social and historical contexts in which philosophers have devised arguments about gods, that attention to these contexts would enable contemporary philosophers to avoid equivocation over the ends of theistic arguments and to gain a better sense of the accomplishments of philosophers of different eras and locations. Clayton argues that it would be beneficial to shift the primary focus of philosophy of religion from the evaluation of tradition-neutral reasons for or against belief in the existence of gods and to the clarification of defensible differences among philosophical and religious traditions. This attention to context and particularity could contribute to the acquisition and refinement of understanding of religions, displaying the constructive (or deconstructive) role of philosophy of religion within religious studies.

While the whole of *Religions, Reasons and Gods* advances the thesis that philosophy of religion needs to be more sensitive to the social and historical context of arguments and less abstractive, to the extent that Clayton achieves his end, it is due to the focus many of the essays have on particular locations of philosophical activity. Indeed, from attending to the multiple uses to which theistic arguments may be put, Clayton discourages contextually insensitive readings of philosophy that might seem to make ancient, medieval, and early modern philosophers foolish in comparison with their present-day critics (reminiscent of Wittgenstein's criticism of Frazer).

In the title chapter of the book, Clayton argues against the interpretive adequacy of abstractive discussions of theistic proofs in the mainstream of philosophy of religion. Clayton observes that an overarching tendency in philosophy of religion is to read theistic proofs as attempting to provide justification for belief (that is, evidence that would be compelling to a skeptic). Instead, Clayton observes: 'A survey of the place and roles of theistic proofs and disproofs within a range of religious traditions, Eastern as well as Western, suggests that in the main they were used to serve intra-traditional ends. Their principal function seems to have been more nearly *explanatory* than *justificatory*' (Clayton, 2006, p. 80). In that chapter, Clayton connects his approach in the philosophy of religion to the later philosophy of Wittgenstein; yet Clayton is quick to note that his own inheritance from Wittgenstein contrasts with some Wittgensteinian philosophers of religion who seem reluctant to allow theistic proofs a legitimate role in religious 'forms of life'. Clayton is fairly coy here about just who he has in mind, but in the final chapter of the book, he mentions Phillips in particular as a figure whose Wittgensteinian philosophy of religion seems to dent the public contestability of religious beliefs. Clayton argues that instead of viewing theistic proofs as 'antecedent attempts to justify the playing' of religious language-games (as some Wittgensteinians do), theistic proofs could 'more plausibly be regarded as *moves within*' such games (Clayton, 2006, p. 81). Clayton here signals a different trajectory by which philosophers of religion might draw on Wittgenstein's philosophy.

As communities around the world have become more interconnected, through economic ties, immigration, and communication technologies, a rich pluralism of religions are now present through many communities. It is in response to this pluralism, and especially the rise in recent decades of 'radical conservatism' in religions that Clayton suggests *defensible difference* as an alternative end for philosophy of religion. Clayton offers defensible difference as an alternative to the aim of seeking consensus in intellectual debate. The ideal of achieving consensus, through the articulation of common ground, Clayton takes to be an illusion, inherited from periods in American and European history in which religious diversity consisted largely of variations on Judaism and Christianity. The search for common ground presupposes that the varied groups present in a community in fact have common interests.

The rationality on display in dialogue aimed at clarifying defensible difference stands in contrast to what Clayton calls 'utopian rationality'. Clayton uses this expression 'to characterize the philosophy of religion typically done within the frame allowed by the Enlightenment project' (Clayton, 2006, p. 180). Utopian rationality is putatively tradition-neutral; utopian reasons are reasons that ought to suffice for anyone within the public sphere. Clayton holds that it is in the context of utopian rationality that theistic arguments in the early modern period came to bear more epistemic weight than they had in traditional contexts. The justificatory role of theistic argument came to be pre-eminent. Another expression Clayton uses to describe this tradition-neutral context for epistemology is 'disembedded foundationalism'; in disembedded foundationalism, other (that is, local, contextually sensitive) uses of theistic arguments are overlooked and arguments are assessed in terms of their capacity to serve *religion in general* as reasons to believe in a *generic* God.

Disputations over correct religious doctrine or fair social policy do not take place in a neutral setting. Clayton does not expect disputes between actors from different cultural or religious points of view to lead to consensus; however, it may be that 'from different motives and disparate grounds', specific limited goals may be visible after the work of clarifying defensible differences despite the lack of a common historical narrative (Clayton, 2006, p. 78). Once these limited goals have become visible, groups may endorse cooperation for their own specific reasons. Clayton also notes in a somewhat hopeful tone that 'clarifying defensible difference may help build up a sense of community and encourage a variety of liberal virtues, including civility toward the stranger and toleration of otherness. It may also contribute to the recognition of cultural and religious diversity as a positive good' (Clayton, 2006, p. 79).

Clayton offers three 'counsels of prudence' for fruitful interpretation. The first begins with Donald Davidson's interpretive principle of charity, the view that in order to perform an interpretation of the linguistic behavior of a community of language users radically different from the interpreter's culture, it is necessary to presume that most of the beliefs of the community in question are true (that is, that the members of the community are rationally competent). Clayton prefers to call this interpretive principle 'the presumption of competence': the idea here is that 'the basic claims of major religious traditions are likely to be justifiable as "true" to members of the community concerned' (Clayton, 2006,

p. 2). Davidson takes the principle of charity to apply in cases of radical interpretation, where no previous knowledge of a culture's language, beliefs, or values is known. Davidson and others hold that interpretation in these circumstances can proceed only with the presumption that most of the beliefs of the community are true. While the interpretation Clayton has in mind does not entail such great epistemic distance, the presumption should still hold that when interpreting the beliefs and practices of a community, it is reasonable to hold that most of the beliefs of the community will be true. After all, if this were not the case then getting about in the world, not to say survival, would be improbable.

The second of Clayton's counsels of prudence is the 'practice of empathy': 'the imaginative participation of the observer in the spiritual and cognitive world of the religious traditions under scrutiny.' Here 'empathy' enables one to understand another in a 'holistic' way; the idea is that beliefs, values, or practices of a tradition are not evaluated discretely or individually but instead in terms of how they hang together, how the beliefs, values, and practices form a 'web of belief', to borrow Quine's expression, that is better assessed in terms of its internal relations. In order to piece together the ends of argument of another philosopher, one must be sensitive to how those aims are expressed in a text; this sensitivity may call for historical or biographical study.

The third counsel is the 'maxim of reticence', which Clayton likens to the phenomenological *epoché*, except that Clayton does not wish to bracket judgment so firmly. This means that Clayton's philosophy of religion wishes to delay, but not derail, normative questions about truth.[4] It is not that Clayton's approach abandons queries into the truth or falsity of religious or philosophical claims; rather he holds that only after presuming epistemic competence and practicing imaginative empathy is it reasonable for the scholar to evaluate the claims of others. While Clayton addresses fellow philosophers of religion, his remarks on being a generous philosophical interlocutor could apply also to interlocutors in other discourses aimed at clarifying defensible difference.

Clayton does not emphasize a moral dimension to these interpretive principles; he explicitly describes these as counsels of *prudence*. Even so, I think a moral 'ought' is implied insofar as failure to observe the counsels would seem to entail indifference to the possibility of misinterpretation or equivocation, rational failures that are surely worth avoiding. Clayton's philosophy of religion, throughout its development as seen in *Religions, Reasons and Gods*, grows out of this appreciation for the goods that can emerge from the practice of responsible interpretation. This is not a responsibility to the projects or purposes of the argument or work to be interpreted but rather a responsibility to search out truth about the object of one's investigation; for Clayton this search should include contextual study such as that indicated by the counsels of prudence.

7.2 Wittgenstein and the ethics of philosophy of religion

Numerous fields, including philosophy, face a crisis today; the crisis is different than that they faced nearly seventy years ago at the end of World War II. The professionalization of academia, already exerting an influence on philosophy during Wittgenstein's lifetime, has proceeded swiftly to question the value of the liberal arts, not as university subjects, but as curriculum that is suitable for college degrees aimed at career preparation. Against this background, the marginalized place of philosophy of religion within many philosophy departments makes the landscape precarious for this subdiscipline. The crisis now faced by philosophy of religion is deep and multifaceted, and it is not my goal to offer a thorough diagnosis of this crisis (in its economic, political, and moral dimensions). Yet surely part of the crisis is exacerbated by the marginalized standing of philosophy of religion within the larger field of philosophy. What I am suggesting is that a philosophy of religion participating in dialectical conversation with Wittgenstein's texts has the opportunity to be more engaged with our diverse world, facilitating conversations across boundaries, that this is an academic and philosophical task of increased urgency. Philosophy of religion might be a field at the vanguard of building connections across the global field of philosophy. What I am suggesting is that philosophy of religion can be thought of as *a* connective tissue among disparate areas of philosophical research.[5] As a connective tissue (there may be others), philosophy of religion can link conversations among those working not just in mainstream analytic and naturalistic philosophy with topics having to do with religions, but also across areas as diverse as comparative philosophy and non-European traditions of philosophy (be they indigenous to particular geographic regions or to Chinese or Indian cultures).

Like Price in the 1940s, some in the early twenty-first century are calling for a program for philosophy of religion that is more responsive to the world in which it is practiced. There are many forms of advice, and given a broad view of the subdiscipline, no doubt this is as it should be. In contemplating the philosophy of religion with an eye to Wittgenstein's ethic of perspicuity, it is not so much that a new program for what the discipline should be emerges, so much as a reconsideration of what the vocation of the philosopher of religion may be. Six points merit reiteration.

First, Wittgenstein was not a figure assimilated into philosophical consciousness in the second and third quarters of the twentieth century once and for all and then transcended by subsequent philosophers; instead Wittgenstein is a philosophical critic with whose texts one may still read dialectically. There are surely many ways in which a philosopher may become a classic figure, but one of them is when the philosopher's writings may be helpful to multiple generations of readers, possessing their own particular projects and problems. Wittgenstein is among this number.

Second, following on the first point, the ethic of perspicuity could provoke philosophers to approach the history of philosophy with a similar scrupulousness; it is possible there will be new lessons to be learned from a great many historical figures. A great lesson given by historians of philosophy is that those who have come before are frequently much more subtle and astute than the lore of philosophy might otherwise suggest. We should guard ourselves against any smug confidence that a figure or era has passed and is now irrelevant to our philosophical concerns; we do not know what lessons we may find useful in the future.

Third, the provocation 'don't think but look!' (Wittgenstein, 2003a, §66) should be brought to the philosophical study of religions. Philosophers of religion have all too often addressed religion *in general* and not the lived religions of actual people. From a historical perspective, this makes sense; after all, one point of origin[6] of the philosophy of religion was in the Enlightenment, when some philosophers sought to find the common essential and rational core around which the revealed religions orbited (a project that, if successful, might have provided rational grounding for religious endeavors as well as for what forms of religious activity might be tolerable politically). Today we are all too aware of the diversity of religious phenomena. When applied to philosophy of religion, Wittgenstein's provocation is concerned with religions as they are practiced, cultivated, debated, and adapted within the lives of people; response to such a provocation would enrich the philosophy of religion immensely, and philosophy of religion could provide much needed wisdom by directing its energies to studying religions in their diversities.

Fourth, Wittgensteinian philosophy of religion could be thought of as philosophical work aimed at addressing confusion, seeking perspicuity, and articulating clarifying connections when helpful at relieving confusion about aspects of religions. In this sense, I see the work of Phillips and Clayton as exemplifying potential paths for Wittgensteinian philosophy of religion, broadly construed. Their philosophies each aim to let religious phenomena speak for themselves and to critique inquiry that silences phenomena in favor of an attractive but illusory systematicity.

Fifth, philosophers may wish to, or need to, add other ends for philosophy of religion to serve (for example, religion-specific ends [like salvation or liberation or edification in piety], secular ends such as pluralistic flourishing, etc.), but these seem to go beyond Wittgenstein's philosophy. Furthermore, religious philosophy aimed at perspicuity may well conflict with elements of Wittgenstein's personal views on religion. Yet this tension should not trouble scholars; Wittgenstein's religiosity, when he expressed his views on Judaism and Christianity, tended away from the metaphysical claims of religious doctrines and towards appreciating the authenticity of religious practice. Wittgenstein's sympathy for religiosities seems to have been related to his conviction that religious beliefs are not like hypotheses or theories; he sought to free religions from inadvertent or ill-advised absorption of empirically reductive forms of rationality. While Wittgenstein had sympathy for the ends that were authentically experienced in religious practices, he did not adopt these ends himself (at least, not for sustained periods of time). Philosophy of religion after Wittgenstein can still perform a service – as a method – in helping clarify these additional ends and whether our projects really answer to these ends.

Sixth, an additional consequence of this reading may be more attention given to the philosopher's own situatedness within a social and historical context. As explored in connection with Chapter 2, some of us may be equal to the philosophical and existential problems that we face through our received language, while many others will not be. (And all of us will not be on at least some occasions – call this human finitude.) This is one reason why human beings need interlocutors, whether they be political, educational, scholarly, moral, or religious interlocutors. Sometimes we cannot or do not overcome our own clichéd or stereotypical thinking on our own; we are in the 'grip of a picture'. Yet, even then, the counsel we gain will only be as good and as wise as the people in our communities, and our willingness to correct or be corrected by those we may otherwise trust will be of critical importance.

7.3 Conclusion

My primary goal in this book has been to elaborate on a reading of some texts from Wittgenstein's corpus along with special attention to Wittgenstein's thought on religion and on approaching the problems arising in twentieth and twenty-first century philosophy of religion (including problems that have arisen from classifying Wittgenstein and Wittgensteinian philosophy of religion as fideistic). One theme that emerges from this study is that the history of philosophy really is philosophy, and a corollary to this would be that the history of philosophy of religion really is philosophy of religion. Studies of the history of philosophy ought to reveal, as Hans Sluga observes in his review of Hacker's *Wittgenstein's Place in Twentieth Century Anglo-American Philosophy*, the contested nature of the discipline. Just as use of the term 'fideism' has shifted over the history of nineteenth to twenty-first century theology and philosophy, as I argued in Chapters 4 and 5, 'Wittgensteinian fideism' and 'Wittgensteinian philosophy of religion' are expressions that have often been used as shorthand for supposedly coherent movements or standpoints in twentieth century philosophy of religion, as I described in Chapter 3. Attending to the historical and social context of philosophical writing shows that the meanings of terms of classification are often disputed, and perspicuous reading should lead scholars to look for subtle differences between critical classifications and the works thus classified. Parallel to this would be that much work in religious studies is philosophical in so far as it contemplates meanings of critical terms and their adequacy for interpreting their putative subject matter. Moving away from a departmental conception of philosophical subdisciplines means that much philosophical work on religions may not bear the label 'philosophy of religion', but it could and perhaps should.

Some hold it is legitimate to criticize generic positions, whether or not anyone actually instantiates the view. Thus it is commonplace to see philosophers refer to the 'global skeptic' in epistemology, the 'moral relativist' in ethics, and the 'realist' in metaphysics. The present book explores a different conception of philosophy, one that sees arguments as being asserted in a time, place, and language. From this conception of philosophy comes an ethic of philosophy: philosophers ought to be scrupulous in their pursuit of perspicuity in the reading of other philosophers and in the formulation of interpretations and arguments. Arguments constructed and presented against generic positions may be useful for the arguer in sharpening claims and reasons, but arguments against generic positions are more than useless as history of philosophy and contextual philosophy of religion: they actively undermine responsible interpretations of particular works.

Wittgenstein's ethic of philosophy should tame the instinct to reach for generality. Scholars of religions nowadays are often at pains to criticize approaches that treat 'religion' as if it were a natural kind term. If the term did possess a coherent essence, then it would be possible to have an empirical science of religion. If it does not, then hermeneutical study of contexts of ascriptions of the term 'religion', and philosophical investigation of problems and puzzles arising from these contexts of ascription, would be helpful approaches. Contexts shift over time, and use of the term 'religion' remains contested in numerous settings. Are Confucianism and Daoism religions? Practitioners and some comparative philosophers frequently shun the term, but religion scholars are more ready to include these traditions within the purview of 'religious studies'. Locations of use or contestation of the term 'religion' are thus legitimate topics of philosophical consideration.

Furthermore, we should resist the inclination to think that there may be eternal philosophical questions regarding religion. If 'religion' is not a natural kind term, then philosophical questions and problems about religions do not remain unchanged over time. While we may find continuity across time or a repetition of a theme from an earlier philosopher, that does not mean that the question is perennial. Theistic arguments are not general, eternal types, despite the fact that one may find ancient philosophers espousing views that show similarities with medieval and early modern theistic arguments. Philosophy of religion after Wittgenstein would recognize that problems have a location of their own that must be understood in order to appreciate the full meaning of those arguments. The work of Clayton has gone a long way towards displaying this dynamic with respect to the uses of theistic arguments across the history of philosophy and different religious and secular contexts.

Paying attention to the local contexts of disputation also, eventually, should involve sensitivity to social and political relationships. My reflection on the work of Stanley Cavell and Annette Baier on attunement and trust in Chapter 6 is a speculative attempt to portray social dynamics that are in play during interpretive ventures (Wittgenstein, 2003a, §43). My goal is not to develop another another theory of religious discourse but rather to show how attending to social and historical contexts of language learning and use – as is involved in studying language-games – can reveal features of interpretive ventures otherwise overlooked when scholars attend only to identifying the truth-claims – and evaluating their truth or falsity – of a given religious community. This approach suggests that Wittgenstein's philosophy supports not an isolationist reading of different ways of life, but rather that particular instances of interpretation will be conditioned by the intellectual resources as well as the moral wills of both the interpreters and those interpreted. Such isolation as there may be is a function of social relationships, involving both shared history, trust, and mistrust.

Having said that, I am reminded of the reflection earlier on in Chapter 2 on Wittgenstein's struggle with his Jewish and Christian religious inheritance. All searching for perspicuity itself begins already within a life with its inherited language, which includes communities, mythologies and philosophical problems alongside. The effort a person may expend in seeking perspicuity will not be sufficient to address all points of confusion or conflict that one faces.

Concerning human finitude, about which a discipline of seeking perspicuity ought to make us aware, what is the proper response? It goes well beyond the scope of this book to answer this question beyond a mere suggestion, but possible answers might involve the exploration and acquisition of virtues such as courage, compassion, resolution, humility, and hope in connection with the duty to pursue clarity. Virtues such as these might also critically inform the scholar's practice of interpretation of religious phenomena. Perspicuous reflection on intellectual and moral virtues such as these could itself well be thought of as a project for a philosophy of religion inspired by reading Wittgenstein.

Ideally, these would not be thought of as virtues cultivated individualistically but cooperatively, as one would when a participant is in a community of trustworthy interlocutors. While Wittgenstein clearly valued genuine friendship and honest conversation, the present author hopes for cooperative philosophical engagement more fitting for our increasingly pluralistic societies and interconnected world. It is a hope not frequently supported in these, if not 'dark' then shall we say 'confusing', times, but this hope nevertheless seems a requirement for a philosophy of religion poised to complement other efforts at promoting human flourishing. Despite having reported that he 'lived a wonderful life', Wittgenstein remained an exile from his world. What I envision for the philosophy of religion is a philosophy perhaps born of exile and alienation but living through engagement and conversation. But I envision this fully aware that historical memory and contemporary politics and economics play significant roles in whether or not the hope in the prospects for conversation may bear out. Yet the alternative to attenuated hope is a failure of nerve at a time in which human beings with their disparate sources of identity have an unprecedented level of contact and at a time when the restructuring of universities seems to be depriving them of the very resources necessary to address complicated conceptual problems arising from cross-cultural contact. The challenge that I argue is worth undertaking *as philosophy of religion* is to venture through the philosophical sensitivities to language and meaning held by an exile and to form a reflective discourse aimed at facilitating conversations across disparate boundaries; this, I take it, is part of the continuing promise of Wittgenstein's philosophy, and it is also a problem as well, for how to read the work of a philosopher not from this time or place.

Notes

Introduction

1. See chapter 8, 'Contested Concepts, Family Resemblances and Tradition' in Glock, 2008.
2. This has been a central topic of dispute within religious studies and cognate academic fields. See Asad, 1993; Taylor, 1998; and Smith, 2004.
3. A recent example of this kind of approach is found in DuBois, 2011. DuBois's book is a good example of the way a perspicuous overview through conceptual genealogy can dispel numerous sources of confusion (for example, the debate over whether it is appropriate to classify a tradition like Confucianism as a religion or not).

1 Problems of Interpretive Authority in Wittgenstein's Corpus

1. According to one bibliography, over 600 books, articles, or theses have been written on topics relevant to Wittgenstein and religion between the 1950s and the year 2000 (Stagaman, Kraft and Sutton, 2001).
2. The editors of that now classic collection in analytic philosophy of religion, *New Essays in Philosophical Theology*, Alasdair MacIntyre and Anthony Flew, chose the name 'philosophical theology' over 'philosophy of religion' for their collection due to the latter's association with 'Idealist attempts to present philosophical prolegomena to theistic theology' (MacIntyre and Flew, 1955, p. viii).
3. Norman Malcolm writes of an encounter with Wittgenstein: 'One time when we were walking along the river we saw a news vendor's sign which announced that the German government accused the British government of instigating a recent attempt to assassinate Hitler with a bomb. This was the autumn of 1939. Wittgenstein said of the German claim: "It would not surprise me at all if it were true." I retorted that I could not believe that the top people in the British government would do such a thing. I meant that the British were too civilized and decent to attempt anything so underhand; and I added that such an act was incompatible with the British "national character". My remark made Wittgenstein extremely angry. He considered it to be a great stupidity and also an indication that I was not learning anything from the philosophical training that he was trying to give me. He said these things very vehemently, and when I refused to admit that my remark was stupid he would not talk to me any more, and soon after we parted... he kept the episode in mind for several years' (Malcolm, 1958, p. 30).
4. These students were Rush Rhees, Yorick Smythies, and James Taylor.

5. Wittgenstein's original entry reads: 'Tortur, von der man nur zeitweise heruntergespannt wird, um für weitere Qualen empfaenglich zu bleiben. Ein furchtbares Sortiment von Qualen. Ein erschöpfender Marsch, eine durchhustete Nacht, eine Gesellschaft von Besoffenen, eine Gesellschaft von gemeinen und dummen Leuten. Tue Gutes und freue dich über deine Tugend. Bin krank and habe ein schlechtes Leben. Gott helfe mir. Ich bin ein armer unglücklicher Mensch. Gott erhöre mich und schenke mir den Frieden. Amen' (Wittgenstein, 1991, p. 68).
6. The first remark comes from *Philosophical Investigations* §23, and the second remark in full reads: 'Grammar tells us what kind of object anything is. (Theology as grammar.)' §373.
7. Both Brian Clack and Paul Engelmann include the poem alongside their respective discussions of Wittgenstein's response to it. (Clack, 1999, pp. 46–7, and Engelmann, 1967, pp. 83–4).
8. Consider for example the anthropologist Clifford Geertz's use of 'forms of life' to depict the deep structure of cultures or the theologian George Lindbeck's use of 'language-games' to articulate the shared cultural and linguistic assumptions religious communities make and that must be acknowledged to support interreligious cooperation.
9. Now considered to be a pivotal move in early analytic philosophy (especially from Frege), compositionality is the idea that terms have meaning insofar as they participate in a proposition.
10. Consider for example Cavell, 1966.
11. See translator's note in Wittgenstein, 1975, p. 352.

2 Wittgenstein, Biography, and Religious Identity

1. See McGuinness, 1988; Monk, 1990; and Malcolm, 1958.
2. Consider Klagge, 2001; and Stern and Szabados, 2004.
3. Tolstoy writes at the beginning of the final chapter of his Gospel narrative, 'Therefore, for him who lives, not the self-life, but a common life in the will of the Father, there is no death. Bodily death is for him union with the Father' (Tolstoy, 1997, p. 201).
4. Indeed, this is a key point of Yaniv Iczkovits's recent comprehensive study of Wittgenstein's approach to ethics in *Wittgenstein's Ethical Thought*, 2012.
5. Consider this remark from 'Movements of Thought': 'Genuine modesty is a religious matter' (Wittgenstein, 2003b, p. 61).
6. See Chatterjee, 2005; and Szabados, 2010.
7. Fergus Kerr argues that while Wittgenstein was not a practicing Catholic, he 'was never free of his Roman Catholic inheritance – for better or worse! "Once a Catholic, always a Catholic," in those days! Most convincingly, perhaps, in this ragbag of anecdotal evidence, he liked James Joyce's book, *A Portrait of the Artist as a Young Man*, singling out the account of the Jesuit retreat sermon ("particularly well done") – an infallible test (we may surely say) of "insider" status, however long disavowed, among Catholics of his generation' (Kerr, 2008, p. 43). While I agree with Kerr that Wittgenstein was never free of his Catholic inheritance, claiming Wittgenstein as a quasi- or lapsed Catholic runs the risk of erasing the Jewish inheritance that also informs Wittgenstein's complicated identity.

8. Consider for example this passage from 1931:

   'Look on this wart as a regular limb of your body!' Can one do that, to order?

   Do I have the power to decide at will to have, or not to have, a certain ideal conception of my body?

   Within the history of the peoples of Europe the history of the Jews is not treated so circumstantially as their intervention in European affairs would actually merit, because within this history they are experienced as a sort of disease, anomaly, & nobody wants to put a disease on the same level as normal life.

   We may say: this bump can be regarded as a limb of one's body only if our whole feeling for the body changes (if the whole national feeling for the body changes). Otherwise the best we can do is put up with it.

   You may expect an individual to display this sort of tolerance or even to disregard such things; but you cannot expect this of a nation since it is only a nation by virtue of not disregarding such things. I.e. there is a contradiction in expecting someone to retain the original aesthetic feeling for his body & also to make the swelling welcome. (Wittgenstein, 1998, p. 18)
9. See Chapter 1, note 3 for Malcolm's recounting of the incident.
10. This point is also discussed by David Stern and Brian McGuinness in their respective essays in Klagge, 2001.

3 A History of Wittgenstein and the Philosophy of Religion

1. Compare Neufeld, 2005 and Amesbury, 2012.
2. Compare Clack, 1999, Arrington and Addis, 2001, Bloemendaal, 2006, and Strandberg, 2006.
3. See, for example, 'Pragmatism's Conception of Truth' in James, 1978.
4. Soames includes a fourth tendency, the tendency towards increased specialization in philosophy; however, it seems to me that this speaks more to the tradition begun by Moore, Russell, and Wittgenstein and less to those three philosophers themselves. See Soames, 2002, p. xv.
5. Consider the following remark from the essay:

   In religion, and in every deeply serious view of the world and of human destiny, there is an element of submission, a realization of the limits of human power, which is somewhat lacking in the modern world, with its quick material successes and its insolent belief in the boundless possibilities of progress. 'He that loveth his life shall lose it'; and there is danger lest, through a too confident love of life, life itself should lose much of what gives it its highest worth. The submission which religion inculcates in action is essentially the same in spirit as that which science teaches in thought; and the ethical neutrality by which its victories have been achieved is the outcome of that submission. (Russell, 1917, p. 31)
6. For more on the changing role of design arguments through the early-modern period, see John Clayton's 'The Debate about God in Early-Modern British Philosophy' in Clayton, 2006.

7. To get a sense of how close this association was in the decades following the publication of the *Tractatus*, see Price, 1935.
8. While religions can of course observe a great deal of systematicity when it comes to theological doctrines, ordinary religious practitioners rarely share this conceptual rigor. This is perhaps why George Lindbeck's 'cultural-linguistic' analysis of inter-religious dialogue in *The Nature of Doctrine* (1984) is unsatisfactory as a theory of religion; it presupposes systematicity that ordinarily rarely exists (that is, systematicity is a possibility for theological elites). Since inter-religious dialogue between theological sophisticates is his aim, perhaps this criticism is beside the point.
9. Ibid., 109ff. This is not to say that mystical thinking and natural theology are opposed – just that much philosophical interest in mysticism in the twentieth century coincided with a relative lack of trust in either metaphysical or natural theology.
10. To borrow an expression from Thomas Nagel's *The View From Nowhere* (1986).
11. Just as famously, Flew adopted something of a deistic attitude around 2004 (see Flew and Habermas, 2004).
12. *On Certainty* was written between 1949 and 1951.
13. In works like *On Religion: Speeches to its Cultured Despisers* (1799), Schleiermacher sought to ground religious faith in experience (that is, the feeling of absolute dependence), rather than in traditional theistic arguments. His philosophical theology has influenced much of the direction of Liberal Protestant theology since the Enlightenment.
14. See Tilley, 2000a, Phillips, 2000, and Tilley, 2000b.

4 The Traditions of Fideism

1. A few books have been written specifically exploring fideism. Evans, 1998; Penelhum, 1983; Popkin, 2003; and Vainio, 2010 are the only book length treatments I am aware of. Hansen, 1993 and Delaney, 1972 each deal with fideism in connection with the primary figure of study. However, with the exception of Vainio's book, none of these mentions the historical origin and development of the term. Helm, 1994 deals with fideism in its final chapter but addresses it in connection with the larger topic in epistemology, the idea of a 'belief policy'.
2. This method is similar to that used by Richard Amesbury in his *Stanford Encyclopedia of Philosophy* article on 'fideism'. There, he offers a brief history not of fideism but of 'the term's (contested) usage within the philosophical literature'. See Amesbury, 2007, 2012.
3. While several scholars suggest possible subclasses of fideism, few of these distinctions have caught on in the literature. I do not dispute that this approach could potentially be useful for certain philosophical or theological purposes. In *Beyond Fideism*, Olli-Pekka Vainio offers a taxonomy of varieties of fideism in Christian theology and philosophy in order to better understand post-foundational theology. While Vainio's strategy for clarifying the meaning of 'fideism' is different than that taken in this chapter, he is careful about avoiding pejorative or otherwise misleading classifications of theologians as fideists.

4. Philosophical discourse does not always register this pejorative connotation of fideism. For example, Ralph Barton Perry's (1912) work on William James in the early twentieth century evinces nothing negative in representing James's thought as being fideistic. Furthermore, Robert C. Fuller's centennial essay on James's 'The Will to Believe' mentions James's thought in connection with fideism without any suggestion that the category might have a negative connotation. See Fuller, 1996.
5. However, note that this does not apply to Penelhum's thought on fideism in general. Like many other philosophers, Penelhum points to figures as early as Tertullian as expressing a fideistic attitude on the relationship between faith and reason (see Penelhum, 1997).
6. The final section of the book addresses what Penelhum considers to be the fideism of Alvin Plantinga and D. Z. Phillips. Not surprisingly, given the confusion surrounding the meaning of 'fideism', both Plantinga and Phillips have rejected the term to classify their own thought. Compare Plantinga, 1983 and Phillips, 1986, 2001, and Nielsen and Phillips, 2005.
7. Technology allowing for the digitization of texts has enabled term-specific searching, and I have thus found uses of 'fidéisme' in Catholic theological sources before the years of 1879–80.
8. American theologian George B. Stevens noted the awkward name for the school of theology in Stevens, 1903. Ménégoz and Sabatier accepted the name but did not invent it themselves, and tended to stay away from it in their publications. However, it is noteworthy that the *Encyclopedia of Religion and Ethics* (1908–27), having no entry for 'fideism', includes one written by Ménégoz for 'symbolo-fideism'.
9. Sabatier writes, 'There are hours when the heresy which suffers, and which seeks and prays, is much nearer the source of life than the intellectual obstinacy of an orthodoxy incapable, as it would seem, of comprehending the dogmas that it keeps embalmed' (Sabatier, 1902, pp. 26–7).
10. See McMahon, 2001.
11. Pope Pius X's encyclical *Pascendi Dominici Gregis* (1907) condemns primarily the modernist theology of Alfred Loisy; however, fideism is also criticized, understood in a way reminiscent of the symbolo-fideism of Sabatier and Ménégoz. See §7.
12. Horton writes in a footnote: 'The "fideism" of Bautain and other Catholic thinkers should be carefully distinguished from the "fideism" of Eugène Ménégoz, the friend and colleague of August Sabatier, which consisted in the doctrine that man is saved "by faith, independently of beliefs." See his *Publications diverses sur le fidéisme*, Paris, Fischbacher. The two fideisms have nothing in common but their anti-intellectualism.' (Horton, 1926a, p. 168)
13. An anonymous reviewer suggests that 'impropriety' or 'inutility' of natural theology is a common theme running through the thought of all those characterized as fideists (both in this chapter and elsewhere in philosophical discourse). Perhaps this is so, but this characterization would need qualification in order to apply accurately to individual cases. It seems to me that the qualifications and subtle distinctions that would follow on such an initial characterization would ultimately be little different from the suggestions I offer here on seeking perspicuity about traditions of usage of 'fideism' as well as the social and historical context of thinkers under study.

14. I do not mean to imply that these are the only uses of the term, but on the basis of this preliminary study, these seem to be the primary traditions of use. Sometimes philosophers distinguish between moderate and extreme variants of fideism. I have not included these modifications because as yet such distinctions have not caught on widely in the literature and rely in some unspecified sense on one or more of these traditions listed. Future work identifying such connections would be helpful.
15. I do not categorize the Catholic modernists as fideists. They did not use the term to describe their own theology, and in the context of Catholic theological discourse, fideism is a charge to be avoided rather than a neutral term of classification. In addition, Ménégoz was at pains to distinguish his theology from modernism. Nevertheless, similarities between the thought of turn of the century French Catholic modernists and the Protestants Ménégoz and Sabatier merit further study and could conceivably complicate the picture I am drawing in this essay. In particular, there is need for further research on what influence Ménégoz and Sabatier may or may not have had on Alfred Loisy, leader of the modernist movement. I am thankful to Professor Han Adriaanse for helpful discussion on this matter.
16. I am indebted to many individuals for helpful comments on various segments of this chapter. I would like to thank in particular Professors Han Adriaanse, Ingolf Dalferth, Juliet Floyd and Alan Olson for constructive criticism of earlier attempts to gain perspective on the nature of fideism. Helpful suggestions were also offered by an anonymous reviewer for *Religious Studies*. All errors and infelicities are mine.

5 On 'Fideism' as an Interpretive Category

1. See, for instance, Fronda, 2010.
2. See for example the work of John Bishop or Duncan Richter.
3. See Reinhardt, 1936, p. 523. Notably, when Reinhardt uses the term, he calls it 'theological terminology'.
4. In this essay, James makes the only reference to 'fideism' that I have found in his writings. The meaning of the term seems essentially to be the same as Perry uses in his analyzes of James's thought.
5. Robert C. Fuller writes, 'James was surely no orthodox believer. He found himself permanently incapable of accepting traditional theism, biblical religion, or the Christian scheme of salvation. He pronounced the specific creeds of the so-called revealed religions "absurd" on scientific, philosophical, and cross-cultural grounds.' (Fuller, 1996, p. 634)
6. James's letters display this influence across many decades, but one of James's letters to Renouvier shows James's indebtedness: 'I sent you a "'New World"' the other day, however, with an article in it called "'The Will to Believe,"' in which (if you took the trouble to glance at it) you probably recognized how completely I am still your disciple. In this point perhaps more fully than in any other; and this point is central.' (James, 1920, p. 44).
7. See also Horton, 1926a, pp. 197–201, where Horton compares the Catholic traditionalist (and so-called fideist) Bautain with James.
8. Richard Amesbury, Christopher Insole and Genia Schönbaumsfeld each question this association. See Amesbury, 2012; Insole, 1998; and Schönbaumsfeld, 2007.

9. These brief descriptions show a remarkable similarity to the four main intuitions that lie behind theories of truth over the last century: correspondence, coherence, pragmatism, and deflationism. See Kierkegaard, 1992, pp. 189–90.
10. See Chapter 4 for more on symbolo-fideism and skeptical fideism.
11. See Buben, 2013; Evans, 1998; and Nelson, 2009.
12. I am grateful for a comment by John Davenport on possible connections between the treatment of truth in the *Fragments* and *Postscript* and that of love in *Works of Love*. See esp. Kierkegaard, 1962, pp. 31–3.
13. See especially Climacus's preface: 'But what is my opinion?' in Kierkegaard, 1985, p. 7.
14. See Amesbury, 2003; Fronda, 2010; Incandela, 1985; Nielsen and Phillips, 2005; Schönbaumsfeld, 2007; and Sherry, 1977.
15. See D. Z. Phillips, 'Religious Beliefs and Language Games', in Phillips, 1994.
16. See Kai Nielsen's entries in Nielsen and Phillips, 2005.
17. Goodman quotes Russell's derisive view of James: 'The scepticism embodied in pragmatism is that which says "Since all beliefs are absurd, we may as well believe what is most convenient"' (Goodman, 2002, p. 13).
18. See Bishop, 2007 pp. 18–19).

6 Religions, Epistemic Isolation, and Social Trust

1. Wolterstorff renders his view of Wittgensteinians thus: 'Characteristic of the Wittgensteinians is their insistence that different language games each have their own distinct "grammar" for *evidence, truth, fact, justification*, and the like' (Wolterstorff, 2009, p. 359). See also Alvin Plantinga's *Warranted Christian Belief*, New York: Oxford University Press, 2000, p. 8n.
2. As early as 1970, Phillips distanced himself from views in the neighborhood of 'Wittgensteinian fideism'; in the essay 'Religious Beliefs and Language Games' (reprinted in Phillips, 1994), Phillips writes 'as one who has talked of religious beliefs as distinctive language-games, but also as one who has come to feel misgivings in some respects about doing so' (Phillips, 1994, p. 56). Given that Phillips does not make great use of expressions such as 'language-game' or 'form of life' in his pre-1970 philosophy, it is difficult to know precisely what Phillips is referring to. I am grateful to Patrick Horn for helpful discussion of this matter.
3. See Diamond's essay 'Riddles and Anselm's Riddle',' in Diamond, 1995.
4. See Putnam, 1995 and 2001.
5. For more on the early modern skeptical crisis and 'skeptical fideism', see Penelhum, 1983, and Popkin, 2003 as well as Chapter 4 of the present book.
6. See 'On Misunderstanding Wittgenstein: Kripke's Private Language Argument' in Hacker, 2001, pp. 268–310.
7. See Horwich, 1998; and Wright, 1992.
8. Here I do not mean to imply that Horwich and Quine do not differ in important ways. For one, they disagree about what they consider to be the proper bearers of truth; for Horwich, propositions are the bearers of truth, while for Quine, sentences are. That said, both agree that the nominalizing function of the truth predicate, observed in Alfred Tarski's Schema T (that is, 'X is true if and only if p', where for 'p' is substituted a sentence and for 'X' is substituted the name of that sentence) says all that needs to be said about truth.

9. I do not wish to imply that the concept of trust exhausts the various preconditions of linguistic collaboration. Surely, language use is also conditioned by the structures of our brains and of the world. However, trust characterizes the collaborative dimensions of language.
10. Much recent work on trust by philosophers has been done by feminist ethicists. See Baier, 1986, 1994, and 2004. See also Friedman, 2004.
11. 'A picture held us captive. And we could not get outside it, for it lay in our language and language seemed to repeat it to us inexorably' (Wittgenstein, 2003a, §115).
12. See Wittgenstein, 2003a, §18.
13. See Carroll, 2010.

7 Wittgenstein's Ethic of Perspicuity and the Philosophy of Religion

1. Martha Nussbaum writes, 'We in the United States cannot be complacent about the health of the humanities, however. Despite continued support from donors, the economic crisis has led many universities to make deep cuts in humanities and arts programming' (Nussbaum, 2010, p. 123).
2. Consider Mulhall's discussion of Anthony Kenny's review of Cavell's *The Claim of Reason* in Mulhall, 2001, p. 1.
3. See Hadot, 1995.
4. However, see Knepper, 2013, for a somewhat critical take on Clayton's long lingering over thick descriptions of religious reason-giving.
5. In this sense, I am in agreement with some of what Wesley Wildman argues in Wildman, 2010 (that is, philosophy of religion as performing a facilitating role in multidisciplinary research on religions).
6. Philosophy of religion likely had multiple points of origin, each contributing to the topics and tone of the subdiscipline. The boundaries of the religious and the rational was one such topic. For a different study of the origins of the subdiscipline, see Taliaferro, 2005.

Bibliography

Amesbury, Richard (2003), 'Has Wittgenstein Been Misunderstood by Wittgensteinian Philosophers of Religion', *Philosophical Investigations*, 26/1, pp. 44–72.

—— (2007), 'Fideism,' in Edward N. Zalta, ed., *Stanford Encyclopedia of Philosophy*, URL = <http://plato.stanford.edu/entries/fideism/>.

—— (2012), 'Fideism,' in Edward N. Zalta, ed., *Stanford Encyclopedia of Philosophy*, URL = <http://plato.stanford.edu/entries/fideism/>.

Appiah, Kwame Anthony (1990) 'Racisms' in David Goldberg, ed., *Anatomy of Racism* (Minneapolis: Minnesota University Press), 3–17.

—— (2006) *Cosmopolitanism: Ethics in a World of Strangers* (New York: W. W. Norton & Co.).

Arrington, Robert L. and Addis, Mark (eds) (2001) *Wittgenstein and Philosophy of Religion* (New York: Routledge).

Asad, Talal (1993) *Genealogies of Religion: Disciplines and Reasons of Power in Christianity and Islam* (Baltimore, MD: Johns Hopkins University Press).

Ayer, A. J. (1936) *Language, Truth, and Logic* (Oxford: Oxford University Press).

Bagger, Matthew C. (1999) *Religious Experience, Justification, and History* (New York: Cambridge University Press).

Baier, Annette C. (1986) 'Trust and Anti-Trust', *Ethics* 96, 231–60.

—— (1994) *Moral Prejudices* (Cambridge: Harvard University Press).

—— (2004) 'Demoralization, Trust, and the Virtues', in Cheshire Calhoun, ed., *Setting the Moral Compass: Essays by Women Philosophers* (New York: Oxford University Press).

Baker, Gordon (2006) *Wittgenstein's Method: Neglected Aspects*, Katherine Morris, ed. (London: Blackwell Publishers).

Bartley, William W. (1973) *Wittgenstein* (Philadelphia: Lippincott Publishers).

Biletzki, Anat (2003) *(Over)Interpreting Wittgenstein* (Boston: Kluwer Academic Publishers).

Bishop, John (2007) *Believing by Faith: An Essay in the Epistemology and Ethics of Religious Belief* (New York: Oxford University Press).

Bloemendaal, P. F. (2006) *Grammars of Faith: A Critical Evaluation of D. Z. Phillips's Philosophy of Religion* (Leuven: Peeters Publishers).

Bouwsma, O. K. (1986) *Wittgenstein: Conversations 1949–1951*, J. L. Craft and Ronald E. Hustwit, eds, (Indianapolis, IN: Hacket Publishing Company).

Bradley, F. H. (1914) *Essays on Truth and Reality* (Oxford: Oxford University Press).

Braithwaite, Richard B. (1955) *An Empiricist's View of the Nature of Religious Belief* (Cambridge: Cambridge University Press).

Broad, C. D. (1929) 'Review: F. R. Tennant, *Philosophical Theology, Vol. I.: The Soul and its Faculties*', *Mind* 38/149, 94–100.

—— (1930) 'Review: F. R. Tennant, *Philosophical Theology, Vol. II.: The World, the Soul, and God*', *Mind* 39/156, 476–84.

Buben, Adam (2013) 'Neither Irrationalist Nor Apologist: Revisiting Faith and Reason in Kierkegaard', *Philosophy Compass*, 8(3), 318–26.

Carnap, Rudolf (1959) 'The Elimination of Metaphysics through Logical Analysis of Language' in A. J. Ayer, ed., *Logical Positivism* (New York: Free Press).

Carroll, Thomas D. (2010) 'The Debate over "Wittgensteinian Fideism" and Phillips' Contemplative Philosophy of Religion' in Ingolf U. Dalferth and Hartmut von Sass, eds, *The Contemplative Spirit: D.Z. Phillips on Religion and the Limits of Philosophy* (Zürich: Mohr Siebeck).

Cavell, Stanley (1966) 'The Availability of Wittgenstein's Later Philosophy', in George Pitcher, ed., *Wittgenstein: The Philosophical Investigations* (Notre Dame: University of Notre Dame Press).

—— (1979) *The Claim of Reason: Wittgenstein, Skepticism, Morality, and Tragedy* (New York: Oxford University Press).

Chatterjee, Ranjit (2005) *Wittgenstein and Judaism: A Triumph of Concealment* (New York: Peter Lang Publishers).

Clack, Brian (1999) *An Introduction to Wittgenstein's Philosophy of Religion* (Edinburgh: Edinburgh University Press).

—— (2001) 'Wittgenstein and Magic', in Robert L. Arrington and Mark Addis, eds, *Wittgenstein and Philosophy of Religion* (New York: Routledge).

Clayton, John (2006) *Religions, Reasons and Gods: Essays in Cross-Cultural Philosophy of Religion*, Anne M. Blackburn and Thomas D. Carroll, eds (Cambridge: Cambridge University Press).

Conant, James (2001) 'Philosophy and Biography', in James C. Klagge, ed., *Wittgenstein: Biography and Philosophy* (Cambridge: Cambridge University Press).

Costello, Diarmuid (2004) '"Making Sense" of Nonsense: Conant and Diamond Read Wittgenstein's Tractatus' in Barry Stocker, ed., *Post-Analytic Tractatus* (Burlington, VT: Ashgate Publishing Co.), 99–126.

Davies, Brian (1982) 'Scarlet O'Hara: A Portrait Restored', *Philosophy*, 57/221, 402–7.

Diamond, Cora (1995) *The Realistic Spirit: Wittgenstein, Philosophy, and the Mind* (Cambridge: MIT Press).

—— (2005) 'Wittgenstein on Religious Belief: The Gulfs Between Us' in D. Z. Phillips and Mario von der Ruhr, eds, *Religion and Wittgenstein's Legacy* (Burlington, VT: Ashgate Publishing), 99–138.

—— (2006) 'Peter Winch on the *Tractatus* and the unity of Wittgenstein's philosophy', in A. Pichler and S. Säätelä, eds, *Wittgenstein: The Philosopher and His Works* (Frankfurt: Ontos Verlag), 133–63.

Delaney, Sheila (1972) *Chaucer's House of Fame: The Poetics of Skeptical Fideism* (Chicago: University of Chicago Press).

Douglas, J. D., ed., (1978) 'Fideism' in *The New International Dictionary of the Christian Church* (Grand Rapids, MI: Zondervan Publishing Co.).

DuBois, Thomas David (2011) *Religion and the Making of Modern East Asia* (Cambridge University Press).

Dunn, Geoffrey D. (2004) *Tertullian* (New York: Routledge).

Engelmann, Paul (1967) *Letters from Ludwig Wittgenstein with a Memoir* (Oxford: Basil Blackwell).

Evans, C. Stephen (1998) *Faith Beyond Reason: A Kierkegaardian Account* (Edinburgh: Edinburgh University Press).

Flew, Anthony (1967) 'Review of *The Concept of Prayer* by D. Z. Phillips', *The Philosophical Quarterly* 17/66, 91–2.

Flew, Anthony and Habermas, Gary (2004) 'My Pilgrimage from Atheism to Theism: An Exclusive Interview with Former British Atheist Professor Antony Flew', *Philosophia Christi* 6/2, 197–211.

Floyd, Juliet (2002) 'Review of Klagge, James C., ed., Wittgenstein: Biography and Philosophy' *Notre Dame Philosophical Reviews* <http://ndpr.nd.edu/review.cfm?id=1137>.

Fouillée, Alfred (1916) *Modern French Legal Philosophy*, Mrs. Franklin W. Scott and Joseph P. Chamberlain, trans. (Boston: The Boston Book Company).

Friedman, Marilyn (2004) 'Diversity, Trust, and Moral Understanding', in Cheshire Calhoun, ed., *Setting the Moral Compass: Essays by Women Philosophers* (New York: Oxford University Press).

Fronda, Earl Stanley B. (2010) *Wittgenstein's (Misunderstood) Religious Thought* (Leiden and Boston: Brill Academic Publishers).

Fuller, Robert C. (1996) '"The Will to Believe": a Centennial Reflection', *Journal of the American Academy of Religion* 64, 633–50.

Gale, Richard M. (1999) *The Divided Self of William James* (New York: Cambridge University Press).

—— (2004) *The Philosophy of William James: An Introduction* (New York: Cambridge University Press).

Gilman, Sander L. (1986) *Jewish Self-Hatred: Anti-Semitism and the Hidden Language of the Jews* (Baltimore: Johns Hopkins Press).

—— (1996) 'Smart Jews in Fin-de-siècle Vienna: "Hybrids" and the Anxiety about Jewish Superior Intelligence – Hofmannsthal and Wittgenstein', *Modernism/Modernity*, 3.2, 45–58.

Glock, Hans-Johann (1996) *A Wittgenstein Dictionary* (London: Blackwell Publishers).

—— (2008) *What is Analytic Philosophy?* (New York: Cambridge University Press).

Goodman, Russell B. (2002) *Wittgenstein and William James* (New York: Cambridge University Press).

Hacker, P. M. S. (1996) *Wittgenstein's Place in Twentieth Century Anglo-American Philosophy* (New York: Blackwell).

—— (2001) *Wittgenstein: Connections and Controversies* (New York: Oxford University Press).

Hadot, Pierre (1995) *Philosophy as a Way of Life*, Michael Chase, trans. (Oxford: Blackwell Publishers).

Hansen, Delbert James (1993) *Fideism and Hume's Philosophy* (New York: Peter Lang).

Harris, James Franklin (2002) *Analytic Philosophy of Religion* (Boston: Springer).

Hasker, William (1995) 'Evidentialism' in Robert Audi, ed., *Cambridge Dictionary of Philosophy* (Cambridge: Cambridge University Press).

Helm, Paul (1994) *Belief Policies* (Cambridge: Cambridge University Press).

Horton, Walter M. (1926a) *The Philosophy of the Abbé Bautain* (New York: New York University Press).

—— (1926b) 'The Theology of Eugène Ménégoz', *Journal of Religion*, 6, 174–94.

Horwich, Paul (1998) *Truth*, 2nd edn (Oxford: Oxford University Press).

Iczkovits, Yaniv (2012) *Wittgenstein's Ethical Thought* (New York: Palgrave Macmillan).

Incandella, Joseph, M. (1985) 'The Appropriation of Wittgenstein's Work by Philosophers of Religion: Towards a Re-Evaluation and an End', *Religious Studies*, 21/4, pp. 457–74.

Insole, Christopher (1998) 'Kierkegaard: A Reasonable Fideist?', *Heythrop Journal*, XXXIX, 363–78.

James, William (1896) *The Will to Believe and Other Essays in Popular Philosophy* (New York: Longmans, Green, and Co.).

—— (1906) 'G. Papini and the Pragmatist Movement in Italy', *The Journal of Philosophy, Psychology and Scientific Methods*, 3/13, 337–41.

—— (1920) *The Letters of William James*, Vol. II, Henry James, ed. (The Atlantic Monthly Press).

—— (1978) *Pragmatism and the Meaning of Truth*, A. J. Ayer, ed. (Cambridge: Harvard University Press).

—— (1985) *The Varieties of Religious Experience*, Introduction by John E. Smith (Cambridge: Harvard University Press).

Janik, Allen and Toulmin, Stephen (1973) *Wittgenstein's Vienna* (New York: Simon and Schuster).

John Paul II (1998) *Fides et Ratio* <papalenclyclicals.net>.

Johnson, R. K. (1984) 'Fideism', in Walter A. Elwell, ed., *Evangelical Dictionary of Theology* (Grand Rapids, MI: Baker Book House).

Kellenberger, James (1984) 'Kierkegaard, Indirect Communication, and Religious Truth', *International Journal for Philosophy of Religion*, 16/2, 153–60.

Kenny, Anthony (1976) 'From the Big Typescript to the Philosophical Grammar' in Jaakko Hintikka, ed., *Essays on Wittgenstein in Honour of G. H. von Wright*. Acta Philosophica Fennica, 1–3 (Amsterdam: North-Holland Publishing Company).

—— (2006) 'A Brief History of Wittgenstein Editing', in A. Pichler and S. Säätelä, eds, *Wittgenstein: The Philosopher and His Works* (Frankfurt: Ontos Verlag), 382–96.

Kerr, Fergus (2008) *'Work on Oneself': Wittgenstein's Philosophical Psychology* (Arlington, VA: The Institute for the Psychological Sciences Press).

Kierkegaard, Søren (1985) *Philosophical Fragments / Johannes Climacus*, Howard V. Hong and Edna H. Hong, trans. (Princeton University Press: Princeton, New Jersey).

—— (1992) *Concluding Unscientific Postscript to Philosophical Fragments*, vol. 1, Howard V. Hong and Edna H. Hong, trans. (Princeton University Press: Princeton, New Jersey).

Kirkham, Richard (1992) *Theories of Truth: An Introduction* (Cambridge: MIT Press).

Klagge, James C., ed., (2001) *Wittgenstein: Biography and Philosophy* (New York: Cambridge University Press).

—— (2011) *Wittgenstein in Exile* (Cambridge, MA: MIT Press).

Knepper, Timothy D. (2013) *The Ends of Philosophy of Religion: Terminus and Telos* (New York: Palgrave Macmillan).

Kripke, Saul (1982) *Wittgenstein on Rules and Private Language* (Cambridge, MA: Harvard University Press)

Kuklick, Bruce (2003) *A History of Philosophy in America, 1720–2000* (New York: Oxford University Press).

L'Abbé Robitaille (1854) 'Qu'est-ce que le traditionalisme?' *L'Ami de la Religion*, 16, (Paris) 661–7.

Linsky, Leonard (1975) 'Review of Wittgenstein's Vienna by Allen Janik and Stephen Toulmin', *Journal of Modern History* 47/4, 699–703.

Leo XIII (1879) *Aeterni Patris*. <papalencylcicals.net>.

Long, Eugene Thomas (2003) *Twentieth Century Western Philosophy of Religion: 1900–2000* (Boston: Kluwer Academic Publishers).

MacIntyre, Alasdair and Flew, Anthony, eds, (1955) *New Essays in Philosophical Theology* (New York: Macmillan Publishing Company).

Malcolm, Norman (1958) *Ludwig Wittgenstein: a Memoir* (New York: Oxford University Press).

—— (1960) 'Anselm's Ontological Arguments', *The Philosophical Review*, 69/1, 41–62.

—— (1977) *Thought and Knowledge* (Ithaca, NY: Cornell University Press).

—— (1982) 'Wittgenstein: The Relation of Language to Instinctive Behaviour', *Philosophical Investigations* 5/1, 3–22.

—— (1989) 'The Groundlessness of Belief', in Terence Penelhum, ed., *Faith* (New York: Macmillan Publishing Company).

—— (1993) *Wittgenstein: A Religious Point of View?* Peter Winch, ed., (Ithaca, NY: Cornell University Press).

Matczak, S. A. (1967) 'Fideism', *New Catholic Encyclopedia* (New York: McGraw Hill).

McCool, Gerald A. (1977) *Catholic Theology in the Nineteenth Century: the Quest for a Unitary Method* (New York: Seabury Press).

McGovern, Ken and Szabados, Béla (2002) 'Was Wittgenstein a Fideist? Two Views', *Sophia* 41/2: 41–54.

McGuinness, Brian (1988) *Wittgenstein A Life: Young Ludwig 1889–1921* (Berkeley: University of California Press).

—— (2002) *Approaches to Wittgenstein: Collected Papers* (London: Routledge).

McMahon, Darrin (2001) *Enemies of Enlightenment: The French Counter-Enlightenment and the Making of Modernity* (New York: Oxford University Press).

Ménégoz, Eugène (1879) *Reflexions sur l'évangile de salut* (Paris: Librairie Fischerbacher, 1879); reproduced in *Publications diverse sur la fidéisme et son application a l'enseignement chrétien traditionnel*, 1 (Paris: Librairie Fischerbacher, 1900–21).

—— (1900–21) *Publications diverse sur la fidéisme et son application a l'enseignement chrétien traditionnel*, 1–5 (Paris: Librairie Fischerbacher).

—— (1908) *Religion and Theology: I. The Triple Theological Distinction…II. Pardon and Righteousness* (London: Williams and Norgate).

—— (1908–27) 'Symbolo-Fideism' in James Hastings, ed., *Encyclopedia of Religion and Ethics* (New York: C. Scribner's Sons).

Monk, Ray (1990) *Ludwig Wittgenstein: the Duty of Genius* (New York: Penguin Books).

Moore, G. E. (1903) 'The Refutation of Idealism', *Mind* 12, 433–53.

—— (1942) 'Autobiography', in P. A. Schilpp, ed., *The Philosophy of G. E. Moore* (Evanston, IL: Northwestern University Press).

—— (1959) *Philosophical Studies* (Paterson, New Jersey: Littlefield, Adams & Co.).

Mulhall, Stephen (2001) *Inheritance and Originality: Wittgenstein, Heidegger, Kierkegaard* (New York: Oxford University Press).

—— (2007a) *Wittgenstein's Private Language: Grammar, Nonsense, and Imagination in Philosophical Investigations, Sections 243–315* (New York: Oxford University Press).

—— (2007b) 'Wittgenstein's Temple: Three Styles of Philosophical Architecture', in Andy F. Sanders, ed., *D. Z. Phillips's Contemplative Philosophy of Religion: Questions and Responses* (Burlington, VT: Ashgate).

Neufeld, Karl-Heinz (2005) 'Fideism', in Jean-Yves Lacoste, ed., *Encyclopedia of Christian Theology, Vol. 1* (New York: Routledge).

Nelson, Eric (2009) 'Religious Crisis, Ethical Life, and Kierkegaard's Critique of Christendom', in *Kierkegaard and the Religious Crisis of the 19th Century* (Toronto: Kierkegaard Circle Sala, Slovakia: Kierkegaard Society in Slovakia).

Nielsen, Kai (1963) 'Can Faith Validate God-Talk?',*Theology Today,* 20, 158–73.

—— (1967) 'Wittgensteinian Fideism', *Philosophy* 42/161, 191–209, reprinted in Kai Nielsen and D. Z. Phillips, eds, (2005) *Wittgensteinian Fideism?* (London: St. Martin's Press).

—— (2001) *Naturalism and Religion* (Amherst: Prometheus Books).

Nussbaum, Martha (2010) *Not for Profit: Why Democracy Needs the Humanities* (Princeton: Princeton University Press).

Ollé-Laprune, Léon (1880) *De La Certitude Morale* (Paris: Belin).

Osborn, Eric (1997) *Tertullian, First Theologian of the West* (New York: Cambridge University Press).

Peirce, Charles S. (1877) 'The Fixation of Belief', *Popular Science Monthly* 12, 1–15.

—— (1908) 'A Neglected Argument for the Reality of God', *Hibbert Journal* 7/1, 90–112.

Penelhum, Terence (1983) *God and Skepticism: A Study in Skepticism and Fideism* (Dordrecht: D. Reidel Pub. Co.).

—— (1997) 'Fideism' in Philip L. Quinn and Charles Taliaferro, eds, *Blackwell Companion to Philosophy of Religion,* 1st edn (Cambridge, MA: Blackwell Publishers).

Perkins, Robert L. (1990) 'Kierkegaard, A Kind of Epistemologist', *History of European Ideas,* 12/1, 7–18.

Perry, Ralph Barton (1912) *Present Philosophical Tendencies: A Critical Survey of Naturalism, Idealism, Pragmatism and Realism together with a Synopsis of the Philosophy of William James* (New York: Longmans, Green, and Co.).

—— (1935) *The Thought and Character of William James,* Vol. II (Boston: Little, Brown and Company).

—— (1938) *In the Spirit of William James* (New Haven: Yale University Press).

Phillips, D. Z. (1965) *The Concept of Prayer* (London: Routledge and Kegan Paul).

—— (1976) *Religion without Explanation* (Oxford: Blackwell Publishers)

—— (1986) *Belief, Change and Forms of Life* (Atlantic Highlands, NJ: Humanities Press International).

—— (1994) *Wittgenstein and Religion* (New York: Palgrave Macmillan).

—— (1999) *Philosophy's Cool Place* (Ithaca: Cornell University Press)

—— (2000) 'Practices, Practice, and Superstition: A Response to Terrence W. Tilley', *Journal of the American Academy of Religion* 68/2, 357–62.

—— (2001) *Religion and the Hermeneutics of Contemplation* (New York: Cambridge University Press)".

—— (2003) 'Wittgenstein, Wittgensteinianism and Magic: a Philosophical Tragedy?' *Religious Studies* 39, 185–201.

—— (2007) 'Locating Philosophy's Cool Place — A Reply to Stephen Mulhall', in Andy F. Sanders, ed., *D. Z. Phillips's Contemplative Philosophy of Religion: Questions and Responses* (Burlington, VT: Ashgate).

Pius X (1907) *Pascendi Dominici Gregis* <papalencyclicals.net>.

Plantinga, Alvin (1967) *God and Other Minds: a Study of the Rational Justification of Belief in God* (Ithaca, NY: Cornell University Press).

—— (1983) 'Reason and Belief in God', in Alvin Plantinga and Nicholas Wolterstorff, eds, *Faith and Rationality: Reason and Belief in God* (Notre Dame, IN: University of Notre Dame Press), 16–93.

—— (2000) *Warranted Christian Belief* (New York: Oxford University Press).

Popkin, Richard H. (1960) *The History of Scepticism from Erasmus to Descartes* (Assen: Van Gorcum & Co.).

—— (1967) 'Fideism' in Paul Edwards, ed., *Encyclopedia of Philosophy* (New York: MacMillan).

—— (2003) *The History of Scepticism: From Savonarola to Bayle* (Oxford: Oxford University Press).

Price, H. H. (1935) 'Logical Positivism and Theology', *Philosophy* 10/39, 313–31.

—— (1945) 'Clarity is Not Enough', *Proceedings of the Aristotelian Society*, 19, 1–31.

Proudfoot, Wayne (1985) *Religious Experience* (Berkeley: University of California Press).

Putnam, Hilary (1992) *Renewing Philosophy* (Cambridge: Harvard University Press).

—— (1995) *Pragmatism: an Open Question* (Cambridge: Harvard University Press)

—— (2001) 'Reply to Jean-Pierre Cometti', *Revue Internationale de Philosophie* 55/4, 457–69.

Quinn, Philip (2005) 'Fideism' in Ted Honderich, ed., *Oxford Companion to Philosophy*, 2nd edn (Oxford: Oxford University Press).

Reinhardt, Kurt F. (1936) 'A Cleavage of Minds', *Commonweal*, vol. 24, 523.

Rhees, Rush, ed., (1984) *Recollections of Wittgenstein* (New York: Oxford University Press).

—— (1997) 'Language as Emerging from Instinctive Behaviour', *Philosophical Investigations* 20/1, 1–14.

Richardson, Alan and MacQuarrie, John (1983) 'Fideism', in Alan Richardson and John Bowden, eds, *The Westminster Dictionary of Christian Theology* (Philadelphia, PA: Westminster Press).

Richter, Duncan (2004) *Wittgenstein at His Word* (New York: Thoemmes Continuum).

Russell, Bertrand (1905), 'On Denoting,' *Mind*, 14, 479–493.

—— (1912) *The Problems of Philosophy* (Oxford: Oxford University Press).

—— (1917) *Mysticism and Logic and Other Essays*, (London: G. Allen & Unwin).

—— (1956) *Logic and Knowledge: Essays, 1901–1950* (New York: The Macmillan Company).

—— (1993) *My Philosophical Development* (London: Routledge).

—— (1999) *The Selected Letters of Bertrand Russell: The Public Years 1914–1970*, Nicholas Griffin, ed., assisted by Alison Roberts Miculan (New York: Routledge).

Sabatier, Auguste (1902) *Outlines of a Philosophy of Religion Based on Psychology and History* (New York: J. Pott and Co.).

Sauvage, G. (1909) 'Fideism', *Catholic Encyclopedia*, Vol. VI (New York: Robert Appleton Company).

Schönbaumsfeld, Genia (2007) *A Confusion of the Spheres: Kierkegaard and Wittgenstein on Philosophy and Religion* (New York: Oxford University Press).

Sherry, Patrick (1977) *Religion, Truth, and Language-Games* (London: Macmillan).

Sluga, Hans (1998) 'What Has History to Do with Me? Wittgenstein and Analytic Philosophy', *Inquiry* 41, 99–121.

Smart, Ninian (1999) *Dimensions of the Sacred: An Anatomy of the World's Beliefs* (Los Angeles: University of California Press).

Smith, Jonathan Z. (2004) *Relating Religion: Essays in the Study of Religion* (Chicago: Chicago University Press).

Soames, Scott (2002) *Philosophical Analysis in the Twentieth Century: Volume 1: The Dawn of Analysis* (Princeton: Princeton University Press).

Stagaman, David J., Kraft, James and Sutton, Kristin (2001) *Wittgenstein & Religion: A Bibliography of Articles, Books, and Theses in the Twentieth Century that Relate the Philosophy of Ludwig Wittgenstein to the Study of Religion and Theology* (Quezon City, Philippines: Office of Research and Publications, Ateneo de Manila University).

Stern, David (2001) 'Was Wittgenstein a Jew?' in James C. Klagge, ed., *Wittgenstein: Biography and Philosophy* (Cambridge: Cambridge University Press).

Stern, David G. and Szabados, Béla, eds, (2004) *Wittgenstein Reads Weininger* (New York: Cambridge University Press).

Stevens, George B. (1903) 'Auguste Sabatier and the Paris School of Theology', *Hibbert Journal*, 1, 553–68.

Strandberg, Hugo (2006) *The Possibility of Discussion: Relativism, Truth and Criticism of Religious Beliefs* (Burlington, VT: Ashgate Publishing).

Strenski, Ivan (2002) *Contesting Sacrifice: Religion, Nationalism, and Social Thought in France* (Chicago: University of Chicago Press).

Szabados, Béla (2005) 'Introduction: Wittgensteinian Fideism 1967–1989', in Kai Nielsen and D. Z. Phillips, eds, *Wittgensteinian Fideism?* (London: SCM Press).

—— (2010) *Ludwig Wittgenstein on Race, Gender, and Cultural Identity: Philosophy as a Personal Endeavor* (Lewiston: Edwin Mellen Press).

Taliaferro, Charles (2005) *Evidence and Faith: Philosophy and Religion since the Seventeenth Century* (New York: Cambridge University Press).

Tanner, Norman P., ed., (1990) *Decrees of the Ecumenical Councils*, 2, (Washington, D.C.: Georgetown University Press).

Taylor, Mark C. (1998) *Critical Terms for Religious Studies* (Chicago: University of Chicago Press).

Tennant, F. R. (1930) *Philosophical Theology, Vol. II.: The World, the Soul, and God* (Cambridge: The University Press).

Tertullian (1931) *Apologeticus and De Spectaculis*, T. R. Glover and G. H. Rendall, trans. (New York: G. P. Putnam's sons).

Tilley, Terrence W. (2000a) 'The Philosophy of Religion and the Concept of Religion: D. Z. Phillips on Religion and Superstition', *Journal of the American Academy of Religion* 68/2, 345–56.

—— (2000b) '"Superstition" as a Philosopher's Gloss on Practice: A Rejoinder to D. Z. Phillips', *Journal of the American Academy of Religion* 68/2, 363–66.

Tillich, Paul (1951) *Systematic Theology, Vol. I* (Chicago: University of Chicago Press).

Tolstoy, Leo (1997) *The Gospel in Brief*, Isabel Hapgood, trans., F. A. Flowers III, ed. (Lincoln, NE: University of Nebraska Press).

Vainio, Olli-Pekka (2010) *Beyond Fideism: Negotiable Religious Identities* (Burlington, VT: Ashgate).

Weininger, Otto (1907) *Sex and Character*, Sixth Edn (New York: G. P. Putnam and Sons).

Wildman, Wesley (2010) *Religious Philosophy as Multidisciplinary Comparative Inquiry* (Albany, NY: SUNY Press).

Williams, Bernard (1992) 'Left-Wing Wittgenstein, Right-Wing Marx', *Common Knowledge* I, 33–42.

Winch, Peter (1990) *The Idea of a Social Science and its Relation to Philosophy* (Atlantic Highlands, NJ: Humanities Press).

Wittgenstein, Ludwig (1965) 'Lecture on Ethics', *The Philosophical Review* 74/1, 3–12.

—— (1967a) *Lectures and Conversations on Aesthetics, Psychology and Religious Belief*, Cyril Barrett, ed. (Berkeley: University of California Press).

—— (1967b) *Zettel*, G. E. M. Anscombe and G. H. von Wright, eds, G. E. M. Anscombe, trans. (Berkeley: University of California Press).

—— (1972) *On Certainty* G. E. M. Anscombe and G. H. von Wright, eds (New York: Harper Perennial).

—— (1975) *Philosophical Remarks*, Rush Rhees, ed. (New York: Barnes & Noble Books).

—— (1979) 'Letters to Ludwig von Ficker', in Allan Janik, ed., Bruce Gillette, trans, *Wittgenstein: Sources and Perspectives*, C. G. Luckhardt, ed. (Hassocks: Harvester Press), 82–98.

—— (1991) *Geheime Tagebücher: 1914–1916* (Vienna: Turia and Kant).

—— (1993) *Philosophical Occasions: 1912–1951*, James C. Klagge and Alfred Nordmann, eds (Indianapolis: Hackett Publishing Company).

—— (1998) *Culture and Value*, Second Edn, G. H. von Wright, ed. (Oxford: Blackwell Publishers).

—— (2001) *Tractatus Logico-Philosophicus*, D. F. Pears and B. F. McGuinness, trans. (London: Routledge Classics).

—— (2003a) *Philosophical Investigations*, G. E. M. Anscombe, ed., 3rd ed. (Malden, MA: Blackwell Publishers).

—— (2003b) *Wittgenstein: Public and Private Occasions*, James Klagge and Alfred Nordmann, eds (Rowman and Littlefield).

Wolterstorff, Nicholas (1998) 'Faith' in Edward Craig, ed., *Routledge Encyclopedia of Philosophy* (London: Routledge).

—— (2009) *Practices of Belief: Selected Essays, Volume 2*, Nicholas Wolterstorff and Terrence Cuneo, eds. (Cambridge: Cambridge University Press).

Wright, Crispin (1992) *Truth and Objectivity* (Cambridge: Harvard University Press).

Index

Printed and bound in the United States of America